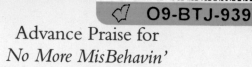
Advance Praise for
No More MisBehavin'

"A sensitive, thoughtful, eminently practical book that will help parents help their children change behavior—and improve the well-being and happiness of the child and the entire family. A wonderful contribution!"
—**Alvin Rosenfeld**, M.D., child psychiatrist and coauthor, *The Over-Scheduled Child*

"The most complete toolkit for coping with behavior I have ever seen. Destined to be a classic for all parents and teachers, *No More MisBehavin'* is powerful and practical."
—**Annie Leedom**, founder and president, www.parentingbookmark.com

"Based on the good old-fashioned idea that kids who behave are happier than those who don't, *No More Misbehavin'* shows parents exactly how to turn their love into *action* with a step-by-step plan for permanently removing bad behaviors. Excellent!"
—**Elaine Hightower**, coauthor with **Betsy Riley**, *Our Family Meeting Book: Fun and Easy Ways to Manage Time, Build Communication and Share Responsibility Week by Week*

"Michele Borba's new book provides parents with an innovative strategy for dealing with children's challenging behaviors. Her suggestions are practical, doable, and proven. Any parent looking for concrete solutions for troubling kid behaviors need look no further. Simply outstanding!"
—**Naomi Drew**, author, *Hope and Healing: Peaceful Parenting in an Uncertain World*

"This book offers hands-on, practical, and effective solutions to everyday problems that all parents encounter from time to time. These strategies are guaranteed to reduce your parenting headaches and help you enjoy your kids! I'll certainly be recommending this book to the parents with whom I work."
—**Dr. Jane Bluestein**, author, *Parents, Teens & Boundaries: How to Draw the Line* and *The Parent's Little Book of Lists: Do's & Don'ts of Effective Parenting*

"*No More Misbehavin's* clear, no-nonsense advice will be a blessing to parents paralyzed by stubborn childhood behaviors ranging from biting to bullying to heel-dragging in the face of chores. This step-by-step, here's-how manual is almost like having Michele Borba as your personal parenting trainer."
—**Tom Lickona**, author, *Educating for Character* and *Raising Good Children*

No More Misbehavin'

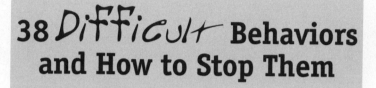

38 *Difficult* Behaviors
and How to Stop Them

Michele Borba, Ed.D.

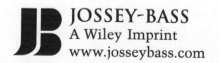

JOSSEY-BASS
A Wiley Imprint
www.josseybass.com

Published by Jossey-Bass
A Wiley Imprint
989 Market Street, San Francisco, CA 94103-1741   www.josseybass.com

Note to the Reader: All of the letters in this book have been received from parents over the past few years. The names of the parents and children, as well as their location, have been changed to protect their privacy.

Jossey-Bass books and products are available through most bookstores. To contact Jossey-Bass directly call our Customer Care Department within the U.S. at 800-956-7739, outside the U.S. at 317-572-3986, or fax 317-572-4002.

Jossey-Bass also publishes its books in a variety of electronic formats. Some content that appears in print may not be available in electronic books.

Library of Congress Cataloging-in-Publication Data

Borba, Michele.
    No more misbehavin' : 38 difficult behaviors and how to stop them/
  Michele Borba.— 1st ed.
      p. cm.
    Includes bibliographical references and index.
    ISBN 0-7879-6617-7 (alk. paper)
    1. Discipline of children. 2. Child rearing. 3. Parenting. I. Title.
  HQ770.4.B67 2003
  649'.64—dc21   2002151368

Printed in the United States of America
FIRST EDITION
PB Printing   10 9 8 7

CONTENTS

PART FOUR
How to Use Consequences   297

PART FIVE
Don't Forget to Tell Your Kids You Love Them!   305

ACKNOWLEDGMENTS

There's a wonderful proverb that says, "A book is like a garden carried in the pocket." I know there were countless people who helped me bring this book to fruition. Each has helped shaped my ideas and the scope of my work. To them all, I express heartfelt appreciation.

To the hundreds of parents who have attended my workshops throughout the years: I am grateful to each one of you for so honestly sharing your concerns, stories, suggestions, and successes.

To the folks at Oxygen Media, especially Anne Patrick and Donna Sher, for your support and the opportunity to work with your moms. All letters in this book are from parents who wrote to my website. Their questions helped me understand which behaviors really trouble parents most, and their honest responses helped me create discipline strategies that stop bad behavior. (I have taken the liberty of tailoring the length of their letters and changing names to protect their privacy.)

To *Parents* editors, especially Diane Debrovner, for the honor of serving on your advisory board and the privilege of speaking with so many great writers about this subject, especially Vicky Mlyniec and Deb Waldman. Special thanks to Leslie Lambert, whose interview with me for her *Parents* article, "From Chaos to Cooperation: A 21 Day Discipline Makeover," resulted in a fabulous friendship and planted the seeds for this book.

To my personal cheerleading squad who have always been there for me: thanks for your loyalty and wonderful support. I'm eternally grateful to Annie Leedom, president of netconnectpublicity.com, for her incredible knock-your-socks-off Internet publicity skills, eternal optimism, and steadfast friendship; Adrienne Biggs, of Biggs Publicity, for her immense support and ingenious ways of finding publicity leads that always turn into gold; Steve Leedom, of nowimagine.net, for creating my gorgeous Web site, www.moralintelligence.com, and having endless patience when talking me through my perpetual computer glitches; Dottie DeHart, at Rocks-DeHart Public Relations, for her fabulous publicity campaigns and never-ending encouragement; Hanoch McCarty, for his incredible humor and constant list of incredible "best" book titles; Francesca Donlan, Gannett journalist, for friendship and writing such wonderful articles; Naomi Drew, fellow writer and comrade, for her empathetic ear and comforting encouragement; Jack Canfield, for being just an e-mail away to offer the perfect advice and help me remember to *laugh;* and Barbara Keane, Judy Baggott, and Patty Service, my true loyal buddies, for always managing to make writing easier by just being so darn fun and available.

To the staff at Jossey-Bass—especially Jesica Church, Beverly Miller, Erin Jow, Jennifer Wenzel, Lasell Whipple, Seth Schwartz, and Amy Scott. Having the fortune to do three books with this dedicated group has been a true privilege. To Alan Rinzler, editor extraordinaire and real cultivator of this book, I send my thanks for so many things: for planting the initial idea, his uncanny ability to pinpoint where a change was needed and provide the perfect suggestions, and his support through every step. Every author should be so lucky to have such an editor.

And finally to my family, the ones who have really made the difference in my life and nourished my growth: my husband and best friend, Craig, for his unending support, patience, and love through every phase of my life; my parents, Dan and Treva Ungaro, for epitomizing that miraculous concept, unconditional love; my mother-in-law, Lorayne Borba, for her continual encouragement and optimism; and the true joys of my life: my sons Jason, Adam, and Zach, for the constant love and fun they bring me. And for all the times they asked, "Aren't you done yet?" well, it's done!

With love to my parents, Dan and Treva Ungaro.
If only every child could be as lucky as I have been,
what a different world it would be!

FOREWORD

Jack Canfield, coauthor of
Chicken Soup for the Parent's Soul®

D iscipline is one of most debated child-rearing topics.
The word alone can churn up unhappy memories:
Crying. Screaming. Yelling. Fighting. Stress. Horrific
headaches. To others, it means cruel and unusual punishment,
totally unhip parenting, or something used only by sadistic,
abusive moms and dads.

Let's face it: discipline has received a bad rap. Even so-
called child experts disagree on the best way to squelch bad
behavior and are markedly different in approaches: time-out,
logical consequences, withholding privileges, ignoring, corporal punishment, lecturing, and grounding. Is it any wonder
parents are so perplexed? Some decide it's easier to put up with
their kids' annoying behaviors; it's just not worth another fight
or ruined evening. Others worry that discipline will permanently ruin their relationship with their kids. Still more figure
it's better letting someone else deal with it. They're too
exhausted or burned out as it is, so why add more stress?

But as much as we may dislike the idea of discipline, as
parents it's something we must do. After all, it's our job to raise

kids who act right, and it's our obligation to intervene so they will. There's no doubt that kids who whine, bite, bully, fight, hit, swear, lie, steal, and act impulsively or mean are not fun to be around. Not for us, not for family and friends, not for school and community, and certainly not for our kids themselves.

The real question is not whether we should discipline, but how to discipline so the misbehavior is stopped for good. What I'm talking about is a permanent behavior makeover, ridding the bad behavior once and for all so you don't have to discipline that behavior ever again. That's a profound child-raising concept and a big secret of good parenting. And that's what this book is all about. It's a unique new approach that will change the way you parent and how you discipline.

This will be the only discipline book you'll ever need to raise good kids. I'm that certain. Why? Because I know Michele Borba and her work. She has a track record that stands miles apart from other parenting experts. She doesn't theorize or speculate or give us a bunch of vague generalities. Instead, she rolls up her sleeves and tells us exactly what to do, moment by moment, step by step, to create permanent change in kids' behavior. Her makeover program with its wonderful activities is so creative and often so much fun that discipline becomes practically a painless process. The best news is that it works!

The ideas, guidelines, specific tips and strategies, and step-by-step makeovers in this book are all culled from parents such as yourself who were frustrated because their discipline attempts didn't work. Bad behaviors continued, family friction grew, and their kids' self-esteem plummeted. When they consistently followed Michele's specific makeover plans, however, their kids' bad behaviors were completely eliminated. They also found their kids more cooperative, better behaved, and fun to be around. What's more, they discovered a change in themselves: they were less stressed and more content in their parenting. What more can you ask?

So here's my advice: don't just read this book, use it! Start a Makeover Journal as Michele suggests, take time to work through her Behavior Makeovers to pinpoint *why* your kid might be using the bad behavior, and then use her steps to stop it. You'll end up with what you want most: a well-behaved kid. There's even a bonus: using these strategies will also help your kid learn good behaviors and strong moral habits. And those are what ultimately will build your kid's reputation as a human being. That's how critical this stuff is! Raising your kids in a loving, secure home and teaching them how to act right is the greatest legacy you can give. I wish you all the best in the most important role of your life!

PART 1

Preparing to
Make Changes

Be not afraid of moving slowly;
be afraid only of standing still.
—Chinese proverb

GETTING STARTED

I can't believe I'm admitting this, but my kid is driving me crazy.
He's ten and basically a good boy, but the way he acts sometimes
makes me wonder if he's had a brain transplant. I've tried sticker
charts, grounding him, taking away privileges, even bribing him.
They work for a while, then he starts doing the same obnoxious
behaviors again. I'm running out of ideas and am at my absolute
wit's end. How do I get my kid to behave—and stay behaving—
while still maintaining my sanity? There has to be a better way!
   —Carolyn, a single mom from Seattle, Washington

"How many times do I have to tell you?"
"That's enough! Stop it!"
"Why can't you just behave?"

Sound familiar? Well, you're not alone. One of the
biggest concerns of parents is how to get their kids to behave.
I know so not only because I'm a mother of three teenagers,
but also a former classroom teacher, expert parenting columnist at Oxygen Media, advisory board member to *Parents*
magazine, and parent workshop leader. Through the years, I've
received hundreds of questions from distraught parents and
have seen two main similarities in all of them.

First, parents almost always ask about the same bad
behaviors. Getting kids to listen, bullying, whining, and talking back have topped their lists. Then they go on to complain
about anger, anxiety, fighting, and on and on. I started keeping track and discovered thirty-eight key bad behaviors that
seemed to trouble them most.

Second, parents want to know how to discipline their
kids, not only to stop the bad behavior on the spot but also
completely eliminate it—and do so without reminders, pleading, coaxing, yelling, threatening, and bribing.

I found I was repeating the same answers over and over
and giving the same behavior tips again and again, until one

parent finally asked, "Can't you write this in a book?" and that's how *No More Misbehavin'* came to be. The letters you read in this book are real ones I've received from parents, and the answers are ones I've given countless times. There's one big difference: although I will give you proven, simple strategies you need to change your child's bad behaviors, I'm asking you to take one more step. Please don't just read these ideas: commit to changing your child's behavior by creating an action plan to help him succeed and then consistently using it until you *do* see change. That's what I call a Behavior Makeover, and that's what this book helps you do.

I'll help you write each plan, but it's you who must carry out it out. And if you do, here's a guarantee: your relationship with your child will improve, your family life will be more harmonious, parenting will be more enjoyable, and your child will behave the way you hope he will. Those are big guarantees, and to achieve them will take work on your part. But isn't that what parenting is all about? After all, we all have one big goal as parents: to raise our kids to be happy, well-behaved, good, and decent human beings. And that's exactly what you'll be gaining when you put into action your Behavior Makeover plans. Let's get started.

HOW TO USE THIS BOOK

All of the strategies you need to help you change your kid's behavior are provided in this book. But after working with hundreds of parents with these ideas, I'm convinced there are a few supplies and ideas that will help your makeover efforts. I strongly recommend you follow the five key tasks of preparation each time you try a new makeover to achieve long-term behavior change:

- *Use a Makeover Journal.* Each makeover poses questions to help you think about your kid's behavior. I urge you to write your thoughts and action plan in what I call a Makeover Journal. It could be a nice leather journal or a plain spiral notebook; either is fine. But be sure to write in it consistently every day. You'll be able to reread your notations, see behavior patterns that you otherwise might have missed, and track your kid's progress. Even the most reluctant parents have found that using a Makeover Journal has been invaluable for their efforts.

- *Talk to essential caregivers.* Consult others who know your child well—family, grandparents, teachers, day care providers, relatives, coaches, scout leaders, Sunday school teachers, ministers, babysitters—to find out their perspective on your child's behavior. For instance: Does your child act the same way with them? What do they think is causing the misbehavior? How do they respond? Does it work? What suggestions do they have? When you develop any makeover plan, share it with them. The more you work together, the quicker you'll be in stopping the problem behavior. Consistency is a critical part of an effective makeover.

- *Track the targeted behavior on a calendar.* An important makeover tool is a monthly calendar. Find one that has space for you to write a few sentences each day about your kid's behavior progress. For instance, note the date the behavior began. Once the makeover begins, every day jot down the number of times your kid displays the misbehavior. If your behavior plan is effective, you'll gradually see a decline in the frequency of misbehaviors, and you'll know your plan is working.

- *Read the resources.* Following each makeover is a list of further reading. Some are for you, and others are for your child. They provide a more thorough background about the behavior and offer more helpful hints for your makeover. Read a selection or two each time you target a behavior to make over.

- *Form a parent support group.* One of the best ways to use this book is by discussing these issues with other parents. You'll realize that other parents' kids have similar behavior problems as yours—which is always a bit comforting—as well as have the chance to hear their suggestions of what works or doesn't work in ridding bad behaviors. So form or join a group. Any size is fine; even one other parent will do. Just make sure you all enjoy one another and will commit to meeting regularly.

HOW EACH BEHAVIOR MAKEOVER WORKS

All of the makeovers in this book follow a general plan that is simple to follow and easy to use. Here are the elements of each makeover:

1. A letter I've received from a concerned parent about a real problem with his or her child's behavior. These letters represent the most common and frequently mentioned behavior problems that I've received.
2. A one- or two-sentence Behavior Tip that provides the essence of a successful approach to changing this behavior.
3. A major section of strategies that have been shown to improve each specific behavior problem. These techniques are culled from empirical research produced by the best professionals, scholars, and practitioners in the field of child development and psychology. Please study these methods carefully and see which ones might apply best for your child.
4. The Behavior Makeover Plan, which shows you how to apply these guidelines to your specific situation. This section is the *key* to creating your own action plan to change your kid's behavior. It asks you to reflect on your own behavior problems, past and present, to help you create the context and make the connection between you and your kid. It will help you understand what's working and

what's not working in your reactions as a parent to your kid's problem so far. Most important, it will ask you to work hard to understand why your kid is acting the way he is. It will encourage you to write your thoughts, responses, and greatest concerns in your Makeover Journal. Next, your job will be to make a plan based on reviewing the strategies in the first section and applying them to your child. Be sure to write this plan in your Makeover Journal.

5. The Makeover Pledge for each behavior problem. This pledge asks how you write exactly what you agree to do within the next twenty-four hours. Then do it. Research has proven that you have a 90 percent greater likelihood of success if you begin your plan within the next twenty-four hours. Don't wait!

6. The Makeover Results, with space to record your child's progress for the next three weeks. Research shows real behavior change takes a minimum of twenty-one days of repetition, so don't give up too soon.

7. Resources, which provide further reading on the problem behavior for parents as well as kids of varying ages.

DID YOU KNOW?

Studies reveal that 85 percent of all parents of children under twelve years of age use spanking when they're frustrated, yet less than 10 percent feel that it is effective. Sixty-five percent of parents surveyed said they'd rather discipline their kids by using consequences and encouraging improved behavior. The reason they resort to spanking instead? They don't know more effective discipline approaches.

PART 2

Behavior Makeover Basics

People who want to move mountains must start by carrying away small stones.
—Anonymous

TAKING THE PLUNGE

"Am I doing enough, or did I do too much?"
"Was I too hard, or should I be stricter?"
"May I should have grounded him. Who knows? Why won't he behave?"

Raising kids is never easy, and especially so these days. We lie awake agonizing over our parenting skills and questioning our choices. But there are a few secrets that will make parenting less stressful and help our kids act the way we want.

The most important discipline secret is this: *Behavior is learned, which means bad behaviors can be unlearned.* Think about it. Kids aren't born obnoxious, rude, defiant, bossy, or selfish. They learn those behaviors. Then the behaviors help them get what they want, so they continue using them.

Keep in mind this critical point: bad behaviors typically don't just go away. To get rid of them, someone has to intervene, and that someone is you. Just telling your kid to stop doing a bad behavior, grounding him, and giving a brilliant lecture, followed by your sternest look, is no guarantee that he will reform. Such discipline techniques are good at halting bad behaviors temporarily, but rarely at eliminating them altogether. That's why kids typically reuse the same old bad behavior again—or a new variation of it—and we're back to square one: pleading, coaxing, yelling, threatening, and bribing them to behave. And once again we're left exhausted, frustrated, discouraged, and questioning our parenting skills.

Remember that our goal isn't just to halt our kid's bad behaviors temporarily; it is to *change these behaviors* so they stop using them. And that's what this book will teach you how to do. It's a new approach to discipline, and it's the approach that will help you change your child's behavior for the long term. You will end up not only with a better behaved kid, but also a much less stressed you who can finally enjoy your relationship with your child. So let's gear up for big changes by looking at a few important points about any behavior makeover.

THE MAIN THINGS TO REMEMBER ABOUT CHANGING YOUR KID'S BEHAVIOR

There are five keys to fixing your child's behavior. These are included in each makeover in this book, but it's important that you recognize them so you can use them any time you attempt a behavior makeover with your kid. Here are those essential five keys:

1. *Target the behavior.* The first part is the most important: you must identify the specific bad behavior that is driving everyone crazy. Granted, your kid may be displaying a number of behaviors that need fixing, but it's best to work on improving only one—and never more than two—behaviors at a time. That way, you can develop a much more specific behavior plan to eliminate the bad behavior, and you'll also be more likely to succeed at your makeover efforts. So don't say, "He's not behaving." Instead, narrow your focus so you target the specific behavior you want to eliminate, like: "He's been talking back."

2. *Make a solid makeover plan.* Once you have identified the bad behavior, you need a solid makeover plan to stop it. The plan must (1) address your kid's behavior, (2) set out exactly how you will correct it, (3) identify the new behavior to replace it, and (4) describe how you plan to teach it. Plans must be specific to the problem and your child's unique needs. I'll give you all the strategies you need and pose the questions to help you create a precise plan for your kid. All you need to do is follow the steps, and then write your ideas in your Makeover Journal.

3. *Establish a consequence.* If your child continues using the misbehavior, the next thing to do is to set a consequence. It must be fair, appropriate to the kid, fit the crime, and be set ahead so your kid is aware of it. Then it must be enforced *each* time your kid uses the misbehavior. A list of consequences is provided on pages 299–300. Please review the list and refer to it for each makeover.
4. *Commit to change.* Even the best makeover in the world won't work unless you really commit yourself to changing your kid's behavior. And then you must be consistent with your plan so you do succeed.
5. *Extend the commitment to twenty-one days.* If you want to eliminate the bad behavior, you must commit to a twenty-one-day trial period. Don't expect to see overnight success; change just doesn't work like that. Behavior change takes a minimum of twenty-one days of repetition, so hang in there. *And don't give up until you do see positive change.* On the unlikely chance that you do not see change, then review your makeover to be sure you have not overlooked another cause. Also, make sure *your* expectations are ones your child is capable of. And if the bad behavior still continues, please do consult with a trained professional—pediatrician, counselor, or child psychologist—to help you with your makeover endeavors.

TEN BEHAVIOR PRINCIPLES
YOU NEED TO KNOW

Since you have bought this book, let's assume things haven't worked as well as you'd hoped in changing your kid's behavior. It's time to try a new approach. We begin by reviewing a few basic principles of Behavior Makeover 101.

Most behaviors . . .

1. *Are learned.* Some behaviors may be influenced by biological factors, but most are learned. For instance, the

shy kid can learn social skills to become more confident in groups, the aggressive kid can learn anger management skills, and the impulsive kid can learn skills and techniques to stop and think before acting.

2. *Can be changed.* Most behaviors can be changed by using proven research-based techniques.

3. *Need intervention.* Don't expect your child to change on his own. His behavior will most likely only get worse without your intervention. Also, don't think poor behavior is just a phase that he'll outgrow. You're just providing more time for your kid's bad behavior to become a habit, and then it will be even tougher to change.

4. *Take time to change.* Behavior change takes time. Don't expect your Saturday night lecture to make more than a dent in your kid's behavior on Sunday. Give you and your kid time. Remember that learning new behavior habits generally take a minimum of twenty-one days of repetition.

5. *Require commitment.* Long-term commitment is necessary for any meaningful and permanent change. There's no getting around it: parenting is tough work.

6. *Must have a substitute.* No behavior will change permanently unless you teach your child another behavior to replace it. Think about it: if you tell your kid to stop doing one behavior, what will he do instead? Without a substitute behavior, chances are he'll revert to using the old misbehavior.

7. *Require a good example.* Behaviors are learned best by seeing it done right, so make sure your own behaviors or examples are ones that you want your kid to emulate. I call that the Boomerang Effect: what you throw out to your child is like a boomerang that comes back to hit you in the face.

8. *Demand practice.* Behavior change requires practice. You'd never tell a child to go out to throw a pass at a game by just handing him a football when the game is

just starting. You would first have helped him practice for weeks before that. The same is true for learning any other new behavior, so practice, practice, practice until he can do the new behavior on his own.

9. *Benefit from encouragement.* Be encouraging every step along the way: from the willingness to try, the first efforts and small successes, the recoveries from setbacks, to the maximum amount of improvement. Behavior change is hard and deserves to be encouraged, acknowledged, and celebrated.

10. *Are never too late to change.* Even if the problem has been going on a long time, don't despair. Help is on the way.

THE TEN C'S OF CRITICAL CHANGE

You will notice certain recurring techniques in virtually every behavior intervention. They are critical in ensuring the success of each makeover so make sure you use them. I call them the ten C's of Critical Change:

1. *Connect calmly with your child.* Any behavior makeover must start by calmly addressing the child. Eliminate any distractions, take a deep breath to get in control, get eye-to-eye, and make sure you have your kid's full attention. Then you can begin.

2. *Clarify your concerns.* Don't assume your child understands what he did wrong. Briefly describe the problem, why it troubles you, and what behavior you expect instead—for example: "When you used that tone, it was disrespectful. I expect you to talk respectfully."

3. *Commit together to work on the problem.* Emphasize your commitment to work with your kid to help him change. Ideally, you need to be on the same team to succeed.

4. *Coach a new behavior to replace the inappropriate behavior so he knows how to use it successfully.* For instance, don't assume

your kid knows how you want him to talk. The whine may have become such a habit that he has forgotten how to talk without it. "I don't listen to whines. Listen to how my voice sounds. It's how I want you to ask for something. Now you try it."

5. *Correct misbehavior as soon as it occurs.* Don't wait. The moment your kid uses an inappropriate behavior is the time to correct it. Behavior corrections are brief; they describe to the child what he did wrong and show how to correct the action: "I know you were angry, but you may not hit. Next time, tell the person that you are mad and what you want."

6. *Check your kid's progress as you continue the makeover.* Alter your plan if needed.

7. *Choose a consequence if the misbehavior continues.* It should be reasonable, appropriate to the child and crime, and announced ahead: "If you bite again, you will to go to time-out for five minutes."

8. *Carry out the agreed consequence.* In the event there's no change or opposition to the behavior makeover, follow through with the agreed consequence. And do so consistently.

9. *Catch your kid's good behavior efforts.* Don't overlook the simplest and often most effective way to change behavior: "That was a respectful voice. That's the kind I listen to. Good job!"

10. *Congratulate your kid's success whenever positive results are confirmed.* Change is hard—and especially for kids—so celebrate his efforts. And don't forget to congratulate yourself!

LOOKING IN THE MIRROR

No behavior problem is just the kid's problem; it's also a family problem. To help your child best, you need to step back and look at the big picture and ask, "What are all the factors that might be causing my child to misbehave?" The place to start is by taking a good, honest look in the mirror. The image you project can have an enormous influence on your child's behavior. After all, our image is reflected back to our kids, and what they see is what they copy. Before you start planning how to change your kid's behavior, take a serious look at your own.

Here are a few parent makeovers to consider. As you seriously review these questions, write your thoughts in your Makeover Journal. They will be the basis of perhaps the most difficult but important makeover: the one you do on yourself.

When you look in the mirror . . .

- The outer image your child and family see radiates from your inner image, so look deeply inward. What do you see? Are you pleased with your image? What concerns do you have? Note them.
- What image do you want your child and family to see? What do they really see? What might you do to improve that image? Write your thoughts.
- How well do you take care of your appearance? Do you walk around the house with your hair uncombed and wear unkempt clothes? How well do you take care of your health? Your stress? Do you go to pieces, have an extra drink, start screaming and yelling when the pressures of family, work, and parenting get to be too much? Or can you hold it together, take a nap, go for a walk, kiss your husband, practice yoga, exercise, or make a joke? How well do you take care of your spirituality? Your intellectual growth? Your interests? Your family? Your relationships? What concerns you most? How do they affect your child? What can you do to nourish the images that are most important to you? Write your plan.
- If your child had only your behavior to watch, what would he see? Which of your behaviors does he copy most? Smoking a cigarette? Gossiping? Reading a book? Exercising? Singing? Putting down friends and neighbors?

Drinking? Telling racial jokes? Swearing? Is it an image that you want your kid to copy? If not, what can you do to improve it so your kid has a better example?

- What are your greatest parenting strengths? Do you listen openly, have a sense of humor, handle frustrations calmly, accept your kid unconditionally? List all of your strengths. Does your child see those strengths? Which of those strengths might enhance your kid's behavior or improve his character? Do you project those strengths to your family regularly? If not, why not? Write what you will do to tune up your strengths.

- What are your parenting weaknesses? What triggers your weaknesses? How do those images affect your kid's behavior? Write how you will make over your most troublesome image right now.

- What behavior problem in your kid are you most concerned about? Why? Do you have the same problem your kid has? Does anyone else in your family have this problem? Did you have it when you were your kid's age? How did your parents react? Did it help? How did people react to you? How did you feel about their reactions? How did you try to solve the problem? Did it work? What didn't work? Why?

- How is your relationship with your spouse or your kid's other parent? Are you presenting the model you'd like your child to copy and use with his kids? Do you fight with your partner in front of your kids? Come to blows? Name-call or insult? Swear? What will you do to improve your relationship with your spouse to help your kid?

- When you look in that mirror, do you see a person who uses your kids as a pawn in your quarrels with your partner? Do you try to get your kids to take sides, confide in them about adult issues, or manipulate them in your own domestic war? Ring any bells? If so, think how it is damaging your child. What will you do to change? Write it.

- Do you think your child might be acting out some of the pain or conflict you can see in that mirror? Is your kid responding to your own behavior or the unresolved conflicts in your relationship? Is he trying to tell you something about yourself or your marriage?

- How do you respond to your child when he misbehaves? How does he react to your response? What message does it send to your kid? Is it effective? If so, why? If not, what could you do to make things better? Describe what steps you're willing to take.

- How was discipline handled in your family as you were growing up? How did it affect your behavior? What is the most common method you use to discipline your child? How effective is it in enhancing her behavior? What improvements would you like to make?

- What would you like your greatest legacy to be for your child? What will you do to ensure that your child attains that legacy? Write a letter to yourself describing your hopes and dreams for your child—the legacy you would like to leave. Reread your letter often.

YOUR OWN BEHAVIOR MAKEOVER

Our daily actions—from our looks, our choices, our words, as well as the way we treat our kids, spouse, friends, colleagues, neighbors—have a major influence on our kid's behaviors in more ways than we ever realize. On the lines that follow, write the most important thing you'd like to change in yourself that would also have a positive influence your child's behavior. Then write an action plan in your Makeover Journal that describes the specific steps you'll take to make that change happen:

_____

_____

_____

PART 3

Thirty-Eight Behavior Makeovers

People seldom improve when they have no model to copy but themselves.
—Anonymous

1

Anger

I 'm really starting to worry about my eleven year old. He's a great kid with a good heart, but has such a temper! Whenever he's upset, he kicks and punches anyone or anything in sight. I've tried withholding privileges, giving lectures, and even spanking him, but nothing's working. He starts middle school soon, and I'm afraid he's going to be the class terror or expelled.

—Kamil, a mom of four from Las Vegas, Nevada

"I'm really worried about him. He gets himself so worked up when he's mad."

"I'm afraid he's going to get in serious trouble: he lashes out so quickly when he's angry."

> **BEHAVIOR TIP**
>
> If we want our kids to be calmer, we need to help them identify why they're upset and teach them anger management skills.

"If she could just tell the other kids she's upset, but she scratches and pinches instead."

Clenched teeth. Rapid breathing. Red face. Teaching kids a new way to cope with their intense feelings is not easy, especially if they have practiced only aggressive ways of dealing with their frustrations. The good news is that although violence is learned, so is calmness. Learning any new habit takes time, especially expressing anger more constructively, so don't give up! If you're consistent, you'll be able to help your kid learn a healthier way to handle anger. You may also be able to help him discover the source of his anger.

FOUR STEPS TO SQUELCH INAPPROPRIATE ANGER

Here are four steps to guide you in squelching inappropriate anger in your kid and teaching him healthier ways to express it.

Step 1. Identify Anger Warning Signs

Explain to your child that we all have our own little signs that warn us we're getting angry and that we should listen to them because they can help us stay out of trouble. Next, help your child recognize what specific warning signs she may have that tell her she's starting to get upset—for example, "It looks like you're tense. Your hands are in a fist. Do you feel yourself starting to get angry?" Anger escalates very quickly; if a kid waits until he is in meltdown to get himself back into control, he's too late—and so are you to try and help him.

Step 2. Recognize Potential Anger Triggers

Every kid has certain cues that trigger deeper frustrations and unresolved conflicts that may resort in angry outbursts. For example, your child may feel unappreciated in your family or inadequate in a competitive classroom environment, or may suffer from low self-esteem. The key is to identify what causes the anger in your kid and help him be aware of it when it occurs.

Step 3. Develop a Feeling Vocabulary

Many kids display aggression such as kicking, screaming, hitting, and biting because they simply don't know how to express their frustrations any other way. They need an emotion vocabulary to express how they feel, and you can help your kid develop one. Here are a few: *angry, upset, mad, frustrated, agitated, furious, apprehensive, tense, nervous, anxious, irritated, furious, ticked off, irate.* When your child is angry, use the words so that he can apply them to real life: "Looks like you're really angry. Want to talk about it?" "You seem really irritated. Do you need to walk it off?"

Step 4. Teach Healthy Anger Management Skills

If you want your kid to handle anger more appropriately, then you must teach her a new behavior to substitute for the inappropriate one she now uses:

- *Use self-talk.* Teach him an affirmation: a simple, positive message he says to himself in stressful situations—for example: "Stop and calm down," "Stay in control," "I can handle this."
- *Tear anger away.* Tell your child to draw or write what is upsetting him on a piece of paper, then tear it into little pieces and "throw the anger away." He can also use the concept by imagining that his anger is slowly leaving him in little pieces.
- *Teach abdominal breath control.* Teach the method with your child sitting in a comfortable position, her back straight and pressed into a chair for support. Show her how to inhale slowly to a count of five, pause for two counts, then slowly breathe out the same way, again counting to five. Repeating the sequence creates maximum relaxation.
- *Teach "1 + 3 + 10."* Explain the formula: "As soon as you feel your body sending you a warning sign that says you're losing control, do three things. First, stop and say: 'Be

calm.' That's 1. Now take three deep, slow breaths from
your tummy. That's 3. Finally, count slowly to ten inside
your head. That's 10. Put them all together and you have
1 + 3 + 10, and that helps you calm down and get back
in control."

Step 5. Use Time-Out When Inappropriate Anger Persists

Although you've taught your child alternative strategies to handle strong emotions, old behaviors take time to replace.
Meanwhile, you can't let your kid continue to display inappropriate anger. Explain that while it's okay to be angry, he must
use words, not his fists, to tell how he feels. If that doesn't work,
refer to pages 299–300 for a list of appropriate consequences.

BEHAVIOR MAKEOVER PLAN

Your behavior is a living textbook to your child, so the first
place to start a behavior makeover is by reflecting on your
own style of responding to anger. These questions might help:
How did your parents handle anger? How do you typically
deal with anger? Where did you learn that style? Does it work
or not work for you? How well are you modeling anger management to your child? How about other members of your

family? What lessons might your kid be learning from these actions? How do you typically respond to your child's anger? Is it effective? What would you like to change? Write your thoughts, and then make a plan for how you will change.

Now it's time to take action to begin making over your child's behavior. Use your Makeover Journal to write down your thoughts and develop your plan:

1. Take a really close look at how well your child controls anger. How our kids act is often a symptom of deeper issues. Here are a few warning signs that mean a child needs a more intensive makeover in anger. How many of these behaviors describe your child?

Anger Warning Signs

_____ Unable to explain how she is feeling when she's upset

_____ Has frequent angry outbursts, even over minor issues

_____ Has trouble calming down when he is frustrated or angry

_____ Turns her anger into a tantrum (for example, by shouting, kicking, swearing, spitting)

_____ Has difficulty bouncing back from a frustrating situation

_____ Frequently fights or hits others

_____ Acts without thinking and many times behaves recklessly

_____ Is often sullen and silent and holds her feelings in

_____ Verbalizes, writes about, or draws pictures of violent or aggressive acts

2. Watch your kid's anger outbursts closely over the next week. Consider tracking the frequency of incidents on a chart or a calendar or in a journal. It may help you tune into what

may be provoking the outbursts. What, if anything, can you do to reduce them? Write down your thoughts.

3. Reread Step One. Notice what physiological signs your child displays *immediately before* he displays anger. Jot down your observations, and then share them with your kid to help him recognize his warning signs.

4. Review Step Two. What are the potential sources of your kid's anger? List them. Which ones can be eliminated? Which ones can be dealt with? Write down your strategy for helping your child deal with inevitable sources of anger.

5. Review Step Three. Does your kid have an adequate emotional vocabulary to express his feelings? If not, plan ways to boost this kind of vocabulary.

6. Review Step Four, and choose an anger management strategy to teach. List the days and times you plan to designate for practice times, and then continue reviewing the technique until your kid can use it without you.

7. The unhealthy way your kid responds to anger must be replaced. Review Step Five. What consequences will you set to help extinguish his incorrect behavior? See pages 299–300.

Anger is normal, but when you see an ongoing trend, when it starts crippling your child's relationships in your family or with others, or when you notice sudden behavior changes that aren't due to illness or medication, *use your instincts and get help.*

➡ See also *Anxiety, Hitting, Temper Tantrums, Yelling.*

MAKEOVER PLEDGE

How will you use the five steps and the Behavior Makeover Plan to help your kid achieve long-term change in handling anger more constructively? On the following lines, write exactly what you agree to do within the next twenty-four hours to begin your kid's behavior makeover.

_____

_____

_____

MAKEOVER RESULTS

All behavior makeovers take hard work, constant practice, and parental reinforcement. Each step your kid takes toward change may be a small one, so be sure to acknowledge and congratulate every one of them along the way. It takes a minimum of twenty-one days to see real results, so don't give up too soon. Remember that if one strategy doesn't work, another will. Write your child's weekly progress on the lines below. Keep track of daily progress in your Makeover Journal.

Week 1

_____

_____

_____

Week 2

_____

_____

_____

Week 3

_____

_____

_____

RESOURCES

Angry Kids: Understanding and Managing the Emotions That Control Them, by Richard L. Berry (New York: Fleming H. Revell Co., 2001). Discusses the root causes of anger in kids and explains ways parents can help them learn techniques for expressing and defusing that anger.

The Angry Child: Regaining Control When Your Child Is Out of Control, by Tim Murphy and Loriann Hoff Oberlin (New York: Clarkson Potter, 2001). Easy-to-follow strategies that help kids manage anger and help parents recognize signs of serious problems.

When Anger Hurts Your Kids: A Parent's Guide, by Patrick McKay (New York: Fine Communications, 1996). A superb guide explaining how parents' anger affects kids and offers ways to regain control.

When I Feel Angry, by Cornelia Maude Spelman (Morton, Grove, Ill.: Albert Whitman & Co., 2000). A gentle book that puts an adorable bunny in a variety of situations that provoke anger. Instead of acting out, the bunny and her friends find constructive ways to deal with the anger. Ages 4 to 8.

Hot Stuff to Help Kids Chill Out: The Anger Management Book, by Jerry Wilde (Kansas City, Mo.: Landmark Productions, 1997). A book that speaks directly to kids and adolescents and provides clear guidelines to help them handle hot tempers more constructively.

Anger Management Workbook for Kids and Teens, by Anita Bohensky (New York: Growth Publications, 2001). Teaches effective coping behaviors to help stop the escalation of anger and resolve conflicts.

Anxiety

I'm really worried about my daughter. She's only ten but already seems so stressed. Right before a test, she's an absolute basket case: she can't sleep, is anxious, and cries. I'm afraid to talk to her before her soccer games—she's so moody. I can't imagine how she's ever going to handle middle school at the rate she's going.

—Raoul, a dad from Kansas City, Missouri

BEHAVIOR TIP

You can help control the amount of anxiety in your kid's life. Be sure your dreams and expectations stimulate and inspire, rather than overwhelm and defeat, her. Also, be sure that bullying, school violence, or tragic world events are not diminishing your child's sense of well-being.

Rapid breathing.
Fear of leaving home.
Pounding heart.
Sleeplessness.

Think stress is just for adults? Think again. Studies show that today's kids are feeling a lot more pressure than we think they are. Stress symptoms are showing up in kids as young as three years of age. Overscheduled days, competition, school, treadmill-paced lives, home problems, scary nightly news, and stressed-out parents are just a few contributors. One thing is certain: stress is part of life, and some kids actually do seem to thrive on it. The critical parenting question is this: *Does the stress stimulate my child or paralyze her?*

FOUR STEPS TO
REDUCE ANXIETY

Use the following as a guide to minimizing your kid's anxiety.

Step 1. Identify Potential Anxiety Triggers
The first step to eliminating anxiety in your child is to see what is causing the pressure. Begin by listening to your kid's concerns and complaints. Don't minimize or dismiss any of her worries. Instead, listen quietly. Then spend a week evaluating your child's daily schedule of school, home, and extracurricular activities (sports, dance, church group, music). How much free time does your child have left?

Step 2. Eliminate Those Stressors That You Can
Cutting out just one thing in your child's weekly activity may make a tremendous difference in reducing her stress and anxiety. It could be an activity that *you* want but may not be a top priority for her.

Step 3. Deal with Stressors You Can't Eliminate

Some stressors are beyond your control. For example, even if you turn off the TV, you child will still hear about devastating world events. But you can help your kid cope with the realities of life by reassuring him that you and the other people in his life are doing their best to keep him safe.

Step 4. Teach Healthy Ways to Deal with Inevitable Anxiety

Anxiety is an inevitable part of life for us all, and kids can learn to use some of the techniques that we adults use to cope with pressure. Here are four anxiety-reducing techniques:

- *Self-talk.* Teach your child to say a statement inside her head to help her stay calm and handle the stress. Here are a few: "Chill out, calm down." "I can do this." "Stay calm and breathe slowly." "It's nothing I can't handle."
- *Elevator breathing.* This one works if your kid has ever ridden in an elevator. Tell him to close his eyes, slowly breath out three times, and then imagine he's in an elevator on the top of a very tall building. He presses the button for the first floor and watches the buttons for each level slowly light up as the elevator goes down. As the elevator descends, his stress fades away.
- *Stress melting.* Ask your kid to find the spot in his body where he feels the most tension—perhaps his neck, shoulder muscles, or jaw. He then closes his eyes, concentrates on the spot, tensing it up for three or four seconds, and then lets it go. Tell him to imagine the stress slowly melting away as he does so.
- *Visualize a calm place.* Ask your kid to think of a place he has been to where he feels peaceful—for instance, the beach, his bed, grandpa's backyard, a tree house. When anxiety kicks in, tell him to close his eyes and imagine that spot, while breathing slowly.

No More Misbehavin'

DID YOU KNOW?

Data show that between 8 and 10 percent of American children are seriously troubled by anxiety. Anxious kids are two to four times more likely to develop depression, and as teens they are much more likely to become involved with substance abuse. The good news is that studies have shown that about 90 percent of all anxious children can be greatly helped by learning coping skills.

BEHAVIOR MAKEOVER PLAN

What kind of life have you created for your child? For instance, do you expect him to excel academically, athletically, artistically, or all the above? Do you expect him to have the most playing time on the field? Do you expect him to have the highest scores on standardized tests? Think how much pressure you're putting on your kid. Is it healthy? What can you do to lighten the pressure before it explodes? What will you do? Write a plan.

Now it's time to take action to begin making over your kid's behavior. Use your Makeover Journal to write down your thoughts and develop your plan.

1. Watch your child a bit closer over the next few days for anxiety. Signs of overload can include a change in sleep patterns, refusal to eat, moodiness, recurring physical ailments, trouble concentrating, restlessness, social withdrawal, nail biting, acting out, aggression, regression to baby-like behavior, nausea, excessive whining, or crying. What signs concern you? List them.

2. Notice what kinds of situations create the most anxiety for him. For instance, is it school violence in the next community, bullying, an upcoming test, world events? List them.
3. What can you to reduce his anxiety? For example, if you determine there's a serious physical threat to his safety, should you move him to a different school? If test taking causes stress because she thinks she'll fail, talk to her teacher, hire a tutor, or help her study. Make an action plan, and then act on it.
4. David Elkind, author of *The Hurried Child,* says one of the easiest ways to reduce stress is by cutting out just one extra activity. If overscheduling is producing stress, decide with your child which activity you will cut. When will you do it?
5. Review Step Four, and decide which one you think will work best with your child. Then rehearse and practice the strategy with your child until she can remember to use the technique during a stressful time.
6. Continue to keep a close watch on your child's stress level. If you don't see change, check with a trained professional.

➡ See also *Anger, Cynicism, Overperfectionism.*

MAKEOVER PLEDGE

How will you use the four steps and the Behavior Makeover Plan to help your child achieve long-term change in reducing stress? On the lines below, write exactly what you agree to do within the next twenty-four hours to begin your kid's behavior makeover.

_____

_____

_____

MAKEOVER RESULTS

All behavior makeovers take hard work, constant practice, and parental reinforcement. Each step your kid takes toward change may be a small one, so be sure to acknowledge and congratulate every one of them along the way. It takes a minimum of twenty-one days to see real results, so don't give up too soon. Remember that if one strategy doesn't work, another will. Write your child's weekly progress on the lines below. Keep track of daily progress in your Makeover Journal.

Week 1

_____

_____

_____

Week 2

_____

_____

_____

Week 3

_____

_____

_____

RESOURCES

Kidstress, by Georgia Witkin (New York: Viking, 1999). What causes kids' stress and practical ideas to alleviate it.

Stress and Your Child, by Bettie B. Youngs (New York: Fawcett, 1995). Stress management strategies for kids to use at home and school.

The Hurried Child: Growing Up Too Fast Too Soon, by David Elkind (Reading, Mass.: Addison-Wesley, 1981). Published over two decades ago, this classic is still pertinent today.

The Over-Scheduled Child: Avoiding the Hyper-Parenting Trap, by Alvin Rosenfeld and Nicole Wise (New York: Griffin Trade, 2001). The authors make a compelling argument against what they consider "hyperparenting" and the impact it has on kids.

Your Anxious Child: How Parents and Teachers Can Relieve Anxiety in Children, by John S. Dacey and Lisa B. Fiore (San Francisco: Jossey-Bass, 2000). Proven ways to help kids handle stress and cope with difficulties more confidently.

Don't Pop Your Cork on Mondays: The Children's Anti-Stress Book, by Adolph J. Moser (Kansas City, Mo.: Landmark Editions, 1988). A wonderfully informative handbook that explores the causes and effects of stress and offers practical approaches for dealing with stress factors. Ages 7 to 12.

Biting

My three year old's preschool teacher told us he bit a little girl three times last week. Apparently, he wants to play with her and bites when she won't let him. If he doesn't stop, he won't be able to attend the school. How do we make him stop biting so he doesn't get expelled when he's only three years old? This is so embarrassing!

—Cindy, a mother of two from Denver, Colorado

"I'm mortified. My neighbor told me my daughter bit her child!"

"When my son's upset, he bites me. I feel like I raising a vampire!"

> **BEHAVIOR TIP**
> Kids usually bite because they lack the ability to handle their frustrations. It's up to us to help find better ways to get their point across.

"There's a boy at my daughter's day care who bites the other kids whenever he's mad. Should my child have a tetanus shot?"

Biting is among the most bothersome and embarrassing kid behaviors. Take comfort in knowing that the behavior is usually temporary and much more common than you may think. Infants and toddlers often bite to relieve teething or gum soreness, or think it's just a game. Preschoolers typically bite because they haven't yet developed the coping skills to deal with stress appropriately or the verbal skills to express their needs. Nevertheless, whatever the reason, the behavior is clearly upsetting to all involved, and it has been known to continue as kids get older if it is not dealt with. Your job is to nip this behavior before it becomes a habit.

FOUR STEPS TO ELIMINATE BITING

You can use the following four steps to squelch biting and other aggressive behaviors.

Step 1. Confront the Biter Immediately, and Set a Consequence

Intervene the minute your child bites. For preverbal kids, label the behavior so they learn the term: "That's biting!" Then in a very stern voice say, "You may not bite people!" Firmly express your disapproval, and quickly remove him from the situation. No matter what you hear from other parents, do *not* bite your kid back! It is not helpful, and in fact, you're only sending him the message that kids aren't allowed to bite but adults are.

If your kid has developed a history of biting, you'll need to take emergency action. Arrange a private meeting with your child and other caregivers (such as teacher, coach, day care worker, babysitter) with whom he's displaying the behavior. Create a consequence everyone understands: this could be the loss of a privilege, time-out, or going home. Then make sure the agreed-on consequence is consistently enforced.

Step 2. Comfort the Victim, and Boost Empathy

Kids always need to know that their biting hurts other people. In the presence of your kid, focus your concern on the victim: "I'm so sorry! That must hurt. What can I do to help?" In this way, you model to your child how to convey sympathy. If possible, find a way to help your child make amends for his misdeed. He might help wash the spot of the bite on the victim, offer the child a tissue or Band-Aid, draw a picture to apologize, say he's sorry, or offer to share a toy with the injured child. Also, apologize to the child's parents on the spot or with a phone call.

Step 3. Teach a New Behavior to Replace the Biting

If your toddler is teething, she's probably biting because of sore gums. In that case, offer something appropriate to bite on to relieve the discomfort: perhaps a frozen juice bar, a hard plastic teething ring, or a chewy toy.

Kids often bite because they haven't developed the verbal skills to communicate their needs or frustrations. Identify what skill your child lacks, and then teach a more appropriate way to respond that will replace the urge to bite. Practice the new skill together until he can successfully use it on his own. One youngster bit because he didn't know how to say he wanted a turn. Once his dad recognized the problem, he taught his son to say, "It's your turn, then it's my turn." The biting quickly stopped. If your child has trouble verbalizing feelings or needs, teach him to say, "I'm getting mad" or "I want to play." Remember to let him know how proud you are when he uses good control.

Step 4. Anticipate Biting Behavior:
The Best Prevention

If your child has developed a pattern of biting, supervise play closely. You can then immediately intervene and stop it before it happens. Put your hand gently over his mouth firmly, saying, "You may not bite. Use your words to tell what you need." Then model how by saying, "I want a turn." Distract a preverbal kid from the situation or offer an alternative: "Would you like to play with the clay or blocks?" You may have to step in a few times before the behavior is stopped, so watch closely, and then intervene immediately.

BEHAVIOR MAKEOVER PLAN

Talk to other parents to see if they are having similar behavior problems with their children. If so, how do they respond when their kids bite? Do they feel their response stops the behavior? If biting is not a new problem, talk to other care-

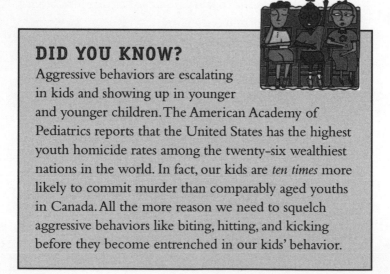

DID YOU KNOW?
Aggressive behaviors are escalating in kids and showing up in younger and younger children. The American Academy of Pediatrics reports that the United States has the highest youth homicide rates among the twenty-six wealthiest nations in the world. In fact, our kids are *ten times* more likely to commit murder than comparably aged youths in Canada. All the more reason we need to squelch aggressive behaviors like biting, hitting, and kicking before they become entrenched in our kids' behavior.

No More Misbehavin'

givers in your kid's world: teachers, day care workers, baby-sitters, his friends' parents. Are they seeing the same behavior? If biting is happening only outside your home, what's different about those other environments? Could he be learning this behavior at school, in the neighborhood, or at day care? Is your child overly frustrated, feeling insecure, or anxious in that environment? Is there a change you could make in your child's environment to stop this behavior?

Now it's time to take action to begin making over your kid's behavior. Use your Makeover Journal to write down your thoughts and develop your plan:

1. How do you typically respond to your kid's biting? Why do you think it isn't working? Next, reread Steps One and Two for more effective ways to respond. Plan what you will do so the next time your kid bites, you'll be ready to act on your plan.
2. Review Step Three. Is there a behavior he needs to learn to replace the biting? If so, think through how and when you will teach him the new skill.
3. Reread Step Four. Watch your kid to see if there's any pattern in his behavior. Consider his mood right before he bites. Do you think he's bored, frustrated, excited, tired, hungry, scared, overloaded, or something else? Once you identify why he's biting, make a plan to reduce what's provoking him to do so. For instance, if he has trouble in larger groups, try a smaller play group until he develops better coping skills, or try limiting the number of kids you invite to the house to play at one time.
4 Keep track of how often your kid bites to make sure the behavior is diminishing over time. If you've consistently used the techniques to end this aggressive behavior and it still persists, get outside help from a professional, especially if your kid is school age.

➡ See also *Anger, Anxiety, Bossiness, Hitting, Temper Tantrums.*

MAKEOVER PLEDGE

How will you use the four steps and the Behavior Makeover Plan to help your kid achieve long-term change? On the lines below, write exactly what you agree to do within the next twenty-four hours to begin your kid's behavior makeover.

_____

_____

_____

MAKEOVER RESULTS

All behavior makeovers take hard work, constant practice, and parental reinforcement. Each step your kid takes toward change may be a small one, so be sure to acknowledge and congratulate every one of them along the way. It takes a minimum of twenty-one days to see real results, so don't give up too soon. Remember that if one strategy doesn't work, another will. Write your child's weekly progress on the lines below. Keep track of daily progress in your Makeover Journal.

Week 1

_____

_____

_____

Week 2

_____

_____

_____

Week 3

_____

_____

_____

RESOURCES

Good Behavior, by Stephen Garber, Marianne Daniels Garber, and Robyn Freedman Spitzman (New York: Villard Books, 1987). An excellent parent resource on what to do about aggressive kid behaviors, as well as dozens more concerns.

Touchpoints: Your Child's Emotional and Behavioral Development, by T. Berry Brazelton (Reading, Mass.: Addison-Wesley, 1992). A reassuring guide written by the renowned pediatrician. A must that should be on every parent's nightstand.

Toddler Taming: A Survival Guide for Parents, by Christopher Green (New York: Fawcett Books, 1998). Practical advice mixed with humor for how to cope with those difficulties that turn your sweet baby into a holy terror.

Bootsie Barker Bites, by Barbara Bottner (New York: Putnam, 1992). Bootsie wants to play games in which she bites—until her friend lets her know her behavior is not appreciated. Ages 3 to 7.

No Fighting, No Biting, by Else Homelund Minarik (New York: HarperCollins, 1987). Delightfully illustrated by Maurice Sendak, this much-loved tale helps kids find out why Rosa and Willy are like two little alligators. Also addresses sibling rivalry. Ages 4 to 8.

Don't Pop Your Cork on Mondays: The Children's Anti-Stress Book, by Adolph Moser (Kansas City, Mo.: Landmark Editions, 1988). Practical, appealing, and popular with kids, it also offers sound strategies for how to handle stress in healthy ways. Ages 7 to 12.

BEHAVIOR 4

Bossiness

We have an eleven year old who has turned out to be very domineering. She dictates to her friends and wants everything to go her way. She might make a great CEO someday, but if she doesn't temper her "overly assertive spirit" now, she's going to end up with no friends at all.
—Eileen, a mother from Manchester, New Hampshire

BEHAVIOR TIP
Bossiness may be an indication of insecurity, low self-esteem, need for approval, poor social skills, and other underlying issues. We can help kids recognize these issues and learn to deal with them with more acceptable behaviors.

"My way or the highway."
"You better come over right now."
"Nobody gets to use this bat except me."

Bossy kids appoint themselves to be in charge. They set the rules, choose the activities, and decide the game plan. And very rarely do they bother listening to their peers' suggestions. Although their dictatorial skills may be the makings of a strong leader someday, right now they are usually highly unappreciated by peers. We can't change a domineering kid's spirit, but we can teach behaviors so they can take their peers' feelings into consideration. In the process, they certainly will boost their "likeability quotient" and social success.

THREE STEPS TO MINIMIZE BOSSINESS

Use the following steps as a guide to help your kid minimize overly domineering behaviors:

Step 1. Expect Cooperative Behavior

Research shows that kids who demonstrate cooperative behaviors—such as sharing, taking turns, and taking into consideration the requests of peers—usually do so because their parents clearly emphasized that they expect this behavior. So take time to spell out your ground rules for sharing and cooperation, and explain them to your child. Then expect that your kid will use them. Here are examples of how parents have spelled out their requirements for less bossiness and more cooperation:

- *Explain taking turns.* If you want your kid to take turns and share, clarify your expectations. For taking turns, you can say, "Let's make sure to take turns when we play. You go first, then it'll be Sally's turn, then mine." For sharing, say, "Share your computer game so Ryan has a chance to play. He doesn't want to just watch you, so switch sides every ten minutes."

- *Set one sharing rule.* One dad passed on his rule: "If it belongs to you and it's in sight, then you must share it."
- *Share only your belongings.* Emphasize that you may share only items that belong to you; otherwise, permission must be granted from the owner. Without permission, it may not be shared: "I'm sorry, we can't play with that. It belongs to my brother, so it's not something I can share."
- *Put away prized possessions.* There are certain possessions that are very special to your child, so putting those items away before a guest arrives minimizes potential conflicts.

Step 2. Teach Strategies to Be More Cooperative

Bossy kids want things to go their way. They don't stop to ponder what the other kid may want. Here are a few strategies to help your kid learn to consider the other kid's desires:

- *Flip a coin.* This one is great when two kids can't decide on rules, who gets to choose what to do, or even who goes first.
- *Teach that the guest goes first.* One simple rule of cooperation is to enforce that the guest always chooses first. If your kid is the host, he must ask his guest to select the first game or activity.
- *Use "Grandma's Rule."* The rule is simple and works like a charm to makes things fairer: "If *you* cut the cake, the other person decides which piece to take." The rule can apply to lots of things—for example: if you chose the game, the other person gets to go first; if you poured the lemonade, the other person chooses his glass first.
- *Use a timer.* Teach kids to agree on a set amount of time— usually only a few minutes—for using an item. Oven timers or sand timers are great devices for younger kids to use. Older kids can use the minute hands on their watches. When the time is up, the item is passed on.

Step 3. Extinguish Bossy Behaviors

The fastest way to increase a good behavior is by "catching" your child acting right, so tune in to your child's actions and reinforce her cooperative efforts. Always remember to describe what she did so she'll be more likely to repeat the behavior: "I noticed how you divided the toys so you both had the same amount" or "I heard you ask Tim what he wanted to play." Reinforcement will gradually help diminish her bossy attitude, replacing it with more cooperative behaviors. If your child continues to display bossy behaviors, then consider applying an appropriate consequence. See pages 299–302.

BEHAVIOR MAKEOVER PLAN

Start by thinking about your own personality. For instance, are you easy-going, domineering, independent, bossy, fun-loving, or a take-charge kind of person? How about your partner? Your other kids? How much of your child's bossy behavior is a result of imitating you or because of other underlying issues? (See the Behavior Tip on p. 40.) Draw two columns on a sheet of paper: one for what you might be modeling and the other for potential emotional or social problems your kid may

DID YOU KNOW?

The National Center for Clinical Infant Program has said that kids' emotional and social abilities are better predictors of school success than the amount of facts a kid knows or whether he or she learns to read early. More important are knowing what kind of behavior is expected, how to control impulsive urges, wait and take turns, ask teachers for help, follow directions, and express needs while getting along with other kids. Does your child need help learning any of these?

be having (like low self-esteem, anger, no friends, or poor social skills). Check the biggest priorities for immediate action. Make a plan by consulting other behaviors in this book and the resources in each section.

Now it's time to take action to begin making over your kid's behavior. Use your Makeover Journal to write down your thoughts and develop your plan.

1. What bossy behaviors does your kid display that bug you? Why do they bug you? What can you do to temper that one annoying behavior? Write a plan.
2. Think about the positive aspects of being bossy. Although you may be seeing only the negative, annoying parts of this trait, how might a domineering personality actually help your child in life?
3. How do you typically react to this bossy trait? How does your kid respond to your reaction? Why has your response not been effective in changing your kid's behavior? Think how responding differently could produce more favorable results.
4. Is your kid aware when she is displaying bossy behavior? If not, develop a quiet signal (pulling on your ear or touching your nose) that only you and your kid are aware of. Each time she displays the behavior, use the code to signal to her that her behavior is inappropriate.
5. Does your kid understand why her bossiness is not appreciated and turns people off? Think how you might explain this so she is more willing to temper her bossy ways. Outline the main points this discussion might cover.
6. Review the three steps, and then choose one or two strategies to teach your kid. Plan to practice the strategy at home several times until he is comfortable using it with peers.

➡ See also *Anger, Anxiety, Lack of Friends, Rudeness, Selfishness.*

MAKEOVER PLEDGE

How will you use the three steps and the Behavior Makeover Plan to help your kid achieve long-term change? On the lines below, write exactly what you agree to do within the next twenty-four hours to begin your kid's behavior makeover.

_____

_____

_____

MAKEOVER RESULTS

All behavior makeovers take hard work, constant practice, and parental reinforcement. Each step your kid takes toward change may be a small one, so be sure to acknowledge and congratulate every one of them along the way. It takes a minimum of twenty-one days to see real results, so don't give up too soon. Remember that if one strategy doesn't work, another will. Write your child's weekly progress on the lines below. Keep track of daily progress in your Makeover Journal.

Week 1

_____

_____

_____

Week 2

_____

_____

_____

Week 3

RESOURCES

Parenting the Strong-Willed Child, by Rex Foreland and Nicholas Long (New York: McGraw-Hill, 1996). A program to help parents of strong-willed kids find positive and managcable solutions to their kids' difficult behavior.

Raising Your Spirited Child: A Guide for Parents Whose Child Is More Intense, Sensitive, Perceptive, Persistent, and Energetic, by Mary Sheedy Kurcinka (New York: HarperCollins, 1992). Redefining the "difficult" kid as "spirited," Kurcinka provides tools to understand your own temperament as well as your child's and then gives readers specific tools to help work with their kids. Also helpful is the *Raising Your Spirited Child Workbook* by the same author.

The Challenging Child: Understanding, Raising, and Enjoying the Five "Difficult" Types of Children, by Stanley I. Greenspan and Jacqueline Salmon (Cambridge, Mass.: Perseus Press, 1996). Calm and reassuring advice that helps parents deal with all types of difficult kids.

Bartholomew the Bossy, by Marjorie Weinman Sharmat and Normand Chartier (New York: Atheneum, 1984). The perfect book to help young kids realize that their bossiness isn't always appreciated. Ages 3 to 8.

Franklin Is Bossy (Franklin Series), by Paulette Boourgeois (Toronto: Kids Can Press, 1994). Franklin the turtle learns that no one likes a bossy friend. Perfect for ages 3 to 7.

Little Miss Bossy (Mr. Men and Little Miss), by Roger Hargreaves (New York: Price Stern Sloan Publications, 1998). Simple text helps youngsters realize the need to treat friends nicer. Ages 3 to 6.

5

Bullied

A boy at school is terrorizing my nine year old—that's the only way I can describe what's happening. He's broken his glasses, threatens to beat him up, trips him in the cafeteria, and calls him horrible names. My son begs to stay home from school and pleads with me not to tell his teacher, who I guess is unaware of this criminal. He says it will only make it worse, and I'm beginning to believe him. I'm heartsick. What do I do?

—Jenny, a single mom from Tampa, Florida

BEHAVIOR TIP

The best way to bully-proof your kid is to help her develop a tough inner strength and strong assertive skills so she'll be less likely to be victimized and can stand up for herself.

"There's a ten year old at camp who put my child through hell."

"My daughter is so afraid of a fourth grader in our neighborhood that she's begging us to move."

"My son can't take this anymore. I'm sending him to another school."

One of the universal dreams we parents have is that our kids will get along with others. The alarming rise in bullying has turned many of our dreams into nightmares: too many kids today are verbally, emotionally, sexually, or physically abused by other children's intentional actions. And data show that bullying is not only increasing but is far more vicious. Although we can't prevent the pain these experiences can cause, we can lessen our kids' chances of becoming victims. Studies say the best way to do that is by empowering kids with strategies to handle bullying.

FOUR STEPS TO HANDLE BULLIES

Use the following steps as a guide to help your kid deal with bullies.

Step 1. Listen Empathically and Gather Facts

The first step is often the hardest for parents: listen calmly to your kid's story without interrupting. Your goal is to try to figure out what happened, where and when the bullying took place, how frequently this is happening, who was involved, whether anyone helped, and why your kid is being targeted. Also find out *how* your kid responded to the bully. These facts will help you find the best way to help your kid deal with his tormentor. Keep a record of these incidents in case you need to meet with school officials, the bully's parents, or law enforcement officers.

Do empathize with your child and take his complaints seriously. Assure him that chances are he did nothing to provoke the incident and that you will help him find ways to feel safe. Please don't blame or belittle his feelings by saying, "There's nothing to be afraid of," or "Just toughen up." Bullying is frightening and humiliating. If you suspect your kid is being bullied and isn't telling you, I've included a few possible indicators. Check the ones that apply to your child:

Warning Signs of Being Bullied

_____   Unexplained bruises or scrapes, torn clothing
_____   Unexplained loss of toys, school supplies, clothing, lunches, or money
_____   Doesn't want to go to school; wants you there at dismissal
_____   Suddenly sullen, evasive, or displays out-of-character behavior
_____   Onset of headaches, stomachaches, or anxiety
_____   Difficulty sleeping, has nightmares or bed wetting, or is overtired
_____   Begins bullying siblings or younger kids
_____   Ravenous when he comes home (lunch money or lunch may be stolen)
_____   Afraid to be left alone or suddenly clingy

Talk to your child if you suspect a problem: he may be embarrassed to tell you. Then decide if you should inform school officials of your concerns. Don't promise your child you'll keep this a secret: you may have to step in to protect his safety.

Step 2. Set a Plan to Ensure Safety

Based on the facts you gathered, you must now plan how to reduce the chances of your kid's getting hurt. Here are a few options you can share with your kid depending on the situation:

- *Stay near others.* Bullying usually happens during unsupervised times, so tell your kid to be near others at lunch, recess, in hallways, or other open areas. There is safety in numbers.

- *Leave the scene.* The safest strategy is often just to leave. Don't say anything to the bully and avoid eye contact. Move toward an adult, a crowd, or older kids if possible.
- *Plan alternate routes.* Decide when and where the bullying most often occurs, and then find safer routes. If it's on the bus, find other transportation. If it's in the park, stay away.
- *Don't retaliate.* Advise him *not* to hit back; it will only increase the risk of getting hurt. Too many kids are carrying weapons, so hit back *only* as a last resort.
- *Use good judgment.* Teach your kid the best safety rule: *always* act on your gut instinct. If you feel you could be in danger, get away fast. Drop your backpack and run.
- *Tell an adult.* Decide which adult is safe to tell: someone who will take the report seriously, deal with the bully, protect your kid, and, if necessary, keep his identity secret.

Step 3. Teach and Then Rehearse Assertiveness

Telling your kid, "Just get him to stop," does not work. Bullies rarely just go away, so offer ways to handle a bully if he must face him, though it's better to avoid him. Then help your child practice any of the following tips that he thinks might work best for his situation:

- *Stay calm and do* not *react.* Bullies love power and knowing they can push other kids' buttons, so *don't* let the bully know he upset you. Pretend you're wearing a special bully-proof vest that bounces his taunts off you so you don't look afraid.
- *Don't look like a victim.* Kids who use assertive posture are less likely to be bullied. Stand tall and hold your head up to appear more confident and less vulnerable.
- *Say no firmly.* If you talk to a bully, use a firm, strong voice (never a whiny, wimpy, or afraid one). Say no to his

demands, or tell him you do not like what he is doing and will not put up with it. Keep repeating yourself until you can walk to an adult who can help.

- *Use a stone-faced glare.* Practice using a mean stare that goes straight through the bully so you seem in control and not bothered.
- *Teach comebacks.* Most bullying is verbal: name calling, insults, prejudicial slurs. Help your kid buffer verbal bullying *before* it turns into physical abuse.

Teased (pp. 267–273) and Negative Peer Pressure (pp. 175–181) offer strategies for combating verbal bullying. Teach your child a few and then practice until he's comfortable using them alone.

Step 4. Boost Self-Confidence

Research conducted by Kaoru Yamamoto, a psychologist at the University of Colorado, found that next to losing the security of family, a kid's biggest concern is losing face with peers. Being bullied dramatically affects your child's self-esteem, so find ways to boost her confidence. Here are a few possibilities:

- *Learn martial arts.* Some kids find that learning martial arts, boxing, or weight-lifting improves their self-confidence. Might this be your kid?
- *Boost social skills.* If a bully targets your child because his social skills need work, coach a few new ones, and then have him join clubs to practice them. See Lack of Friends (pp. 145–152).
- *Find a friend.* Help your child find at least one friend. See Lack of Friends (pp. 145–152).
- *Develop a talent.* Find an avenue—such as a hobby, interest, sport, or talent—that your kid enjoys and can excel at. Then help her develop the skill so her self-esteem grows.

DID YOU KNOW?

Bullying can cause long-term emotional distress. A survey conducted by the American Association of Suicidology found an alarming trend: more than 20 percent of the high school students surveyed said they had seriously considered attempting suicide in the preceding twelve months. Bullying, teasing, and peer rejection topped the reasons they considered suicide.

BEHAVIOR MAKEOVER PLAN

First, review your own behavior. Do you model the behavior of a victim, or do you stand up for yourself? Victim behavior is learned. So is there a behavior you'd like to change to improve your example to your kid? Is so, what will you commit to doing? Write down your plan.

Next, talk to other parents about how prevalent bullying is in your community and school. Find out if their kids are being bullied, who the bullies are, where the bullying is happening, and what, if anything, they are doing to help their kids. If bullying is a problem in your child's school, consider creating a parent group to discuss your concerns with the administration and teachers.

Now it's time to take action to begin making over your kid's behavior. Use your Makeover Journal to write down your thoughts and develop your plan:

1. Reread Step One. Listen carefully to your child's story, or if you suspect your kid is being bullied, ask. Try to find a pattern to the bullying. For instance, is it happening usually at the same time or place? List what you discover.

2. Review your notes from Step One, and then reread Step Two. Is there at least one thing you can do to make your kid safer? Develop a plan.
3. Review Step Three. Read also Teased (pp. 267–273) and Negative Peer Pressure (pp. 175–181). How can you help your kid be more assertive? Do you encourage your child to assert himself and be independent, or do you encourage compliance and dependence? Write a plan of how to help your kid learn to stick up for himself. Make sure you rehearse the strategy.
4. Review Step Four. How does your kid respond to the bully? He may not be able to tell you the answer, so try to observe his social interactions a bit more closely. Is there anything he does that might increase the likelihood that he will be a victim? What about behaviors that might set off the bully? List your ideas, and then develop a plan to eliminate those behaviors and boost your child's assertiveness.
5. Review Step Four, and consider your child's self-esteem. What could you do to boost his confidence? Write a plan.

There are times when we should not put all the responsibility on a child to stop a bully. That's when adult intervention may be the *only* way to handle the situation. Use your instinct so your child does not get hurt. If there's even the possibility your child could be injured, step in.

➡ See also *Anxiety, Negative Peer Pressure, Lack of Friends, Shyness, Teased.*

MAKEOVER PLEDGE

How will you use the four steps and the Behavior Makeover Plan to help your kid achieve long-term change? On the following lines, write exactly what you agree to do within the next twenty-four hours to begin your kid's behavior makeover.

_____

_____

_____

MAKEOVER RESULTS

All behavior makeovers take hard work, constant practice, and parental reinforcement. Each step your kid takes toward change may be a small one, so be sure to acknowledge and congratulate every one of them along the way. It takes a minimum of twenty-one days to see real results, so don't give up too soon. Remember that if one strategy doesn't work, another will. Write your child's weekly progress on the lines below. Keep track of daily progress in your Makeover Journal.

Week 1

_____

_____

_____

Week 2

_____

_____

_____

Week 3

_____

_____

_____

RESOURCES

Coping with Peer Pressure, by Leslie Kaplan (New York: Rosen, 1987). Ideas for helping kids learn to stand up for themselves.

Your Child: Bullying, by Jenny Alexander (Boston: Element, 1998). A practical guide written by the mother of a bully victim that discusses whole family initiatives for dealing with bullying.

Your Child—Bully or Victim: Understanding and Ending School Yard Tyranny, by Peter Sheras and Sherill Tippins (New York: Simon & Schuster, 2002). Strategies for both victims and bullies.

Liking Myself, by Pat Palmer (San Luis Obispo, Calif.: Impact Publishers, 1977). A great source of ideas for helping kids ages 5 to 9 learn assertiveness skills.

Stick Up for Yourself! Every Kid's Guide to Personal Power and Positive Self-Esteem, by Gershen Kaufman and Lev Raphael (Minneapolis, Minn.: Free Spirit Publishing, 1990). A wonderful compilation of strategies to boost kids' self-esteem and decision making. Ages 9 to 12.

The Mouse, the Monster and Me! by Pat Palmer (San Luis Obispo, Calif.: Impact Publishers, 1977). Assertiveness concepts for 8 to 12 year olds.

Why Is Everybody Always Picking on Me: A Guide to Understanding Bullies for Young People, by Terrence Webster-Doyle (New York: Weatherhill, 2000). Provides bully-proofing ideas. Ages 9 to 12.

Bullying

My son's teacher told us that Scott has been bullying other kids. A few parents complained that he threatened their kids and called them names that I'm embarrassed to repeat. He also stole their lunches and ripped up their work. Apparently he's doing such a good job of tormenting them that they don't want to go to school. I feel terrible: last year's teacher told me similar stories, and I didn't believe her. I don't know what to do. Unfortunately, Scott's dad thinks this behavior is "manly." Please help!

— Jerri, a mother of two sons from Vancouver,
   British Columbia

"Why should I care how he feels? He's just a little suck-up."

"He's such a wimp—he deserved it!"

"I hit him. So what? Nobody likes him anyway."

BEHAVIOR TIP

There is only one key to combating bullying: *the behavior must never be tolerated.* Bullying is learned; therefore, it can be unlearned. Don't wait!

Bullying has increased dramatically over the past decade. A recent study found that 80 percent of middle school students have bullied a classmate within the past thirty days. Do be aware that because only 15 percent of bullies fit the stereotype of someone who physically hurts others, many parents don't suspect their child is a bully. Other kids sure do: bullies also maliciously tease, threaten, name-call, hit, spread nasty rumors, sexually harass, or intimidate victims, and their efforts are *always* intentional. Bullies can be male or female, urban or rural, rich or poor, and be popular or lack friends. Their one commonality is their immense ability to wreak havoc on their victims' self-esteem. There's also another often-overlooked victim in terms of long-term self-damage: the bully. If not stopped, kid tormentors all too often become adult abusers who bully their offspring, spouse, colleagues, and neighbors, thereby alienating loved ones and friends and business relations they do really care about, and also punishing themselves with isolation, lost privileges, lost opportunities, and peer group contempt. What's more, one in four end up with criminal records.

FOUR STEPS TO SQUELCHING BULLYING BEHAVIORS

Use the following steps as a guide to eliminating bullying in your kid.

Step 1. Recognize That Your Kid Is a Bully

The first and most important step to eliminating bullying behaviors is to admit your kid has a problem. Data show that this behavior does not go away on its own: you must intervene. Here's a list of warning signs of kids who are bullies. Check the ones that apply to your child:

_____   Uses aggressive behaviors: shoves, hits, kicks, says mean or insulting names

_____   Impulsive: easily frustrated or quick to react; may break things when upset

_____   Thinks aggression is an acceptable way to solve problems

_____   Need to dominate or control others

_____   Humiliates or makes fun of others and sees nothing wrong with this behavior

_____   Is cruel with pets or other kids; often rough with toys or possessions

_____   Lacks empathy: insensitive to others' feelings and concerns

_____   Takes no responsibility for actions; shows little remorse; blames others

_____   Deliberately provokes or annoys other people

_____   Self-centered: concerned about his own pleasure, not about others

_____   Friends who have been over don't come back or return a phone call

Step 2. Set a Zero Tolerance for Bullying, and Use a Consequence If It Continues

Your child must learn that bullying is totally unacceptable, and it's up to you to teach him. This is time for serious talk. Begin by explaining firmly your disapproval of his behavior. Never allow him to take his cruel actions lightly, blame others, or dismiss them as a joke. If he says, "It wasn't any big deal!" Respond: "It was a *very* big deal to her. You caused her a lot of pain. Don't ever treat anyone that way again." Then tell him that any time you see or hear that he is acting like a bully, there will be a consequence. Pages 299–300 offer a list; once you have selected one, inform your child. Tell him you will also be in contact (daily, if needed) with all immediate caregivers in his life—relatives, teachers, baby-sitter, day care—so you can monitor his behavior. Be sure to ask them to inform you of any bullying. Everyone must be on-board and consistent in enforcing the stipulated consequence if you are to squelch this behavior. *Be vigilant, and don't give in!*

Step 3. Promote Empathy and Concern for Others

One powerful way to squelch bullying is by nurturing empathy. Think about it: if you can feel how your victims might feel, treating them cruelly would be unthinkable. Empathy is teachable; that means you can increase your kid's feeling for others. Here are ways:

- *Switch roles.* Bullies need to realize that their actions hurt, so ask him to imagine being the victim. "Pretend you're that boy. Tell me what you think he's thinking. How does *he* feel?"
- *Gain a new point of view.* Find ways for your kid to encounter different perspectives: visit—even better, volunteer at—a homeless shelter, pediatric ward, center for the blind, nursing home, juvenile hall, or soup kitchen. The more your kid experiences different views, the more likely she will be to empathize with others.
- *Demand reparations.* Studies show that parents who call attention to the harm done by the kid and encourage reparations increase their kid's concern for others. Require your kid to do something to ease his victim's emotional pain and make amends for his behavior—for instance, sincerely apologize, repair or replace damaged property, pay for any financial damages, tell peers to befriend her.

Step 4. Model Self-Control and Conflict Management

Data show that bullies believe that aggression is an acceptable way to solve conflicts and often show little remorse for their cruel behavior. It's up to you to prove him wrong and show him appropriate alternatives to remedy problems peacefully. Here are a few possibilities:

- *Teach self-control.* Bullies tend to be impulsive and aggressive, so teach him suitable ways to control his impulses and anger. (See also Anger, pp. 18–25; and Impulsivity, pp. 129–136.) Praise him when he shows any attempts to control his aggressive behaviors and act in a considerate way.
- *Monitor media consumption.* Be aware of the ratings for violence on television, music, movies, and video games. Set clear standards for what you will allow your kid to watch, and stick to them.
- *Express disapproval for violence.* Whenever you see or hear violent and cruel actions displayed on TV, movies, nightly news, musical lyrics, video games, as well as in real life, firmly voice your disapproval and state your reasons to help him learn new beliefs.
- *Watch out for negative peer influence.* Steer him away from overly aggressive friends.
- *Teach conflict resolution skills.* Studies show that bullies often solve problems aggressively because they don't know other options. Fighting (pp. 94–101) and Hitting (pp. 108–114) offer conflict resolution strategies; teach them to your kid. Also, model peaceful resolution. If your kid sees you using dialogue rather than force to get your needs met, he'll be more inclined to do the same.

BEHAVIOR MAKEOVER PLAN

Bullying is a learned behavior, so start by seriously reflecting as to where your child may be learning it. Think of your home environment. Do you and your spouse fight in front of your kids? Do you fight emotionally? Physically? Has your child seen you smash furniture, get in a pushing contest, or come to blows? Are your kids' aggressive behaviors condoned?

DID YOU KNOW?

Bullies are on a crash course with the future. Leonard Eron, a University of Michigan psychologist, tracked more than eight hundred eight year olds over four decades. He first identified the 25 percent who showed bullying behaviors. By age thirty, one in four of those kids had an arrest record. Eron also found that even the aggressive kids without criminal records had difficulties. Although they were as bright as the other kids, they achieved less educationally, occupationally, and personally. Studies also show that kids who bully in elementary school are more likely to be involved in sexually harassing and physically aggressive behaviors in adolescence, as well as commit date violence in their first relationship, join gangs, and become juvenile delinquents. The time to stop bullying is now. It is usually *not* a behavior that kids outgrow.

Is bullying portrayed as a positive trait such as "assertive" or "manly" instead of unacceptable and cruel? Are violent images from television, video games, musical lyrics, and the Internet allowed in your home? Now think of outside influences. Are your child's friends overly aggressive? If you want to change your child's behavior, you must also alter the factors that teach him that bullying is acceptable. What can you change that you have control over? Write your plan, and then commit to putting it into action.

Now it's time to take action to begin making over your kid's behavior. Use your Makeover Journal to write down your thoughts and develop your plan.

1. Review Step One, and take a good look at your kid. Why does he feel a need to bully others? For instance, does he lack friends? (See Lack of Friends, pp. 145–152.) Does he need to control others? (See Bossiness, pp. 40–46.) Is she mean? (See Meanness, pp. 167–174.) Find out what is underlying your kid's need to bully, and then fix it. Write down ideas, and then create a plan.
2. Review Step Two so you can set a clear consequence if bullying continues. See pages 299–300 for a list of consequences, and then plan what you will say to your kid. Also, set times to contact all other immediate caregivers in your kid's world: relatives, teachers, day care providers, and others. Think through how you will monitor your kid's daily behavior (if necessary) when you are not present. For instance, could the teacher send a note that briefly reports any bullying problem? What else?
3. Review Step Three. Write how you will boost empathy and when you will begin your plan.
4. Review Step Four. Write a long-term plan as to how you will help your kid learn acceptable alternatives to aggression.
5. Bullying is a behavior that must be closely monitored. If you do not see positive changes in your child's behavior in the next few weeks, seek the help of a professional. There may be underlying psychological reasons that require therapy or other forms of intervention. Remember: *Do not give up.*

➡ See also *Anger, Fighting, Hitting, Impulsiveness, Meanness, Selfishness.*

MAKEOVER PLEDGE

How will you use the four steps and the Behavior Makeover Plan to help your kid achieve long-term change? On the lines below, write exactly what you agree to do within the next twenty-four hours to begin your kid's behavior makeover.

_____

_____

_____

MAKEOVER RESULTS

All behavior makeovers take hard work, constant practice, and parental reinforcement. Each step your kid takes toward change may be a small one, so be sure to acknowledge and congratulate every one of them along the way. It takes a minimum of twenty-one days to see real results, so don't give up too soon. Remember that if one strategy doesn't work, another will. Write your child's weekly progress on the lines below. Keep track of daily progress in your Makeover Journal.

Week 1

_____

_____

_____

Week 2

_____

_____

_____

Week 3

_____

_____

_____

RESOURCES

Odd Girl Out: The Hidden Culture of Aggression in Girls, by Rachel Simmons (New York: Harcourt Brace, 2002). A brilliant book that skewers the stereotype of girls as the kinder, gentler gender.

Keys to Dealing with Bullies, by Barry Edwards McNamara and Francine McNamara (Happauge, N.Y.: Barron's, 1997). Profiles bullies and their victims, describes patterns underlying causes, and offers suggestions for dealing with bullying.

Your Child—Bully or Victim: Understanding and Ending School Yard Tyranny, by Peter Sheras and Sherill Tippins (New York: Simon & Schuster, 2002). Strategies for victims and bullies.

The Bully Free Classroom: Over 100 Tips and Strategies for Teachers K–8, by Allan L. Beane (Minneapolis, Minn.: Free Spirit Press, 1999). Packed full of ideas to squelch bullying behaviors—a must for every educator.

And Words Can Hurt Forever: How to Protect Adolescents from Bullying, Harassment, and Emotional Violence, by James Garbarino and Ellen deLara (New York: Free Press, 2002). A must-read for all parents and educators to help readers understand the cruelty and violence perpetrated by bullies in schools.

BEHAVIOR 7

Chore Wars

I can't stand my eight and ten year olds' constant bickering about doing chores. At this point, it's just easier for me to make their beds or take out the trash than go through their usual daily battle. I know other parents require chores, so what's their secret?

—Joslyn, a mom of two from Tarrytown, New York

"Not now, Mom."

"Maybe I'll do it later."

"My allowance doesn't cover that."

BEHAVIOR TIP

The earlier you expect your kids to take an active role in helping around the house, the easier you'll find it is to get them to cooperate.

Oh, how times have changed! Five decades ago, nearly all families could count on their kids to help around the house, with no payment expected. A recent TIME/CNN poll found that 75 percent of people surveyed said kids today do fewer chores than they did when they were young. There's no denying that today's families are different: most parents and kids are overscheduled and stressed to their limits, and home priorities have dramatically changed. The fact is, though, that chores *do* help kids develop responsibility, cooperation, and an old-fashioned work ethic. Studies also show that doing chores increases the likelihood that kids will become contributing family members who really do enjoy helping out around the house.

FOUR STEPS TO MINIMIZE CHORE BATTLES

The following steps will help guide you in avoiding chore wars.

Step 1. Specify Chores and Delegate Responsibilities

The first step to ending family chore wars is to identify the jobs you want to assign. One of the best ways to do this is by gathering all the troops and brainstorming together all the ways they can help out. Chore specifics such as the number of jobs per kid, how chores are assigned, when they're to be completed, and how long jobs are allocated—daily, weekly, or monthly—are things your family can negotiate. Some experts suggest assigning each child three daily chores (for example, making the bed, putting dishes in the dishwasher, and putting toys away) and one weekly chore (such as watering flowers or plants, sorting and folding laundry, stacking magazines, dusting). Another possibility is for each kid to choose a job he likes and doesn't like, or assign one easier chore per kid (emptying trash) and one harder one (cleaning up after dinner one night a week). Matching chores to your child's natural interests also helps to keep conflict down. If your kid loves to be outside, then weeding, watering, or raking might be good selections. Even children as young as three years old can help around the house by picking up toys or feeding pets.

Do adjust chore requirements for younger kids so they're not overwhelmed. The tricky part is distributing chores so little kids as well as older family members are assigned responsibilities aimed at their ability and everyone is contributing his fair share. Then make sure everyone is very clear about which person is expected to do what and when.

Step 2. Teach How to Do the Chore, Then Expect Completion

This may well be the most important as well as most neglected. Go through each chore step by step at least once with your kid so that she clearly knows how to do it, or have an older sibling teach a younger one. Then observe your kid doing the job to make sure she can handle it. It's also a good idea for the first few times to ask her to show you her work when she's finished so you can make sure it's done right. This is the time when you can correct any sloppiness. If after your instruction you notice that she still has trouble doing the task to your satisfaction, consider whether your expectations are realistic. If not, break the chore into smaller parts so she can succeed.

When you're sure she's capable of the task, expect her to do it on her own. *Whatever you do, don't do any task your child can do for herself.* She'll never learn to be responsible if she knows you'll finish the job for her and acknowledge her for a job well done.

Step 3. Set Deadlines for Task Completion and Consequences for Incompletion

As in any other job, chores should have specified times of completion. Make sure your kids are clear on your expectations, and then be consistent. Most kids, especially younger ones, need reminders. Charts using words or pictures that list job assignments and completion dates are helpful. Even non-readers can "read" their chores chart with pictures of what they are expected to do. Kids can then mark off their chores as they are completed. Of course, some occasions—such as a kid's birthday, illness, athletic tournament, or upcoming school test—warrant flexibility. Otherwise, be consistent with the schedule. Inconsistency lessens the importance of the jobs in kids' minds and can diminish their motivation to complete them.

Step 4. Set a Consequence for Incompletes

If the task isn't completed, there should be a consequence. The most effective ones (that change kids' behavior) are related to the chore. For instance, if your kid doesn't put her dirty clothes in the hamper, she won't have clean ones and must wait until the next wash cycle. If kids are paid for chores, withhold their allowances. One family has a "chore jar" filled with slips of paper listing extra jobs if kids haven't completed what they should have done. Offenders pull a chore and then complete their assigned chores as well as the new one before doing anything recreational. One of the easiest consequences is to enforce one family rule: work first, then play. Kids know that homework and chores must be done before watching TV, playing video games, using the telephone, or playing with friends. Whatever you decide, *be consistent with your policy.*

BEHAVIOR MAKEOVER PLAN

Start by thinking about when you were growing up. Were you responsible for doing chores in your home? If so, which ones? Studies have shown that kids a few decades ago were responsible for doing much more around the house than kids are today. What's changed in our lifestyles that's causing the decline in chores?

Next, think about the whole issue of chores. How important is it for your kids to do them? Carefully think

DID YOU KNOW?

Elizabeth Crary, author of *Pick Up Your Socks . . . and Other Skills Growing Children Need,* surveyed hundreds of families and found that young kids were able to handle a wide variety of household chores though usually needed help from parents. She also found that if parents expect their kids to do chores by themselves at first, they're likely to give up in frustration. So if you want your kid to succeed, first show *exactly* how to do the task right.

about *why* you want your kids to do chores. Write your thoughts. They will help motivate you to resolve your chore battles at home.

Now it's time to take action to begin making over your kid's behavior. Use your Makeover Journal to write down your thoughts and develop your plan.

1. Reflect on what the key issues are that are triggering your kids to wage war over chores. List them. Is there one thing you can do to ease the battles? Also think about whether all kids as well as adult members of the family do their fair share of household work. Could a lack of fairness be triggering tension? What might you do to make things more fair?
2. Reflect on how well you've assumed your responsibilities. For instance, have you taught your kid how you expect him to do the task? Do you help him plan when and how to do the job? Do you praise him each time he follows through? Does *your* behavior need a tune-up? If so, how will you change? Write your plan.

3. Reread Step One, and list the chores you'd like your kids to do. Here are possibilities:

List of Possible Chores

_____ Set and clear the table: fold napkins, rinse off dirty dishes, put dishes in dishwasher, put clean dishes back in cupboards

_____ Clean the car: clean out trash, vacuum, wash exterior, clean windows

_____ Gardening: weed, water plants, rake leaves, mow lawn, sweep patios

_____ Bedroom: dust, make the bed every day, put toys away

_____ Bathroom: wash counters and sinks; clean showers, toilets, tub; fold towels

_____ Pets: feed, take on walks, brush, bathe, clean out the cage

_____ Laundry: put dirty clothes in hamper, empty the hamper, sort lights and darks, fold clean laundry

_____ Recycling: stack magazines and papers

_____ Windows and mirrors: clean using a spray bottle

_____ Dust furniture, vacuum

4. Decide whether you plan to pay for chore completion. If so, will it be the same amount for each child, per chore, or a flat weekly payment?
5. Agree if chore assignments are to be changed weekly, daily, bimonthly, or monthly. Are Sundays considered a day off or part of the schedule? Find a schedule that's manageable for your family's lifestyle, post it on a chart, and stick to it.
6. Think how you will explain your plan to your kids. Write out your plan, and then implement it.

➡ See also *Defiance, Doesn't Listen.*

MAKEOVER PLEDGE

How will you use the four steps and the Behavior Makeover Plan to help your kid achieve long-term change? On the lines below, write exactly what you agree to do within the next twenty-four hours to begin your kid's behavior makeover.

_____

_____

_____

MAKEOVER RESULTS

All behavior makeovers take hard work, constant practice, and parental reinforcement. Each step your kid takes toward change may be a small one, so be sure to acknowledge and congratulate every one of them along the way. It takes a minimum of twenty-one days to see real results, so don't give up too soon. Remember that if one strategy doesn't work, another will. Write your child's weekly progress on the lines below. Keep track of daily progress in your Makeover Journal.

Week 1

_____

_____

_____

Week 2

_____

_____

_____

Week 3

RESOURCES

Didn't I Tell You to Take Out the Trash? Techniques for Getting Kids to Do Chores Without Hassles, by Foster W. Cline and Jim Fay (Golden, Colo.: Love and Logic Press, 1996). Focuses on the importance of chores and tools for getting kids to do them without hassles.

Chore Wars: How Households Can Share the Work and Keep the Peace, by James Thornton (Berkeley, Calif.: Conari Press, 1997). Strategies to ease chore battles and boost cooperation.

Pick Up Your Socks . . . and Other Skills Growing Children Need, by Elizabeth Crary (Seattle, Wash.: Parenting Press, 1990). Well-structured content for parents to assist their kids in developing skills and then developing self-motivation.

Chores Without Wars: Turning Dads and Kids from Reluctant Stick-in-the-Muds to Enthusiastic Team Players, by Lynn Lott and Riki Intner (Roseville, Calif.: Prima Publishing, 1998). Topics include how to persuade all family members to pitch in, distribute chores fairly, and encourage responsibility.

Home Allowance and Chore Kit: Larry Burkett's Money Matters for Kids: Ages 6–16, by Larry Burkett (Colorado Springs, Colo.: Chariot Victor Publishers, 2000). Written from a Christian perspective, it addresses how to teach kids to contribute to the family without expecting to be paid. Ages 4 to 8.

A Child's Book of Responsibilities, by Marjorie R. Nelsen (Longwood, Fla.: Partners in Learning, 1997). Ten child-centered categories illustrated in a clever book. Kids flip the cards themselves to the "I did it" pocket when they are finished. Ages 3 to 7.

8

Cynicism

O ur twelve year old used to be a positive kid. Lately, we've seen a change in his attitude that's really concerning us. Last week, he wouldn't come with us to deliver meals to people with AIDS because he said they're all going to die anyway. He's become so negative and cynical about everything. How do we get the old kid back? This one is not fun to be around.

—Jane, a mother of five from Albuquerque, New Mexico

"Why bother? It won't make any difference."

"No matter who's elected class president, my opinion still won't matter."

"Why pray? The world's going to blow up anyway."

BEHAVIOR TIP

The first step to helping your kid develop a more positive outlook on life is to curtail any of your own negative thinking. You just may be passing it on for her to catch.

Cynical kids tend to focus on the bad parts of events, find only the inadequacies in themselves and others, and put everything and everyone down. Kids aren't born pessimistic and negative; research shows this behavior is learned. And today's world is fertile for breeding the seeds of cynicism. Need evidence? Just tune into popular musical lyrics, and listen to the despair. Newspapers and the nightly news further cement in kids' minds that the world is a bad, hopeless place. It's no wonder that many kids are pessimistic. Changing a kid's negative attitude is not easy. The good news is that because negativity is learned, it can also be unlearned. The sooner you start, the easier it will be to make over this behavior.

SIX STRATEGIES TO SQUELCH CYNICISM

Here are six strategies to guide you in squelching negative attitudes that corrode kids' behavior:

1. *Accentuate the positive.* The first step to eliminate cynicism is captured in the lines of a great old song: "You have to accentuate the positive to eliminate the negative." Begin your kid's makeover by stressing a positive outlook in your home. You might consider starting your dinner with a Good News Report in which each member reports something good that happened during the day. Look for inspiring news stories, books, and videos, and share them so your child sees the good parts of life instead of just the downside.

2. *Notice negative thoughts.* Because your kid forms much of his attitude from listening to others, tune into the kinds of statements family members say. Are *you* in need of an attitude makeover? A simple way to begin is by saying more positive messages out loud so your kid overhears them.

3. *Monitor negative media consumption.* Pay attention to what your kid listens to and watches, such as TV shows, the Internet, musical lyrics, video games, and movies. How much of it is providing a cynical outlook on life? Are any changes needed? If so, put restrictions on specific media or entertainment that might be contributing to your child's negative, cynical views.

4. *Point out cynicism.* A big reason many kids don't change their behavior is simply that they don't see their behavior as inappropriate. Help your kid recognize how often he is cynical by pointing it out. Be careful not to be negative when you do so. Create a code that only you and your kid are aware of that means he's uttered a negative comment—such as pulling on your ear, touching your elbow, or pointing your thumb downward—and then use it whenever he's cynical.

5. *Turn negatives into positives.* A great rule to combat cynicism is called: "One Negative = One Positive." Whenever a family member says a negative comment, the sender must turn it into something positive. If your kid says, "This is stupid. Why do we have to do this?" encourage him to turn the statement into something positive: "Okay, if I clean my closet, I'll have some room." Enforcing the rule gradually diminishes negative statements—but you must be consistent.

6. *Counter with a balanced view.* Cynical kids can seem as if they're trapped in a "gloom-and-doom" thinking pattern and see only the bad side of any situation. As the habit becomes more prominent, they often blow negative happenings out of proportion and downplay the importance of positive ones. A way to thwart your child's negative thinking is to provide a more balanced view of the world. For instance, if your kid didn't make the soccer team and is positive that "everyone" thinks she's a bad player, you could counter with a different perspective: "I know you're disappointed about not making the team. Remember you're a good skier and roller-blade pretty well, too."

DID YOU KNOW?

Kids today are ten times more likely to be seriously depressed compared to a child born in the first third of the twentieth century. Martin Seligman of the University of Pennsylvania and author of *The Optimistic Child* found that helping youngsters become more optimistic and less cynical not only helps protect them from depression but also to be less frequently depressed, more successful at school and on the job, better able to bounce back from adversity, and even physically healthier than cynical people. He also found that optimism can be nurtured and cynicism can be reduced. So how are you squelching cynicism in your kid?

BEHAVIOR MAKEOVER PLAN

Reflect on your childhood. Did you think of yourself as a positive or cynical person? How about now? How did your parents respond if you were cynical? Do you think today's kids are more cynical than when you were growing up? Why or why not? If you were a kid today, what kind of an attitude would you have about the world? How do you think we can help our kids see their world as a more positive place?

Now it's time to take action to begin making over your kid's behavior. Use your Makeover Journal to write down your thoughts and develop your plan.

1. Think about how you respond to your child's cynical behavior. Could your response be stoking his cynicism?

Typical parental responses that provoke pessimism in kids all end in "ing": insulting, judging, humiliating, threatening, and yelling. If any of these fits your parenting style, how will you change your usual response? Write a plan.

2. Think what might be provoking his cynicism. When did the behavior begin? Were there any new events that happened around the same time—a new teacher, school difficulties, relationship frictions, a hectic schedule, a family change—that might have triggered the behavior? Do particular situations or people cause the behavior to flare up? Are there times of the day or circumstances when you don't see pessimism? Why or why not? Is there any particular thing your child expresses pessimism about? Write down any patterns you notice.

3. Eliminate more serious causes. For instance, could your child be anxious about something, depressed, or suffering from low self-esteem? Did he experience a traumatic event that could be triggering negative feelings about the world? Substance abuse could be another trigger. If you think any of these could be provoking negativity, seek help from a trained professional. Talk to other adults who know your child well. What will you do?

4. Review the six strategies to squelch cynicism, and choose one to help your kid shift from pessimism to a more optimistic outlook. Plan your steps as to how you will use the strategy with your kid.

5. Cynicism is a learned behavior. The key question is where he is learning it. Be sure to take a serious look at your behavior and that of other members of your family to make sure that isn't the source. Then make the commitment to replace the negativity. Now write down the steps you'll take to turn the behavior around.

➡ See also *Anger, Anxiety, Put-Downs.*

MAKEOVER PLEDGE

How will you use the six strategies and the Behavior Makeover Plan to help your kid achieve long-term change? On the lines below, write exactly what you agree to do within the next twenty-four hours to begin your kid's behavior makeover.

_____

_____

_____

MAKEOVER RESULTS

All behavior makeovers take hard work, constant practice, and parental reinforcement. Each step your kid takes toward change may be a small one, so be sure to acknowledge and congratulate every one of them along the way. It takes a minimum of twenty-one days to see real results, so don't give up too soon. Remember that if one strategy doesn't work, another will. Write your child's weekly progress on the lines below. Keep track of daily progress in your Makeover Journal.

Week 1

_____

_____

_____

Week 2

_____

_____

_____

Week 3

RESOURCES

Positive Self-Talk for Children: Teaching Self-Esteem Through Affirmations, by Douglas Blouch (New York: Bantam Books, 1993). A wonderful guide that instructs parents, step by step, how to help toddlers to teens turn off the negative voice within and activate the powerful "yes" voice.

Raising Positive Kids in a Negative World, by Zig Ziglar (New York: Ballantine Books, 1996). Ziglar, a popular motivational speaker, offers sensible guidelines on raising positive, happy kids.

The Optimistic Child, by Martin Seligman, Karen Reivich, Lisa Jaycox, and Jane Gillham (Boston: Houghton Mifflin, 1995). A wonderful guide offering parents specific tools to teach kids of all ages life skills that transform helplessness and negativity into mastery and bolster genuine self-esteem.

"I Think I Can, I Know I Can!" by Susan Isaacs and Wendy Ritchey (New York: St. Martin's Press, 1989). A guide to help kids learn to replace negative thinking patterns with positive self-talk.

Positively Mother Goose, by Diane Loomans, Karen Kolberg, and Julia Loomans (New York: H. J. Kramer, 1991). These rhymes are a delightful twist on the traditional Mother Goose tales. The authors have turned the old rhymes into new positive, affirming ones. For young ones.

The Pushcart War, by Jean Merrill (New York: Dell, 1984). A satire on a garbage strike in New York City and how negativity began to spread. For upper grades.

Defiance

M y kid is driving me crazy! He never does what I ask him to. He argues, refuses to do anything I ask him, and tells me I'm unfair. If I push the issue, World War III breaks out. I don't have the energy to deal with him now—and he's only twelve. What happens when he's a teenager? HELP!

—Alan, a dad of two kids from Madison, Wisconsin

"None of my friends have to. Why should I?"
"You can't make me!"
"I'm not doing it, so don't even bother asking."

BEHAVIOR TIP

Defiant behavior should never be tolerated, but that doesn't mean we shouldn't try to understand what's causing a kid to act this way.

Every kid disobeys his parents from time to time. But when they consistently do not do what we ask, then they've crossed the line. These kids are not only not doing what we want, but are defying a parent's authority. Paul Coleman, a psychologist and author of *How to Say It to Your Kids,* calls noncompliance "disobedience with attitude." Under no circumstances should your kid get off the hook for this behavior. Ignoring noncompliance, giving in, or wearing down and doing your request for him will have deadly costs to both your family harmony and your kid's character development.

THREE STEPS TO MINIMIZE DEFIANCE

Use the following steps as a guide to squelch defiant behavior and boost cooperation in your kid:

Step 1. Spell Out Your Expectations for Compliance

Wait until you're both calm, and then discuss your concerns. Tell your kid that from this point on, you expect him to obey. Say: "Listen to my tone. If I sound serious or say 'I'm serious,' I mean it." HINT: Please make sure your kid clearly knows your "serious tone." Don't make any assumptions. Model it. Explain that if he doesn't do what you ask, there will be a consequence. Then explain the consequence (review Step Three). To make sure he understands, have him repeat what you said. It's a good idea to put your agreement in writing, and both of you sign it. A young child can draw the contract. Put the contract in a safe place so you can rely on it later if needed.

Suppose your kid has a legitimate excuse for not complying with your request (the possibility does exist). You might say: "If you really have a good reason that you can't do what I ask you, tell me in a respectful tone right then. Maybe you have a science test the next day and need a reprieve from your chores so you can study. Or you're right in the middle of an important phone call about your homework assignment and you need an extra five minutes. I might consider those legitimate. Listen to how I ask respectfully." Then model to him how to ask respectfully.

When the time comes when his request is legitimate and respectfully stated, my advice is to comply. But he also needs to know that you won't be granting too many reprieves. There should be a good reason for him not to do what you ask. Just make sure he states his request respectfully.

Step 2. State Your Request Firmly and Calmly

Now the time has come when you want your kid to do something. First, *make sure you have his attention* (review Doesn't Listen, pp. 88–93, for pointers) and then state your request firmly and calmly. The fewer words you say, the better. To be absolutely sure he knows what you want use the Rewind Method: Give the directions, and then your kid "rewinds" (repeats) what you just said back to you.

Here are ways to say your request that also help reduce verbal power struggles with kids:

- *Broken record technique:* Firmly tell why you want her to comply, and then state your position: "Dinner is at six o'clock: you need to come to the table now." Calmly repeat your request word for word each time your kid tries to argue.
- *Offering choices:* Giving just a bit of leeway sometimes breaks down a resister—for example, "Your chores need to be done today. Would you like to finish them before dinner or after?"
- *Compromise:* "You're supposed to do your homework now, but you're working so hard on your dribbling. Do you agree to do your homework in half an hour?" Don't ever let your kid force you into a compromise you don't think is fair or appropriate.

Step 3. State Your Ultimatum, Including the Consequence for Defiance

Suppose your kid still refuses to comply. Stay calm, which is not easy when you're dealing with resistance. Take a deep cleansing breath to get *yourself* calm, and then tell your kid in a controlled but firm tone that this is your bottom-line statement and there is no more negotiating. WARNING: *Do not* plead, argue, bargain, beg, or coax. Your kid may try every trick in the book to break you down: argue, turn your words around, and call you unfair and other luscious names. His goal is to wear you down. So be thick-skinned, and *do not let him get to you.* Giving in puts you right where he wants you, and he wins again. Don't let him. If your kid doesn't obey your request within seconds, then the agreed consequence must follow immediately. And if he still doesn't comply with your request or doesn't complete the stipulated time-out length correctly, you now go to Code Red, the highest level of punishment. See pages 299–300 for potential consequences.

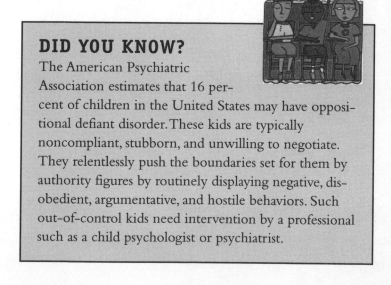

DID YOU KNOW?

The American Psychiatric Association estimates that 16 percent of children in the United States may have oppositional defiant disorder. These kids are typically noncompliant, stubborn, and unwilling to negotiate. They relentlessly push the boundaries set for them by authority figures by routinely displaying negative, disobedient, argumentative, and hostile behaviors. Such out-of-control kids need intervention by a professional such as a child psychologist or psychiatrist.

BEHAVIOR MAKEOVER PLAN

Imagine a video camera was filming your child's most recent defiant episode. Play it in your mind so you can replay the interaction. What was your request? Was it reasonable? What was your kid doing at the time? Did you get his attention first? How did you state your request? Was it respectful? How did your kid respond to you? How did you respond to his reaction? Jot down notes as you rethink the scene. Was there one thing you could have done differently that might have prevented the outcome? If so, how can you apply that the next time?

Next, ask yourself if there is any kind of pattern. For instance, is your kid totally defiant to all your requests or just some? If so, which ones does he agree to do? What might be causing the difference? Is he defiant with other adults besides you? If so, who? If not, why not?

Now it's time to take action to begin making over your kid's behavior. Use your Makeover Journal to write down your thoughts and develop your plan.

1. Reread Step One, and prepare yourself to meet with your kid. Make sure all your expectations are fair and reasonable. At this point, you want your kid to do *anything* you ask him to do, so limit the number and select only those you really care about. Once he starts complying, you can slowly add more requests.
2. Review Step Three, and then decide on the consequence you'll apply if your kid refuses your next request. Determine also your Code Red consequence: something your kid really craves and you can control that can be removed as a privilege. See pages 299–300 for possibilities. Make sure you announce to your child the consequence for continued defiance.

3. Review Step Two carefully. Practice how you'll interact with your kid the next time he refuses to obey. What will you do to stay calm and firm and not back down?
4. How are you at following through? Remember that once you explain your expectations and your kid does not comply, you *must* follow through. If you have any problems with this issue, reflect on what you can do differently, and then write down your plan.

➡ See also *Anger, Bossiness, Cynicism, Doesn't Listen, Talking Back.*

MAKEOVER PLEDGE

How will you use three steps and the Behavior Makeover Plan to help your kid achieve a long-term change in defiance? On the lines below, write exactly what you agree to do within the next twenty-four hours to begin your kid's behavior makeover.

_____

_____

_____

MAKEOVER RESULTS

All behavior makeovers take hard work, constant practice, and parental reinforcement. Each step your kid takes toward change may be a small one, so be sure to acknowledge and congratulate every one of them along the way. It takes a minimum of twenty-one days to see real results, so don't give up too soon. Remember that if one strategy doesn't work, another will. Write your child's weekly progress on the following lines. Keep track of daily progress in your Makeover Journal.

Week 1

_____

_____

_____

Week 2

_____

_____

_____

Week 3

_____

_____

_____

RESOURCES

Children Who Say No When You Want Them to Say Yes, by James Windell (New York: Macmillan, 1996). A parent tool for handling stubborn, oppositional kids through adolescence.

From Defiance to Cooperation: Real Solutions for Transforming the Angry, Defiant, Discouraged Child, by John F. Taylor (Roseville, Calif.: Prima Publishing, 2001). Constructive ways to channel defiant, oppositional energy and determination with easy-to-implement suggestions.

Parent in Control, by Gregory Bodenhamer (New York: Fireside, 1995). Using common scenarios to demonstrate specific parenting techniques, a one-time probation officer offers a straightforward tested program for maintaining control over adolescents without harsh discipline.

Parenting the Strong-Willed Child, by Rex Forehand and Nicholas Long (New York: McGraw-Hill, 1996). A program to help parents of strong-willed kids find positive and manageable solutions to their children's difficult behavior.

The Explosive Child, by Ross W. Greene (New York: HarperCollins, 1998). Sound parenting suggestions for dealing with easily frustrated, "chronically inflexible" kids.

Treating the Unmanageable Adolescent: A Guide to Oppositional Defiant and Conduct Disorders, by Neil Bernstein (Northvale, N.J.: Aronson, 1996). Although aimed at clinicians, this guide offers invaluable suggestions for dealing with the out-of-control older child.

BEHAVIOR 10

Doesn't Listen

O kay, I admit it: Ryan, my eleven year old, doesn't respond whenever I ask him to do something. And I know he's not deaf: he hears the TV perfectly and keeps talking to his friends on the phone. I'm getting really tired of saying, "How many times do I have to tell you?"

— Barbara, a mom of two sons,
   from Calgary, Alberta, Canada

"Did you take the trash out?" Silence.
"Did you do your homework?" Leaves the room.
"Did you feed the dog?" Starts burning a new CD.

BEHAVIOR TIP

One of the fastest ways to get kids to pay attention is by doing one simple thing: talk less, not more. They're more likely to hear what you really want them to hear.

A lot of kids seem to be excelling at selective listening these days. Oh, they can hear the TV, their friends, and even the most obscure musical lyrics just fine. But when it comes to responding to certain parental inquiries or requests, it's a whole different story. If you've resorted to using threats, bribes, or yells to try to get your kid's attention, take heart: you're not alone. *Parents* magazine polled moms and dads about their toughest discipline challenge, and the hands-down winner was, "My kid doesn't listen to me."

SIX TIPS TO GET YOUR KID TO LISTEN THE FIRST TIME

Use the following tips as a guide to getting your kid to listen to you *the first time.*

1. *Model good listening.* Kids can't learn to be good listeners if they don't have good models to copy. So make sure you show your kids what you expect them to do by being a good listener yourself. Show them that you listen to your spouse, your friends, and, most important, to them. An old proverb is a great reminder: "We have two ears and one mouth for a reason." Listen to your kid twice as much as you talk!

2. *Talk respectfully.* The fastest way to tune kids out is using these communication blocks: criticizing, ordering, preaching, opinion giving, judging, threatening, yelling, and pleading. Ask yourself how you'd like to be talked to if you were a kid, and use that as your model.

3. *Attention first, then talk.* Get your kid's attention, and make sure he's looking at you before you speak. You might gently lift your kid's chin up so he looks into your eyes or give a verbal cue to get his attention: "Please look at me, and listen to what I have to say." When you're eyeball to eyeball, you'll have his full attention: this is the time to make your

request. Using the same technique each time you really want their attention will cue your kids to listen.

4. *Give a warning.* Sometimes it really is hard for kids to shift gears, especially if they're involved in something that interests them. Besides, he really may not hear you. So give a time limit: "I'll need your help in two minutes" or "I need to talk to you in a minute. Please be ready."

5. *Lower your voice tone.* Instead of raising your voice, lower your tone. Nothing turns a kid off faster then yelling, so do the opposite: talk more softly, not louder. It usually catches the kid off-guard, and he stops to listen. Teachers have used this strategy for years because it works.

6. *Keep it short, sweet, and specific.* Kids are more receptive if they know they don't have to hear a lecture, so keep your requests short and to the point: "Please make your bed before you go outside." "You need to get ready to go to school now." Limiting your request to fewer words also helps. Sometimes saying one word does the trick: "Homework!" "Chores!"

DID YOU KNOW?

Mary Budd Rowe, a noted educator, discovered that children need "wait time"—more time to think about what they hear—before speaking. So whenever you ask a question or give a request, remember to *wait at least three seconds* for your child to think about what she heard. She will absorb more information, be more likely to respond, and probably give you a more complete answer.

BEHAVIOR MAKEOVER PLAN

Think how you feel when you are truly listened to. Think about wonderful listeners you know. What makes them good listeners? What behaviors could you copy? Kids can't learn to listen if they don't see adults around doing the same thing, so tune into *your* behavior. What kind of an example are you setting for your child?

Now it's time to take action to begin making over your kid's behavior. Use your Makeover Journal to write down your thoughts and develop your plan.

1. Consider whether you are guilty of using the eight communication blocks with your kid: criticizing, ordering, preaching, opinion giving, judging, threatening, yelling, and pleading. If you are, what will you do to change *your* behavior? Make a plan.
2. Review the six tips to get your kid to listen the first time, and choose one or two to try. How do you plan to use them? Write about this. Remember that change in behavior is rarely instant, so experiment with the same strategy several times before trying another.
3. If your child seems to have problems hearing (and not just hearing *you*), consult a pediatrician to make sure there isn't a physical condition.

➡ See also *Defiance, Rudeness, Talking Back.*

MAKEOVER PLEDGE

How will you use the six tips and the Behavior Makeover Plan to help your kid achieve long-term change in listening? On the following lines, write exactly what you agree to do within the next twenty-four hours to begin your kid's behavior makeover.

_____

_____

_____

MAKEOVER RESULTS

All behavior makeovers take hard work, constant practice, and parental reinforcement. Each step your kid takes toward change may be a small one, so be sure to acknowledge and congratulate every one of them along the way. It takes a minimum of twenty-one days to see real results, so don't give up too soon. Remember that if one strategy doesn't work, another will. Write your child's weekly progress on the lines below. Keep track of daily progress in your Makeover Journal.

Week 1

_____

_____

_____

Week 2

_____

_____

_____

Week 3

_____

_____

_____

RESOURCES

How to Talk So Kids Will Listen and Listen So Kids Will Talk, by Adele Faber and Elaine Mazlish (New York: Avon, 1982). A practical, highly readable book for helping parents learn to communicate more effectively with their kids.

Cool Communication, by Andrea Frank Henkart and Journey Henkart (New York: Perigee, 1998). A much-needed perspective told from both the parent and teen side on how to boost communication and understanding.

P.E.T. Parent Effectiveness Training, by Thomas Gordon (New York: Signet, 1975). A book that belongs on every parent's bookshelf. Gordon sets out a proven method to help improve communication between parents and their children.

Nobody Listens to Andrew, by Elizabeth Guilfoile (New York: Scholastic, 1967). A classic. Andrew tries to tell everyone there is a bear in his bed. The problem is that no one listens to him. Ages 4 to 7.

The Basic Connection, by Mary Micallef (Redding, Calif.: Good Apple, 1996). A nonfiction book with advice on good listening. Ages 5 to 11.

Dealing with Someone Who Won't Listen, by Lisa K. Adams (New York: Rosen Group, 1998). Explains to kids what to do when someone doesn't listen to them. Ages 5 to 10.

BEHAVIOR 11

Fighting

I'm beginning to feel like a referee: my kids are constantly fighting, and I'm constantly having to tell them what to do. I know
I'm not helping them by solving their own problems, but frankly
it's a lot easier telling them what to do than listening to their crying, yelling, and arguing. There has to be a better way, so what is it?
I'm exhausted.

—Jake, a dad of two from Salt Lake City, Utah

"Mavis won't be my friend. I threw sand at her when
she took my shovel."

BEHAVIOR TIP

Learning how to deal with problems in the comfort of
your home is the best place for kids to learn by trial
and error. Keep reinforcing a realistic approach to help
your kids solve problems until they can confidently do
so on their own.

"Kevin and I were benched all recess because the teacher heard us fighting about the game."

"Tim asked *my* girlfriend to go out, so I'm not talking to him again!"

On a day-to-day basis, the problems our kids face are tough: prejudice, sibling conflict, academic and youth sport pressures, rejection by friends, cliques and gangs, bullying, trying to get along, as well as the frustrations of just growing up. These are issues we used to think affected only older kids; the fact is that they are having an impact on our children at younger and younger ages. Although we can't protect our kids from problems, frustrations, and heartaches, we can arm them with tools to handle them better. The more we help them learn to resolve conflicts peacefully, the greater the likelihood is that they'll develop into more self-sufficient and resourceful individuals able to deal with any issue—and do so *without our guidance.*

FIVE STEPS TO REDUCING CONFLICTS

Use the following steps as a guide to help your kid minimize fighting and learn to solve problems peacefully. Each letter in the acronym STAND represents one of the five steps in conflict resolution and helps kids recall the process.

Step 1. S = Stop and Calm Down
The first step to conflict resolution is teaching kids to calm down and tune into their feelings. The reason is simple: it's impossible to think about how to solve a problem if you're upset. Once in control, you can begin to rationally figure out why you're upset and then find an answer to your dilemma. So teach your kid to take a slow, deep breath to calm down or walk away until he's calm. If emotions are high between the two kids, do intervene: "I see two angry kids who need to calm down so they can figure out how to solve their

problem." You might need to separate the kids until their anger is under control.

Step 2. T = Take Turns Telling What the Problem Is

The important thing here is to enforce these critical rules:

- No put-downs or name-calling.
- Listen to each other respectfully.
- Do not interrupt. Each person gets a chance to talk.

You might ask each kid to say what happened, summarize each view, and then end with, "What can you do now to solve this problem?" Make suggestions only when the kids really seem stuck.

Tell kids to start their explanations with the word *I* instead of *you* and then describe the problem and how they want it resolved. This helps the speaker focus on the conflict without putting the other child down—for instance, "I'm ticked because you never give me a turn. I want to use the computer too." If emotions are high, give kids the option of writing or drawing their view of the problem instead of saying it to each other. This is particularly helpful for younger or less verbal children. The goal should be to help each child try to feel what it's like to be in the other kid's shoes. One way to do this is to have each youngster put into words what the other child has said.

Step 3. A = List the Alternatives to Resolving It

Kids need to think of alternatives so they have ways to find a resolution. Whether your child is a preschooler or an adolescent, the basic rules of thinking of solutions are the same:

1. Say the first thing that comes into your mind.
2. Don't put down anyone else's ideas.
3. Change or add onto anyone's idea.
4. Try to come up with ideas that work mutually for both sides.

No More Misbehavin'

Don't offer help unless they really seem stuck! To keep kids focused, say they must come up with five solutions before you return. Then leave for a few minutes. Stretch the time depending on the children's age and problem-solving skills.

Step 4. N = Narrow the Choices

Narrow the options to a few choices. Here are two rules to help kids get closer to resolving the problem:

1. Eliminate any solutions that are unacceptable to either child because they don't satisfy their needs.
2. Eliminate any solutions that aren't safe or wise.

Step 5. D = Decide the Best Choice and Do It!

This final step helps kids learn how to make the best decision by thinking through the consequences of their choices. You can teach children to think about the consequence of their remaining choices by asking, "What might happen if you tried that?" Another way to help kids decide on the best choice is

DID YOU KNOW?

Well over one thousand studies, including reports from the Surgeon General's Office and the National Institute of Mental Health, have concluded that exposure to TV violence causes aggressive behavior in some kids, as well as increasing their tendency to favor using physical aggression to resolve conflicts. The American Psychological Association estimates that televised violence *by itself* contributes to as much as 15 percent of all kids' aggressive behaviors. Are you monitoring your child's TV viewing?

by helping them weigh the pros and cons of each remaining possibility: "What are all the good and bad things that might happen if we chose that?" "What is the one last change that would make this work better for both of us?" Once they decide, the two kids shake on the agreement or take turns saying, "I agree."

BEHAVIOR MAKEOVER PLAN

Take a minute to think about how you solved problems when you were a kid. Did your parents teach you how to solve problems? Do you have a method for solving problems in your relationships or at work today? Is this a skill you are able to model to your children, or do you need to do some more work on it yourself?

Now it's time to take action to begin making over your kid's behavior. Use your Makeover Journal to write down your thoughts and develop your plan.

1. Think about how your child typically reacts to a problem. Does she stay calm, or does her body tense up? Does she confront the problem, or does she walk away from it? Does she coolly try to solve the problem, or does she become so anxious that she needs help calming down? If any of these is her typical response, there might be an immediate need for her to learn Step One: Stop and Calm Down. Write a plan.

2. Review Step Two with your child. This is a hard step for many kids to learn, so maybe the best way is for you to model it by telling a story about one of your own problems. Then show your kid how to listen when she tells you her side of the story. Ask questions to help her fill in the important details, and then model repeating back what your child told you so you can model being in her shoes.

3. Review Steps Three and Four with your child. Encourage your kid to think of solutions to any problem, and remind her to say anything that comes to her mind, no matter how wild and crazy it may seem to her.
4. Review Step Five, and help your child practice weighing consequences. Try to find teachable moments throughout the day that you could use as examples of how everyday conflicts get resolved without fighting.

➡ See also *Anger, Bossiness, Cynicism, Hitting, Put-Downs, Sibling Battles, Yelling.*

MAKEOVER PLEDGE

How will you use the five steps and the Behavior Makeover Plan to help your kid achieve long-term change? On the lines below, write exactly what you agree to do within the next twenty-four hours to begin your kid's behavior makeover.

_____

_____

_____

MAKEOVER RESULTS

All behavior makeovers take hard work, constant practice, and parental reinforcement. Each step your kid takes toward change may be a small one, so be sure to acknowledge and congratulate every one of them along the way. It takes a minimum of twenty-one days to see real results, so don't give up too soon. Remember that if one strategy doesn't work, another will. Write your child's weekly progress on the following lines. Keep track of daily progress in your Makeover Journal.

Week 1

_____

_____

Week 2

_____

_____

Week 3

_____

_____

_____

RESOURCES

Conflict Resolution: Communication, Cooperation, Compromise, by Robert Wandberg (Mankato, Minn.: Lifematters Press, 2000). Helps teens and young adults learn critical life skills to resolve conflicts.

Peaceful Parents, Peaceful Kids: Practical Ways to Create a Calm and Happy Home, by Naomi Drew (New York: Kensington, 2000). If you're going to buy one book on creating a harmonious home, this should be it. Drew is an expert, and her ideas are practical.

Getting to Resolution: Turning Conflict into Collaboration, by Steward Levine (San Francisco: Berrett-Koehler, 1998). Step-by-step guidelines through the process of resolving conflicts.

Getting to Peace: Transforming Conflicts at Home, at Work, and in the World, by William Ury (New York: Viking Press, 1999). A renowned expert on negotiation and peacemaking offers tips on how to achieve peace at home, at work, and in the community so we can live together peacefully.

Conflict Resolution: The Win-Win Solution, by Carolyn Casey (Berkeley Heights, N.J.: Enslow Publishers, 2001). Strategies for dealing nonviolently with peers, parents, teachers, and others. For ages 12 to 15.

We Can Work It Out: Conflict Resolution for Children, by Barbara Kay Pollard (Berkeley, Calif.: Tricycle Press, 2000). A straightforward format to help kids learn skills to handle fourteen difficult situations, such as anger, teasing, hitting, and excluding. For ages 5 to 8.

BEHAVIOR 12

Giving Up Easily

W e watch our eleven-year-old daughter, and we worry. She's sweet, kind, and smart, but at the first sign something looks hard, she gives up. She'll never be able to survive this dog-eat-dog world of ours if she keeps quitting. At this rate, she'll never recognize what's she's capable of achieving. Is there anything we can do to help her?

—Danielle, a mother of two from Berkeley, California

BEHAVIOR TIP

Perseverance is one of the important success traits we can help our kids develop. We can make an immense difference in our children's potential if we emphasize effort and stress that "it's not good enough just to start; you have to finish."

"This is too hard. I quit."
"That's going to take too long. I want to watch TV."
"I can't do that. I'm going home."

The old proverb "Always at it wins the day" is a telling example of how important perseverance can be in our children's lives. It's not only the effort kids put into learning new things, but often it's their persistence that matters most. That attitude is what will help them through all sorts of ups and downs in childhood as well as adulthood. Their accomplishments no doubt will steadily grow, because they'll be more willing to try new tasks and stick with them until they succeed. If our kids are to survive and succeed in this competitive world, they must learn to hang in there, especially in challenging times, and not quit. And if they quit, they will be greatly shortchanged from experiencing the exhilarating feeling that comes from recognizing only after you finish something really hard, "I did it!"

FIVE TIPS TO MINIMIZE
A GIVING-UP ATTITUDE

Use the following tips as a guide to help your kid learn "stick-to-it-ness":

1. *Define the word* perseverance. Take time to explain that *perseverance* means "not giving up" or "hanging in there until you complete the task you started." Use *perseverance* frequently to help your children understand how important the trait is in their lives. When your child sticks to a task, point it out: "There's perseverance for you. You hung in there with your work even though it was hard." Make the word your family theme for the month.
2. *Model effort.* Take a pledge to show your kids how you don't give up on a task even when things get difficult.

Before starting a new task, make sure your child overhears you say, "I'm going to *persevere* until I succeed." Modeling the trait is always the number one teaching method, so consciously tune up perseverance in your behavior.

3. *Start a family "never-give-up" motto.* Develop a family motto that reminds your kids of your basic code of expected behavior: "Never give up!" Begin by brainstorming together possible perseverance anthems, such as, "Try, try, and try again, and then you will win," "In this family, we finish what we start," "You'll never succeed if you give up," and "Quitters never win." Choose one, and have your kids write the selected motto on index cards that they put on the bulletin board in their bedroom or tape to the refrigerator. It's now your family's guiding belief.

4. *Use encouraging language.* The kinds of words we say to our children can help them learn the value of effort and get into the habit of completing what they start. Here are a few phrases you can use with your child: "Don't quit!" "I know you can do it! Don't give up!" "Hang in there. Don't stop!" "It's usually harder at the beginning." "Almost! Try again." "You'll get it. Keep at it!"

5. *Create a "Stick-to-It Award."* Ask your kid to help you find a stick at least the length of a ruler to acknowledge perseverance. Print "Stick-to-It Award" across the stick with a black marking pen. Now tell everyone to be on alert for family members who show special persistence for the next month. Each night, have a family gathering to announce the names of family members who didn't give up and print their initials on the stick with the marking pen.

BEHAVIOR MAKEOVER PLAN

Think about your own behavior. How are you at sticking to tasks without quitting? How about your spouse? How about your parents? Was this trait modeled to you as you were grow-

No More Misbehavin'

DID YOU KNOW?

Stanford professor Lewis Terman studied fifteen hundred gifted kids for several decades and found that high intelligence was a poor predictor of success. Only a small portion of the highly intelligent group did succeed. What did those who succeeded have in common? They had all learned the value of perseverance and not giving up, and they had all learned it before they left high school. It was that trait that was most critical in helping them succeed.

ing up? Now think about your family: Are you and your spouse modeling perseverance to your kids? If so, how? If not, how could you tune this up in your behavior? Start by thinking of daily activities that might become teachable moments to model perseverance. For instance, doing the bills can be a great lesson if you announce to your kids, "I have a lot of bills to do tonight. I'm going to sit here until they're done." Write a few ideas about how you could model perseverance to your kids.

Now it's time to take action to begin making over your kid's behavior. Use your Makeover Journal to write down your thoughts and develop your plan.

1. Think about your kid. What things does he tend to give up on? This may take time to make an accurate appraisal, so keep observing. Make a list and keep adding to it.
2. Reread the list. Do you notice a pattern? For instance, you may see that he gives up easily on his math homework. Why? Does he have an adequate attention span? Is the assignment at his knowledge level? Does he write down homework assignments? Or suppose your preschooler can't finish a game of Candy Land. Is she too easily frustrated?

Giving Up Easily

Can she tolerate losing? Play detective, and try to discover the cause. Once you understand it, write your plan to help.
3. Reread the five tips for minimizing a giving-up attitude. Choose the ones you would like to try with your kid. Write what you will do help him succeed.

➡ See also *Anxiety, Impulsivity, Overperfectionism.*

MAKEOVER PLEDGE

How will you use the five tips and the Behavior Makeover Plan to help your kid achieve long-term change? On the lines below, write exactly what you agree to do within the next twenty-four hours to begin your kid's behavior makeover.

_____

_____

_____

MAKEOVER RESULTS

All behavior makeovers take hard work, constant practice, and parental reinforcement. Each step your kid takes toward change may be a small one, so be to sure acknowledge and congratulate every one of them along the way. It takes a minimum of twenty-one days to see real results, so don't give up too soon! Remember that if one strategy doesn't work, another might. Write your child's weekly progress on the lines below. Keep track of daily progress in your Makeover Journal.

Week 1

_____

_____

_____

Week 2

_____

_____

_____

Week 3

_____

_____

_____

RESOURCES

I Think I Can, I Know I Can! by Susan Isaacs and Wendy Ritchey (New York: St. Martin's Press, 1989). A wealth of practical ways to nurture confidence in children.

The Confident Child: Raising Children to Believe in Themselves: A Compassionate, Practical Guide, by Terri Apter (New York: Bantam Books, 1998). Clear-cut thoughtful strategies for parents who want to promote self-confidence in their kids.

The Parent's Little Book of Lists: Dos and Don'ts of Effective Parenting, by Jane Bluestein (Deerfield Beach, Fla.: Health Communications, 1997). A gold mine for parents offering simple tips to build successful and confident children.

Positive Self-Talk for Children, by Douglas Blouch (New York: Bantam Books, 1989). A wonderful reference on teaching self-esteem and bouncing back from mistakes through affirmations.

Horton Hatches the Egg, by Dr. Seuss (New York: Random House, 1940). The classic story of an elephant who is determined to keep his word—no matter what happens! Ages 6 to adulthood.

Comeback! Four True Stories, by Jim O'Connor (New York: Random House, 1992). The tale of four famous athletes who overcame serious injuries or debilitating conditions through effort, perseverance, and a "never-give-up attitude." Ages 8 to 11.

13

Hitting

W e're really concerned that our son might be turning into an eight-year-old Mike Tyson. Whenever he's frustrated, he resorts to hitting, punching, and kicking the person he's with. He's been in two fights at school just this month. We haven't a clue as to how to stop his aggressiveness.

—Will, a father of three from Toronto, Ontario, Canada

"I had to hit him. He called me a name."

"I didn't sock him *that* hard."

"She hit me first."

BEHAVIOR TIP

Kids who hit haven't learned appropriate substitutes for frustrations and anger. So teach your kid a positive alternative so he doesn't have to resort to hitting.

Most kids resort to hitting at one time or another. Hitting may be the only way they know to take matters into their hands. Although anger and frustration certainly are normal feelings, using hitting to express them is not. It very quickly becomes a habit, and one that can be tough to break. Studies also show that kids who hit today are much more likely to grow up to be the bully, spousal abuser, or violent parent. Stop this behavior now.

FOUR STEPS TO ELIMINATE HITTING

Use the following steps as a guide to squelch hitting in your kid:

Step 1. Set a Zero Tolerance for Hitting

Find a calm, uninterrupted time to discuss your concerns about hitting. Be serious and firm so your child understands you are not pleased with his behavior, and explain why you disapprove. If your child is older, discuss the possible serious consequences: injury to the victim or himself, getting into trouble, suspension from school, developing a poor reputation, loss of friends. Take time to listen to your kid's reasons for his hitting behavior. Don't judge; just listen. You may discover causes that you weren't aware of. Offer to help remedy any legitimate concerns. Then do spell out that hitting will not be tolerated, and explain the consequence any time he resorts to using the behavior: "If I see you hitting your sister again, you will stop playing and go to time-out for fifteen minutes" or "If I hear that you hit someone again, you will be grounded for the day." See a list of appropriate consequences on pages 299–300 that are suited to your child's age and temperament.

Step 2. Teach Acceptable Alternatives to Hitting

Just telling your kid not to hit does not teach her what she should do instead. Help her learn appropriate ways to handle frustrations without resorting to hitting. Brainstorm a few acceptable alternatives: "Let's think of what you could do instead of hitting." Then choose one, and teach it to your child. Rehearse it again and again until she learns it. Here are possibilities:

- *Deal with the anger.* Pound clay, hit a pillow, or punch a punching bag.
- *Use an "I want" statement.* Tell the other person what you want him to do. The statement must focus on the problem: "You took my toy, and I want you to give it back." Name-calling and put-downs are not allowed.
- *Say how you feel.* Children with limited language skills can say how they feel to their offender: "I'm mad" or "I'm really, really angry."
- *Go to a calm spot.* Ask your kid to help you set up a place where he can go to gain control. Put a few soothing things there such as books, music, pens, and paper, and then encourage him to use the spot to cool down.
- *Leave the scene.* Whenever you feel the urge to fight, walk away. It's always safer.

Step 3. Reinforce Peaceful Behaviors

One of the simplest ways to change kids' behavior is to catch them being good. It's also the technique most parents do the least. Any time you notice your child handling a difficult situation calmly, expressing his frustrations without hitting, or using self-control, acknowledge his behavior and let him know you appreciate his efforts: "I noticed you were really mad, but you walked away to calm yourself. That's really a good sign." "You used your words to tell your friend you were upset. Good for you!" Remember that behaviors that are reinforced are the ones that kids will continue to use. It's also one of the best ways to have those desirable actions become a behavior habit.

Step 4. Enforce the Agreed Consequence for Hitting

So what do you do if your child continues to hit? First, stop, breathe, and cool off before reacting, and then enforce the preagreed consequence. Do not lecture, and above all, *do not hit your aggressive kid*. That sends a huge double message: "It's okay for adults to hit, but kids may not." Instead, take a young tyke's hands and say: "You may not hit people. You need to go to the calm-down chair for five minutes." For an older youngster, firmly state the punishment: "We agreed that hitting is not allowed. You may not watch TV for the evening" (or whatever the consequence was). The child is expected to obey. If he does not, the consequence is doubled.

BEHAVIOR MAKEOVER PLAN

The American Academy of Pediatrics recently posted this troubling fact: of the twenty-six most industrialized countries of the world, kids in the United States are the most aggressive. What might be causing this trend? What can parents do to help kids become more peaceful?

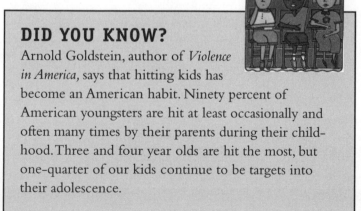

DID YOU KNOW?

Arnold Goldstein, author of *Violence in America,* says that hitting kids has become an American habit. Ninety percent of American youngsters are hit at least occasionally and often many times by their parents during their childhood. Three and four year olds are hit the most, but one-quarter of our kids continue to be targets into their adolescence.

Experts agree that aggression is learned. Where might your kid be learning aggressive behaviors? Reflect on your example: How well do you model calmness under fire to your kid? How do you respond without violence to stresses or pressures in your life? Also, how do you and your spouse typically respond to your kid's aggressive behaviors? For instance, do you remain calm, yell, criticize, scold, lecture, or spank? Could your reaction be triggering your kid's reaction? If so, what will you do to change your behavior so you model calmness to your kid? Write a plan, and then commit to it.

Now it's time to take action to begin making over your kid's behavior. Use your Makeover Journal to write down your thoughts and develop your plan.

1. Take a serious look at your kid's aggressive behaviors. How frequently is he engaging in hitting or other explosive behaviors? Keep a record on your calendar of how often he exhibits this behavior. Note also the time of day. Is there a pattern of where, when, and with whom he is prone to hit? Is he exhibiting this behavior elsewhere? If so, talk to his other caregivers.
2. When did this hitting behavior start? What might be triggering it? List possibilities, and then reread the list. Is there anything you can do to alter your kid's environment to reduce stress and frustrations?
3. Review Step One, and determine the consequence the next time your kid hits. Then plan how you will explain your concerns and the consequence to your kid.
4. Review Step Two. What will you do to help your kid learn a substitute behavior for hitting? Select one or two alternatives to teach, and then commit to reviewing the new behavior until your kid uses it instead of hitting.
5. Read Step Three, and plan how you will acknowledge your kid's peaceful behaviors.
6. Be prepared for backsliding. The longer your kid has been hitting, the longer it will take to make over this behavior.

So review Step Four, and reflect on how you will respond the next time your child hits.

7. If you still notice no change in your kid's aggressive behaviors in a few weeks, seek the help of a trained professional.

➡ See also *Anger, Anxiety, Biting, Fighting, Impulsivity, Meanness, Poor Sportsmanship, Sibling Battles, Temper Tantrums.*

MAKEOVER PLEDGE

How will you use the four steps and the Behavior Makeover Plan to help your kid achieve long-term change? On the lines below, write exactly what you agree to do within the next twenty-four hours to begin your kid's behavior makeover.

_____

_____

_____

MAKEOVER RESULTS

All behavior makeovers take hard work, constant practice, and parental reinforcement. Each step your kid takes toward change may be a small one, so be sure to acknowledge and congratulate every one of them along the way. It takes a minimum of twenty-one days to see real results, so don't give up too soon. Remember that if one strategy doesn't work, another will. Write your child's weekly progress on the lines below. Keep track of daily progress in your Makeover Journal.

Week 1

_____

_____

_____

Week 2

_____

_____

_____

Week 3

_____

_____

_____

RESOURCES

From Defiance to Cooperation: Real Solutions for Transforming the Angry, Defiant, Discouraged Child, by John F. Taylor (Roseville, Calif.: Prima Publishing, 2001). Easy-to-implement suggestions for improving life with a rebellious and argumentative kid.

Hands Are Not for Hitting, by Martine Agassi (Minneapolis, Minn.: Free Spirit Publishing, 2002). Perfect tool for helping preschoolers recognize there are more peaceful ways to solve problems than hitting.

Lost Boys: Why Our Sons Turn Violent and How We Can Save Them, by James Garbarino (New York: Free Press, 1999). Must reading for anyone concerned about preventing the surge of aggression in violence in our youth.

The Explosive Child, by Ross W. Greene (New York: HarperCollins, 1998). Good advice for parents who are living with out-of-control kids.

Winning Cooperation from Your Child! A Comprehensive Method to Stop Defiant and Aggressive Behavior in Children, by Kenneth Wenning (Northvale, N.J.: Aronson, 1999). A range of techniques to promote cooperative behavior for oppositional, defiant, and aggressive kids.

14

Homework Battles

S *even o'clock around our house might as well be called "trauma city." It's when our three kids, ages seven, ten, and twelve, are supposed to start their homework. In reality, it's the time when the arguing, wailing, and pleading start. Sometimes I can't tell who does those behaviors more: my husband and me or our kids. So how do I get my kids to do their homework without a world war?*

—Susan, a mother of three from Truckee, California

"But you helped me last week!"

"Can't you write a note and say I'm sick?"

"But I did almost all of it. It's not due until tomorrow morning!"

BEHAVIOR TIP

Recognize that your role in homework is as a helper, not a doer. Once you get your role straight, your battles are half over. The responsibility rests in your kid's hands, not yours.

Research says doing homework enhances not only children's learning but also essential skills they will need to succeed in school and in life, such as organization, problem solving, attention span, memory, goal setting, discipline, and persistence. But sometimes in our quest to help kids succeed, we get carried away and provide *too much* help. Or maybe we haven't exerted tough enough standards to make sure our kids finish their work as required and do the very best they can.

EIGHT STRATEGIES TO EASE HOMEWORK PAINS

Use the following strategies as a guide in helping your kid become a more successful and independent learner:

1. *Create a special homework spot.* To help your kid gain a sense of the importance of homework, set aside a special place just for him to work. Any place that has good lighting and is reasonably quiet is fine. Then have your kid help stock it with necessary supplies, such as pens, pencils, paper, scissors, a ruler, a calculator, and a dictionary. If you don't have a desk, store supplies in a plastic bin or box. It will help your kid get organized.
2. *Know the teacher's expectations.* Check with the teacher periodically throughout the year so you're clear on her homework expectations. For instance, when are test dates communicated? When is library day? Are there spelling tests each week? When are book reports due? Are reports to be typed or handwritten?
3. *Set a routine from the beginning.* Select a time that works best for your kid—after school, before dinner, after dinner— and then stick to it. You may want to post your agreement in a visible place. Drawing a clock face of the time is helpful for younger kids.

No More Misbehavin'

4. *Communicate that homework is not an option.* From the beginning, maintain a firm, serious attitude. Your kid needs to know that homework has to be done well. There is no choice.

5. *Teach planning skills.* Show your kid how to make a list of what needs to be done each night in order of priority. He can then cross each item off as it is done. A young child can draw a different task on paper strips, put them in the order he plans to complete them, and then staple the packet together. Each time a task is finished, your child tears off a strip until no more remain.

6. *Offer help only when it's really needed.* If your kid is having difficulties, help her understand the work by making up similar problems and showing her step by step how to do it. Then watch her try to do one on her own. Asking her to show you her completed work at the end of each row or section is another way to ensure she's following the directions correctly but not relying on you for every detail.

7. *Divide the assignment into smaller parts.* Breaking up homework into smaller chunks is often helpful for kids who have difficulty sticking to a task or seem overwhelmed with an assignment. Just tell your child to do "one chunk at a time." You can increase the size of the "work chunks" gradually as your child's confidence increases.

8. *Set a consequence for incompletion.* If you find out the homework isn't getting done, and done with the quality you expect, announce a consequence. For instance, if work isn't finished by a predetermined time (ideally, the same time each night), your child knows he will lose a desired privilege either that evening or the following day.

BEHAVIOR MAKEOVER PLAN

Talk to other parents. How do they feel about their kids' homework load? Ask what tips (if any) they have for minimizing nightly homework hassles. If you know parents of kids in your

DID YOU KNOW?

Data show the greatest benefits of doing homework are seen at the high school level, especially when students do at least five to ten hours of homework each week. The same is true for middle schoolers. Anything less demanding does not result in kids' learning more. Homework in the elementary school years has been found to have relatively little effect on academic achievement but will have a positive effect because it develops critical learning skills. Janine Bempechat, of the Harvard Graduate School of Education and author of *Getting Our Kids Back on Track,* states: "Homework, over time, serves to foster qualities that are critical to learning: persistence, diligence, and the ability to delay gratification" and is "increasingly necessary as a feature of school success" as students advance to high levels of schooling.

child's class, find out how their kids are managing the assignments. Do they think the tasks are too hard, too easy, or just right? This information will help you assess your kid's abilities.

Now it's time to take action to begin making over your kid's behavior. Use your Makeover Journal to write down your thoughts and develop your plan.

1. Think about the underlying causes of your homework battles. First, determine if your child is really capable of doing the homework. For instance, are the tasks above his abilities? Is he easily distracted? Does he have the skills needed to achieve success? Writing a list of your concerns will help you develop a plan to deal with them.

2. If the tasks are really too difficult (or so easy he's bored), set up a conference with his teacher to find out her or his perspective. Does your child need tutoring? Is the class too hard? Is the reading (or math) group too difficult? What changes can be made to ensure your kid does succeed? Write a plan.

3. Think how you are reacting to these battles. Are you hovering, pleading, correcting, signing, bribing, protecting, demanding? If so, how will you change your reaction so it doesn't hinder your relationship with your kid?

4. Now comes the big question: How much of the work is your kid doing on his own? Remember that homework is for your kid, not you. Your job is to guide, not do. Reflect on what's not working, and then make a plan to turn it around.

5. Reread the eight strategies. Then choose the two that might help your kid the most. Write out the steps you'll take to ensure that you succeed.

6. If you find your child is really having a difficult time with homework or your relationship with him is suffering, consider hiring a tutor. Ask your teacher or other parents for recommendations. HINT: Don't overlook a high school student as a possible tutor.

➡ See also *Giving Up Easily, Hooked on Rewards, Overperfectionism, Short Attention Span.*

MAKEOVER PLEDGE

How will you use the eight strategies and the Behavior Makeover Plan to help your kid achieve long-term change? On the lines below, write exactly what you agree to do within the next twenty-four hours to begin your kid's behavior makeover.

_____

_____

_____

MAKEOVER RESULTS

All behavior makeovers take hard work, constant practice, and parental reinforcement. Each step your kid takes toward change may be a small one, so be sure to acknowledge and congratulate every one of them along the way. It takes a minimum of twenty-one days to see real results, so don't give up too soon. Remember that if one strategy doesn't work, another will. Write your child's weekly progress on the lines below. Keep track of daily progress in your Makeover Journal.

Week 1

_____

_____

_____

Week 2

_____

_____

_____

Week 3

_____

_____

_____

RESOURCES

Ending the Homework Hassle, by John K. Rosemond (Kansas City, Mo.: Andrews McMeel Publishing, 1990). Demonstrates ways to help kids learn to work on their own and take responsibility for getting the work done themselves.

Seven Steps to Homework Success: A Family Guide for Solving Common Homework Problems, by Sydney Zentall and Sam Goldstein (Plantation, Fla.: Specialty Press, 1999). A guide to help kids achieve homework success by teaching them to do the work with you assisting only if needed.

How to Help Your Child with Homework: Every Caring Parent's Guide to Encouraging Good Study Habits and Ending the Homework Wars, by Marguerite Cogorno Radencich and Joeanne Shay Schumm (Minneapolis, Minn.: Free Spirit Publishing, 1997). Broken down into subject and age appropriateness, gives ideas galore for parents of elementary and middle school students.

The Homework Handbook: Practical Advice You Can Use Tonight to Help Your Child Succeed Tomorrow, by Harriett Cholden, John A. Friedman, and Ethel Tiersky (Lincolnwood, Ill.: Contemporary Books, 1998). Comprehensive treatment of a worrisome topic that offers practical advice to parents.

How to Do Homework Without Throwing Up, by Trevor Romain and Elizabeth Verdick (Minneapolis, Minn.: Free Spirit Publishing, 1997). Hilarious cartoons and text provide helpful homework tips and insights. Ages 9 to 12.

The Study Skills Handbook (Grades 4–8), by Judith Dodge (New York: Scholastic, 1994). Teaches kids strategies they need to be effective and organized learners.

15

Hooked on Rewards

*W*henever *my five year old picks up his toys or waits without interrupting me when I'm on the phone, I give him a little treat like candy or a quarter. But now, whenever I ask him to do anything, he says, "What'll you give me?" I think my idea is backfiring: he expects to be rewarded. Now what?*

— Amy, a single mom with one child from
  Lincoln, Nebraska

"What do I get if I do it?"
"How much will you give me?"
"I won't do it for less than ten dollars."

BEHAVIOR TIP

Rewards and incentives don't always bring about the behavior changes we hope for. In fact, rewards can backfire. The more kids receive them, the more they seem to expect.

Heard these words lately from your darling offspring? If so, the chances are that your kid is suffering from a widespread kid epidemic called "hooked on rewards." They expect the gold stars, stickers, or money for a job well done. The danger is that instead of developing internal motivation, these kids end up with a highly developed external dependence system that relies on someone else to acknowledge their actions. One of our most important parenting tasks is to help our kids become self-reliant and recognize that they have control over their lives and the choices they make. Although we may relish the role of cheering our kids on to success, in the end our kids have to be their own cheerleaders and learn to count on themselves, not on us.

SIX STRATEGIES TO WEAN KIDS FROM EXTERNAL REWARDS

Use the following strategies as a guide to help your kid become responsible for reinforcing his own behavior and not expect something in return:

1. *Stop giving material rewards for every little thing.* Take a firm stand against unnecessary incentives. Expect your kid to help out at home and do the best she can in school and other activities. This is the only way your child will learn to be self-reliant, independent, and self-motivated.
2. *Switch your pronouns from I to you.* One of the easiest ways to wean kids away from external control is simply to change the pronouns in your praise: switch your *I* to *you*— for example:

   I statement: "I'm really proud of how hard you worked today."
   You statement: "You must be really proud of how hard you worked today."

This switch takes the emphasis off your approval and puts more on the child's acknowledging her appropriate actions. It also helps kids begin to regulate their own actions.

3. *Encourage internal praise.* Point out what they did that deserved merit, and then remind them to acknowledge themselves internally (to use self-talk). Suppose your son has difficulty being a good sport when his soccer team loses. This time he really made an effort not to blame everyone for the loss. At a private moment, encourage him to acknowledge his success: "John, you really made an effort not to say anything negative about the other team today. You were being a good sport. Did you remember to tell yourself that you did a great job?"

4. *State what you see.* The very next time your kid does something noteworthy, keep your wallet closed. Instead, state a simple judgment-free comment: "You rode your bike all by yourself!" or "Wow, you really put a lot of work into this report. Good for you!" Or simply smile and say, "You did it."

5. *Ask questions to boost internal pride.* Instead of being so quick to reinforce your kid, find out what pleased her about the job she did. "How did you learn to balance yourself without the training wheels?" or "What was the hardest part about writing that report?" Nurture your kid's internal motivation by putting the success back inside her corner.

6. *Keep an Accomplishment Journal.* Give your kid a small journal. At least once a week, ask him to spend a few minutes writing (or drawing) his successes. Explain that the true definition of success is a four-letter word spelled g-a-i-n. It is any improvement, big or small, that your kid thinks he has made. The simple routine helps kids slowly recognize that they are their own best behavior guide and reinforcer.

BEHAVIOR MAKEOVER PLAN

Start by thinking about your childhood. Did your parents give you monetary rewards or incentives for a job well done? Talk

to other parents: Do they pay kids for good grades, doing
chores, good efforts, or contributing around the house? How
valuable do you think such rewards are for improving kids'
behavior? What about your kid's behavior?

Are there determinants to using behavioral incentives?
If so, what are they? Is there a point where you've gone too
far in offering incentives for good behavior? How would you
know it's too far? How do you draw the line? Where is your
line? Write down where you stand, so you can review it any
time you might waver from your belief.

Now it's time to take action to begin making over your
kid's behavior. Use your Makeover Journal to write down
your thoughts and develop your plan.

1. Take a good look at your kid's behavior. When were you
   first concerned that your kid was becoming hooked on
   rewards? Write your concerns.
2. How will you start weaning your kid away from expecting
   a reward each time he achieves or even does something
   you ask? Going completely "cold turkey" is probably

unreasonable, so what might a reasonable first step be? Write it.

3. How will you explain your new behavior standards to your kid? Plan what you will say.
4. Plan how you will react the next time your kid asks, "What do I get?"
5. Review the strategies, and then choose one or two you'd first like to experiment with. Reflect on how you'd use the strategy with your kid, and write down your plan.
6. Continue to use the strategies until you see change in your child's behavior.

Of course, there are special occasions when you may want to show your appreciation and respect by giving an appropriate present. And because your gift isn't an everyday event, it will much more appreciated.

➡ See also *Materialistic, Selfishness.*

MAKEOVER PLEDGE

How will you use the six strategies and the Behavior Makeover Plan to help your kid achieve long-term change? On the lines below, write exactly what you agree to do within the next twenty-four hours to begin your kid's behavior makeover.

_____

_____

_____

MAKEOVER RESULTS

All behavior makeovers take hard work, constant practice, and parental reinforcement. Each step your kid takes toward change may be a small one, so be sure to acknowledge and congratulate every one of them along the way. It takes a minimum of twenty-one days to see real results, so don't give up too soon. Remember that if one strategy doesn't work, another will. Write your child's weekly progress on the lines below. Keep track of daily progress in your Makeover Journal.

Week 1

_____

_____

Week 2

_____

_____

Week 3

_____

_____

RESOURCES

Kids Are Worth It! Giving Your Child the Gift of Inner Discipline, by Barbara Coloroso (New York: Morrow, 1994). A wonderful resource of parenting ideas to develop internal motivation.

Punished by Rewards, by Alfie Kohn (Boston: Houghton Mifflin, 1993). A strong argument regarding raising kids on rewards and how it robs them of developing strong inner motivation.

Raising a Responsible Child: How Parents Can Avoid Overindulgent Behavior and Nurture Healthy Children, by Elizabeth M. Ellis (Secaucus, N.J.: Carol Publishing Group, 1995). Ways to help your child become more self-sufficient and independent, no matter what his current maturity level.

Too Much of a Good Thing: Raising Children of Character in an Indulgent Age, by Daniel Kindlon (New York: Hyperion, 2001). How to set the right balance between helping kids and overindulging them.

Impulsivity

I'm so concerned about my middle schooler that I can't sleep. She makes such quick and thoughtless decisions when she's with her friends. The other night she and her friends left a sleepover at one in the morning to go to a 7–11 and get sodas and magazines. I'm scared she's going to do something really stupid and get in major trouble or even get hurt. She's a smart kid and makes great grades, but once she turned twelve, I think she started losing IQ points. What can I do?

—Rebecca, a mother from Shaker Heights, Ohio

BEHAVIOR TIP

You can help your kids make safer and wiser decisions by showing them how to pause and think about their choices and possible consequences before they act.

Running after a ball into the street.
Tripping a friend as he goes down the hall.
Skateboarding off the end of a pier.

The habit of not being able to wait can produce long-term negative results. In 1960, Walter Mischel, a psychologist at Stanford University, conducted the now-famous marshmallow test. Mischel challenged a group of four year olds: Did they want a marshmallow immediately, or could they wait a few minutes until a researcher returned, at which point they could have two marshmallows? Mischel's researchers then followed up on the children upon their high school graduation and found that those who had been able to wait for those marshmallows years before at age four were now far more socially competent. They were more personally effective, self-assertive, and better able to deal with the frustrations of life. The one-third who waited longest also had significantly higher Scholastic Aptitude Test scores by an average of two hundred points of the total verbal and math scores combined than the teens who couldn't wait when they were four years old. Those results clearly revealed the importance of helping kids develop the ability to cope with behavioral impulses. And with the range of issues facing our kids, tuning up this behavior could well be one that also saves their lives.

THREE STEPS TO REDUCE IMPULSIVITY

Use the three following steps: (1) Stop, (2) Think, and (3) Act Right to help your kid be less impulsive and learn to stop to think *before* he acts. The first initials of each part spell STAR. Help your kid remember the STAR way to stay out of trouble.

Step 1. Stop and Freeze Before Acting
The first part to helping your kid restrain impulses is the most important: you must help them to learn to stop and freeze

before acting. The split second she takes to freeze and *not* act on an impulse can make a critical difference, especially in stressful or potentially dangerous situations. Stopping is not easy for many kids to learn, particularly for those who are younger or more impulsive. At first, you may have to physically restrain your child by gently but firmly putting your hands on her shoulders and saying, "Stop and freeze." Continue doing so as situations arise until she can stop on her own.

You might also help your kid develop a special response that reminds her to freeze, such as putting a pretend stop sign or red light in front of her eyes or just saying, "Stop and freeze" inside her head.

Step 2. Think of the Possible Consequences of a Wrong Choice

The second step in helping kids control impulses is getting them to think about their stressful situation and the possible consequences of a wrong choice. The easiest way to train thinking is by teaching your child to quickly look around him, see what's happening, and then ask himself such questions as: Is this right or wrong? Is this a good idea? Can someone get hurt? Is this safe? Could I get in trouble? Even very young kids can learn this step. Your child will need you at the beginning to remind him of the questions, so you will need to ask your child the questions repeatedly at first. When he hears you asking the same question or two over and over, he will begin using them inside his own head without your prodding. Here are four strategies you can teach that help kids think through possible consequences:

- Tell her to pretend she is a fortune-teller who can look into the future. Then ask, "What do you see happening if you did that?"
- Teach your kid to ask himself, "If I did that now, will I still feel okay about it tomorrow?" If the answer is no, he should not do it.

- Teach one critical decision-making rule: "If you're not comfortable, don't do it." If she ever feels she may later regret making a particular decision, she should always eliminate that choice.
- Tell an older kid to use his gut instinct: "If you feel it isn't right, is unsafe, or you could get in trouble, chances are you will. Act on what your instincts tell you. They're usually right."

Step 3. Teach How to Act Right

This last step helps your kid recognize that she alone is ultimately responsible for her actions. Responsible kids not only think before they act but also accept whatever happens— without making excuses, blaming, or spouting out rationalizations—even if the outcome turns out to be not safe or wise. The point is that all kids are bound to make unwise decisions sometimes; that's part of life. If your child did make an unwise decision, use it as an opportunity to help her think through what she did wrong so she can make a better choice the next time. Here are a few questions you can use to help her sort out what happened following one of her impulsive decision-making episodes:

"What did you want to happen? What happened instead?"
"At what point did you think it might turn out right?"
"Did you think about saying no? What made you keep going?"
"What could you do the next time so it won't happen again?"

BEHAVIOR MAKEOVER PLAN

Think about your kid's behavior. Jot down a few notes to help you develop your makeover plan. Here are questions to consider: What does he do that you consider impulsive? How

long have you noticed these impulsive behaviors? Does he
display this behavior in environments other than your home?
If so, where? Why? Are there certain situations or people who
incite his impulsivity? Why? Talk to other caregivers for your
kid to see if their observations match yours.

What strategies, if any, have you already tried to help
your kid control his impulses? Why do you think they were
unsuccessful? Is there anything you might do differently?
Write it down.

Now it's time to take action to begin making over your
kid's behavior. Use your Makeover Journal to write down
your thoughts and develop your plan.

1. Is your kid capable of controlling his impulses? If you have
   any concerns, consult a medical doctor. Even if he is diagnosed with an attention problem, he still needs to learn to
   control his impulses so he doesn't rely on medication.
2. Reread Step One, and choose one technique to teach your
   kid. Write your plan on the calendar, noting when you will
   begin.
3. Reread Step Two, and think through how you might use
   the strategies with your kid. Plan exactly what you will do
   and say, so that when the opportunity comes, you'll be able
   to use the strategy without referring to this book.

4. Review Step Three. Think of a recent impulsive decision your kid made that you could turn into a teachable moment. Your aim is not to lecture but to guide your kid so she recognizes at what point her actions took a wrong turn, and then help her think through what she might have done instead. Plan what you will say.
5. Once you teach an impulse-control strategy to your kid, you must help her practice it, over and over and over, until it becomes second nature. Only then will she be able to use the method during a trying time. Work those practice times into your daily schedule, and continue until you see she can use it without your guidance.

➡ See also *Anger, Anxiety, Fighting, Negative Peer Pressure, Short Attention Span.*

MAKEOVER PLEDGE

How will you use the three steps and the Behavior Makeover Plan to help your kid achieve long-term change? On the lines below, write exactly what you agree to do within the next twenty-four hours to begin your kid's behavior makeover.

_____

_____

_____

MAKEOVER RESULTS

All behavior makeovers take hard work, constant practice, and parental reinforcement. Each step your kid takes toward change may be a small one, so be sure to acknowledge and congratulate every one of them along the way. It takes a minimum of twenty-one days to see real results, so don't give up too soon. Remember that if one strategy doesn't work, another will. Write your child's weekly progress on the lines below. Keep track of daily progress in your Makeover Journal.

Week 1

Week 2

Week 3

RESOURCES

The resources that follow are written primarily for children with attention deficit disorders. They are included here because the strategies work for any impulsive child.

Driven to Distraction, by Edward Hallowell and John J. Ratey (New York: Touchstone, 1994). An excellent resource on attention deficit disorder and attention deficit–hyperactivity disorder.

Raising a Thinking Child, by Myrna B. Shure (New York: Holt, 1994). A valuable resource full of ideas for teaching problem solving and feeling identification to children 3 to 7 years of age.

Ritalin Is Not the Answer, by David Stein (San Francisco: Jossey-Bass, 1999). Another excellent resource on attention deficit disorder and attention deficit–hyperactivity disorder and techniques for managing behavior without medication.

Raising Huckleberry Finn: A New Narrative Approach to Working with Kids Diagnosed ADD/ADHD, by David Nylund (San Francisco: Jossey-Bass, 2000). A new drug-free strategy for treating playful, adventuresome, restless, and rebellious kids.

Talking Back to Ritalin, by Peter Breggin (Monroe, Me.: Common Courage Press, 1998). Interesting reading for any parent faced with the dilemma of whether to use Ritalin.

The Myth of the A.D.D. Child, by Thomas Armstrong (New York: Dutton, 1995). Useful, practical drug-free strategies to help kids with short attention spans.

17

Intolerance

My eleven-year-old son just told me he doesn't want any African American friends. He wouldn't elaborate, and I'm totally surprised because I've been telling him about accepting people for who they are since he was little. I'm curious: Could he have learned this prejudice in school or from his friends in the neighborhood?

—John, a dad with two kids from San Diego, California

BEHAVIOR TIP

Hatred and intolerance can be learned, but so too can sensitivity, understanding, empathy, and tolerance. Although it's certainly never too late to begin, the sooner we start, the better is our chance of preventing insidious, intolerant attitudes from taking hold.

"Blondes are dumb!"

"Jews are all rich."

"Chinese are all smart."

Figures show that American youth are displaying intolerant actions at alarming rates and at younger and younger ages. Researchers say that most hate crimes are committed by youth younger than age nineteen, and following the September 11, 2001, terrorist attack on America, FBI reports reveal a surge in racism aimed at Arab Americans. Kids are not born hateful; they learn prejudice. If children are to have any chance of living harmoniously in this multiethnic twenty-first century, it is critical that parents model and nurture a healthy appreciation of differences and diversities.

FOUR STEPS TO SQUELCHING INTOLERANCE

Here are four steps you can use that will help curtail bigotry while at the same time influencing your kids to treat others with tolerance.

Step 1. Embrace Diversity

Inexperience or lack of information are two of the most common reasons that children develop stereotypes or insecurities about others. Encourage your child, no matter how young, to make friends with individuals of different races, religions, cultures, genders, abilities, and beliefs. Expose him to positive images—including toys, music, literature, videos, public role models, and examples from TV or newspaper reports—that represent a variety of ethnic groups. Also, involve your child in programs in school, after school, or even at a summer camp that foster diversity. Make sure you display openness to people who represent a range of positive diversities so that your child imitates how you respect differences.

Step 2. Emphasize Similarities

Encourage your child to look for what he has in common with others instead of how he is different. Anytime your child points out how she is different from someone, you might say, "There are lots of ways you are different from other people, but there are probably even more ways that you are the same." "Yes, Gabriella's skin is a different color from yours. But she fights with her brother, she loves her mom and dad, she tries to look nice, she wants to have friends who like her, she's cares about basketball—just like you." Help her see how similarities outweigh differences.

Step 3. Refuse to Allow Discriminatory Comments

Your kid may make prejudicial comments or repeat discriminatory jokes—for example, "Those guys are a bunch of fags," "Hey, did you hear the one about the Polack who . . . ?" or "Those Asian kids are all such brainy nerds. They'll all get into whatever college they want!" How you respond to these statements sends a clear message to your child about your values. When you hear such comments, emphasize your discomfort, and verbalize your displeasure: "That's a biased comment, and I don't want to hear it." Your child needs to hear your discomfort so that she knows you really walk your talk. It also models a response she should imitate if prejudicial comments are made in her presence.

Step 4. Squelch Stereotypical Messages

An important part of ending prejudice is helping kids tune into the way they generalize about other people or groups. Be sure they listen for any sweeping categorical statements they or another person might make, such as "You always . . . ," "They never . . . ," or "They're all . . . ," because chances are that what follows is an intolerant stereotype. Sara Bullard, author of *Teaching Tolerance,* suggests you tell your kids that whenever someone in the family makes such a sweeping statement, another family member should gently remind the speaker by saying, "*Check that!*" For example if your kid says, "Asian kids always get good grades," a sibling could respond: "Check that! I know an Asian kid in my class who is flunking math."

When you're clear as to why your kid expresses such intolerant views, challenge his prejudicial feelings with more accurate information. For example, if your child says, "Homeless people should get jobs and sleep in their own houses," you might counter, "There are many reasons homeless people don't work or have houses. Some of them are ill. Some can't find jobs. Houses cost money, and not everyone can pay for a house or an apartment."

BEHAVIOR MAKEOVER PLAN

Can you think of specific instances when your parents demonstrated intolerance toward anyone when you were growing up? What were some of your parents' prejudices? Do any of those remain with you today? Do you feel you are passing any of these on to your child? If so, which ones? Take time to reflect

DID YOU KNOW?
Gordon Allport, a Harvard social psychologist, explored the roots of intolerance and published the results in his renowned classic, *The Nature of Prejudice*. He found that children who grow up to become tolerant are generally raised in families where three conditions prevail: strong parental love and warmth, consistent discipline, and clear models of moral behavior. When children's needs in these areas are not met, intolerance develops.

on how you might be projecting those outdated ideas to your child. Then make a conscious attempt to temper them so that they don't become your child's prejudices.

How many friends of other ethnicities or cultures do you invite to your home or include in your family activities? Should you make a greater effort to have a more diverse group of friends? If so, how will you accomplish that?

Now it's time to take action to begin making over your kid's behavior. Use your Makeover Journal to write down your thoughts and develop your plan.

1. Take a good look at how your kid treats others who are different from him. For instance, does he show disrespect or anxiety toward people because of their differences—race, religion, sexual orientation, beliefs, appearance, age, gender, disabilities, or culture? Does she make comments or jokes that put another group or person down or focus on their negative traits?
2. Tune into your child's culture, and monitor what he watches, reads, and listens to. Be particularly aware of music, movies, video games, and TV shows that can spread hateful negative stereotypes. Make a plan to stop the source.
3. Reread Steps One and Two. Ask yourself how you could expose your kid to more positive images that represent a variety of ethnic groups. Find simple ways to broaden your child's exposure to diversity.
4. Reread Step Three, and plan what to do when a relative, colleague, or family friend makes a prejudicial comment or repeats a discriminatory joke in your kid's presence. Rehearse exactly what you'll say no matter to whom it must be said.
5. Reread Step Four, and review the strategies for squelching stereotypical messages. Practice the technique a few times with your kid, and then remind yourself each day to review the strategy. Look for natural opportunities to use the strategies throughout the day, such as while you're watching TV, reading together, or car-pooling.

Each day, hundreds of new sites are posted on the Internet that promote racial supremacy, hate, intolerance, and bigotry, and kids can easily access them. This is a good time to tell your kids that these sites do not represent the views of your family. Then remind them how much discrimination hurts. To be on the safe side, always keep your computer in a visible location, take advantage of any parental controls offered by your Internet server, and install child-protection software that blocks access to hate sites.

➡ See also *Anger, Meanness, Negative Peer Pressure, Put-Downs, Rudeness.*

MAKEOVER PLEDGE

How will you use the four steps to improve tolerance and the Behavior Makeover Plan to help your kid achieve long-term change? On the lines below, write exactly what you agree to do within the next twenty-four hours to begin your kid's behavior makeover.

_____

_____

_____

MAKEOVER RESULTS

All behavior makeovers take hard work, constant practice, and parental reinforcement. Each step your kid takes toward change may be a small one, so be sure to acknowledge and congratulate every one of them along the way. It takes a minimum of twenty-one days to see real results, so don't give up too soon. Remember that if one strategy doesn't work, another will. Write your child's weekly progress on the lines below. Keep track of daily progress in your Makeover Journal.

Week 1

_____

_____

_____

Week 2

_____

_____

_____

Week 3

_____

_____

_____

RESOURCES

I'm Chocolate, You're Vanilla, by Marguerite Wright (San Francisco: Jossey-Bass, 1998). Great tips on how kids who are born color-blind can be protected from learning prejudice and intolerance.

40 Ways to Raise a Nonracist Child, by Barbara Mathias and Mary Ann French (New York: HarperPerennial, 1996). A simple guide for helping parents talk openly with their kids about racism and respect for racial differences.

Teaching Peace: How to Raise Children to Live in Harmony—Without Fear, Without Prejudice, Without Violence, by Jan Arnow (New York: Perigee Books, 1995). Ways to encourage tolerance and respect in kids.

Teaching Tolerance, by Sara Bullard (New York: Doubleday, 1996). Solid research-based suggestions for raising more open-minded, tolerant, and empathetic children.

Angel Child, Dragon Child, by Michele Maria Surat (New York: Scholastic, 1983). About a young Vietnamese girl who arrives at her new American school and faces taunts by her classmates for her cultural differences. Ages 4 to 8.

My Dream of Martin Luther King, by Faith Ringgold (New York: Crown Publishers, 1995). An interpretation of Martin Luther King's legacy and the civil rights movement that poignantly urges that intolerance, hatred, and prejudice be replaced by love, tolerance, and dreams. Glorious! Ages 8 to 12.

BEHAVIOR 18

Lack of Friends

My ten-year-old daughter is always complaining that she has no friends and that all of her classmates are mean to her. So I volunteered to go on the class field trip to see if the kids really were unkind. Watching how she interacted with them showed me a whole different story. She's demanding, always wants her own way, and really has no idea of how to be a friend. Is there anything I can do to help her?

—Harold, a single dad from Fort Worth, Texas

BEHAVIOR TIP
There can be many different reasons that a child has few or no friends. As parents, we can help identify why they lack friends and teach them skills to improve their social competence.

145

"Why wasn't I invited?"
"Nobody likes me!"
"Kevin says I'm too bossy."

Friends play an enormous role in our kids' lives. Our real parenting goal should not be to try to produce popular kids, but to help them gain the confidence they'll need to deal successfully with any social situation. After all, that's a major part of what life is all about. The good news is that friendship-making skills can be taught. By teaching your kid one new skill at a time and practicing it together over and over until he can use it on his own, you can help him improve his friendship-making skills.

FOUR STEPS TO HELP GAIN FRIENDS

Here are four steps you can use as a guide to help you boost your kid's social skills and enhance his ability to be a better friend.

Step 1. Target Behaviors That Prevent Friendship

Identify what skills your kid lacks that may be hindering him from having friends or being a good friend. Remember that the ability to make and keep friends uses social skills, and they are all learned. You can teach them to your kid. Following is a list of behaviors often displayed by children needing a boost in friendship-making skills. Check areas that concern you, and compare your notes with other adults who know your child well.

Warning Signs of Friendship Problems

_____ Doesn't take turns
_____ Acts like a poor loser
_____ Rarely cooperates

_____ Shows little empathy for others' feelings
_____ Lacks the skills to play the game
_____ Acts too competitively
_____ Acts too immature for the group
_____ Acts too mature for the group
_____ Hoards toys and doesn't share
_____ Acts discourteously
_____ Always make excuses when losing
_____ Stands too close to (or too far from) other kids
_____ Acts bossy; always wants his own way
_____ Uses a sulky, unhappy expression
_____ Criticizes too often
_____ Interrupts; never listens to others
_____ Barges into an activity too quickly
_____ Doesn't how to initiate or end a conversation
_____ Doesn't know how maintain a conversation
_____ Doesn't know how to join a group; hangs back
_____ Doesn't pay attention to the group
_____ Doesn't use eye contact
_____ Quits before the game is over
_____ Gets upset and angry easily
_____ Uses a whiny, unfriendly, or loud voice
_____ Switches rules midstream

Step 2. Select and Coach New Friendship Skills

Choose one or two problems from the list of warning signs, and replace them with friendship skills. For instance, if she is demanding and uncompromising, your goal is to teach her how to get what she wants by meeting other kids halfway. Find a private moment to role-play the new skill to your child. Talk with her about why the skill is important, and then be sure she can show you how to do the skill correctly. It's helpful to go with your child to a public place such as a playground or schoolyard where she can observe other kids using the skill. Seeing the skill in action helps your kid copy it, so she can try it on her own.

Step 3. Find Opportunities to Practice the Skill and Offer Feedback

Just telling your kid about the skill is not enough. She needs to try it out with others. The best kids for your child to practice with are those she doesn't already know and are younger or less skilled. Then keep the practice session short, and stand back at a comfortable distance. Evaluate any problems your kid might be having in the group and make suggestions only privately—*never* in front of other kids. "How did it go?" "What did you say?" "How do you think you did?" "What would you do differently next time?" Don't criticize what your child didn't do; instead, praise what your child did right. As soon as your kid feels comfortable with one skill, she's ready to learn another.

Step 4. Provide Better Social Opportunities for Your Kid to Make Friends

There are many ways that parents can help their kids have friends. Here are just a few:

- Befriend other adults who have kids the same age as yours.
- Provide interactive toys, games, and sports equipment.
- Teach your kid how to encourage others. Kids like to be around kids who accept them and build them up. Brainstorm a list of supportive statements such as, "Great idea!" "Super!" "Nice try!"
- Introduce your kid to a hobby, sport, or activity that he can share with other kids.

BEHAVIOR MAKEOVER PLAN

Start by thinking about when you were growing up. Who were your best friends when you were your child's age? Did you make friends easily? What were some of the social skills you used that helped you make and keep your friends? Where did you learn them? Which social skills were harder for you? Do you think it's harder for kids to make friends today than when you were growing up? Why or why not?

Now it's time to take action to begin making over your kid's behavior. Use your Makeover Journal to write down your thoughts and develop your plan.

1. Take a good look at your kid's friendship-making skills. Observe your kid interact with peers without his being aware you're watching. Watch him in different social settings—for instance, on the playground, in a backyard, in an athletic event, at school, with one child and then with a group of kids, and with younger kids and older kids.
2. Watch kids whom your child would say are well liked. Tune into their friendship-making skills. What do they do that helps them be popular? Talk to other parents about what skills they think are important in helping kids make and keep friends.

3. Identify the friendship-making skill your child lacks from the Warning Signs of Friendship Problems. Compare your notes with other adults who know your child well.
4. Choose one friendship-making skill to teach your child. Plan how you will rehearse and practice the strategy just as he would use the skill with a peer.
5. When he feels comfortable enough with the new skill, encourage him to try it with another child. Encourage his friendship-making endeavors, and remind him that learning new skills takes work.
6. Review Step Four. Choose a strategy and write the steps you'll take.

➡ See also *Bossiness, Fighting, Negative Peer Pressure, Shyness, Tattling, Teased*.

MAKEOVER PLEDGE

How will you use the four steps to improve your kid's friendship-making skills and the Behavior Makeover Plan to help your kid achieve long-term change? On the lines below, write exactly what you agree to do within the next twenty-four hours to begin your kid's behavior makeover.

_____

_____

_____

MAKEOVER RESULTS

All behavior makeovers take hard work, constant practice, and parental reinforcement. Each step your kid takes toward change may be a small one, so be sure to acknowledge and congratulate every one of them along the way. It takes a minimum of twenty-one days to see real results, so don't give up too soon. Remember that if one strategy doesn't work, another will. Write your child's weekly progress on the lines below. Keep track of daily progress in your Makeover Journal.

Week 1

_____

_____

_____

Week 2

_____

_____

_____

Week 3

_____

_____

_____

RESOURCES

Good Friends Are Hard to Find, by Fred Frankel (Pasadena, Calif.: Perspective Publishing, 1996). Written by the director of the UCLA Parent Training and Social Skills Programs, this parent guide is invaluable. It lays out step by step how to help kids from 5 to 12 years old make friends and solve relationship problems.

"Nobody Likes Me": Helping Your Child Make Friends, by Elaine K. McEwan (Wheaton, Ill.: Harold Shaw Publishers, 1996). A handy, practical guide of ways to boost young kids' friendship-making skills.

Teaching Your Child the Language of Social Success, by Marshall P. Duke, Stephen Nowicki Jr., and Elisabeth A. Martin (Atlanta, Ga.:

Peachtree Books, 1996). Easy-to-use parent guide that includes ways to help kids improve their nonverbal skills to enhance relationships with others.

Why Doesn't Anybody Like Me? A Guide to Raising Socially Confident Kids, by Hara Estroff Marano (New York: Morrow, 1998). Helpful hints for parents on fostering traits of popularity at any age.

Cap It Off with a Smile: A Guide for Making and Keeping Friends, by Robin Inwald (Kew Gardens, N.Y.: Hilson Press, 1994). Simple, practical ideas about friendship making for young kids. Ages 3 to 5.

How to Lose All Your Friends, by Nancy Carlson (New York: Viking Press, 1994). A hilarious tale that offers advice on the kinds of things to do if you don't want to have any friends. Ages 5 to 9.

19

Lying and Cheating

I have a seven-year-old son who keeps telling small lies, like say-ing he took out the garbage or just hit a home run. I try to talk to him about the consequences of lying and that more trouble will come from lying than telling the truth. He seems to hear me, but then it happens again. Any suggestions?
—Andy, a father of two from Des Moines, Iowa

Copying an essay from the Internet as a paper for school. Saying she finished her homework but actually lost it. Blaming a friend for breaking the window.

BEHAVIOR TIP

Our role is to explain to our kids the importance of telling the truth so other people will trust them and admire their character.

Facts confirm that lying and cheating are on the rise among today's youth. Since 1969, the percentage of high school students who admitted cheating on a test has increased from 34 percent to 68 percent. Plagiarism among college students has become so rampant that many professors have to rely on a specially designed Web site to scan their students' papers to validate originality. And it isn't just the big kids: teachers say that cheating is prevalent even in the early grades. Sure, little kids don't have the experience or cognitive ability to understand that dishonesty and lying are wrong, but that doesn't mean we should condone their truth stretching. The good news is that parents *do* play a significant role in nurturing honest behaviors and strong consciences in their kids. Let's make sure we use that role wisely so our kids do turn out right.

SEVEN TIPS TO REDUCE DISHONESTY

Use the following tips as a guide to help you minimize your kid's "truth stretching" and help her become more honest:

1. *Expect and demand honesty.* Parents who raise honest kids expect their kids to be honest—and even demand that they do. Repeatedly spell out your expectations for honesty: "Everyone in our family is always expected to be honest with one another."
2. *Reinforce honesty.* Certainly we should tell our kids that it is important to tell the truth. We also should let them know how much we appreciate their truthfulness: "I really appreciate your honesty. I can count on you to say the truth."
3. *Use moral questioning.* Asking the right questions can be an important tool for enhancing kids' consciences and honesty. Here are a few to ask your kid if she lies or cheats:

   "Was that the right thing to do?"
   "Why do you think I'm concerned?"

"If everybody in the family [class] always lied [or cheated], what would happen?"
"If you don't follow through on your word, what will happen to my trust in you?"
"How would you feel if I lied to you?"
"How do you think I feel to be lied to?"

4. *Don't overreact when truth is stretched.* That's tougher said than done, but kids often use such behaviors as lying to get our attention. If your child does, stay calm so you can get down to the important issue: why he lied and what he plans to do to remedy the mistruth.
5. *Teach the difference between real and make-believe.* Deal with a young kid's "exaggerated truth" by explaining the difference between a real story (*really* true) and a make-believe story (you wish were true but really isn't). Whenever you suspect your kid might be fabricating a tale, say, "Is that real or make-believe?" The terms are less threatening than "telling a lie," and usually kids will admit their statements were make-believe.
6. *Explain why dishonesty is wrong.* When your kid lies or cheats, approach the subject head-on and help guide his conscience by explaining why it's wrong. Don't assume your kid understands the consequences; young children especially don't fully grasp why it's wrong. Reasons for being honest include these: dishonesty gets you in trouble, people won't trust you, you get a bad reputation, it can become a habit, it hurts other people, cheating isn't fair to other students who did study.
7. *Set a consequence for repeat dishonesty.* If dishonesty or cheating continues, it's time to set a consequence. The best ones help kids think how they'll change their misbehavior. Here are a few options: Write or draw a letter of apology to the victim. Write an essay or paragraph discussing at least five reasons dishonesty or cheating is bad (younger tykes could draw two reasons). Kids who cheat on tests or plagiarize

reports should be required to redo the assignment. If dishonesty continues, spend some serious uninterrupted time with your kid (if needed, go away for the weekend together) in an effort to come to an agreement on how further dishonesty will be prevented. Then spell out a clear consequence for future lying: the loss of a desired privilege or grounding.

BEHAVIOR MAKEOVER PLAN

Reflect on how well you model honesty for your family. For instance, do you tell white lies? Order from the kid's menu for kids under age twelve when your kid is thirteen years old? Do you return the extra money if a clerk makes a mistake when giving you change? Tell your kid to say you're not there if your boss phones? Do you buy a ticket for a "child under twelve" even though your kid is older? Brag about cheating on your tax return? Write a note excusing your kid's tardiness by claiming she was ill if she misses school because she oversleeps? Any time you stretch the truth, you're actually giving your kid permission to do it also. If you notice your example of truthfulness needs tuning up, what will you do to be a better model? Write your plan for being a better model of honesty.

Now it's time to take action to begin making over your kid's behavior. Use your Makeover Journal to write down your thoughts and develop your plan.

1. Seriously reflect on your kid's behavior. Usually when behaviors such as lying, stealing, fighting, or meanness suddenly emerge, they are set off by feelings of rejection, jealousy, frustration, hurt, or anger toward an adult. It could also be a fear of punishment or of letting a parent down. Asking kids why they're behaving a certain way usually doesn't work; they usually don't know the reason for their actions. So play detective. Here are some questions to consider. When did the lying start? What type of issues does he lie about? Who does he lie to—for instance, to everyone or just certain individuals? Why? What might be triggering your kid to lie? Write down your thoughts.

2. How important is it to you for your kid to be honest? If this is a trait you value, how will you let your kid recognize its importance? Write down the steps you'll take to ensure he turns out honest and trustworthy.

3. Review the first six strategies, and choose at least two. Write how you plan to use the strategy to boost your kid's honesty quotient.

4. If your kid continues to lie, review Tip Seven. Talk to other adults who know your kid well. Are they seeing the same pattern? What do they feel is the underlying cause? Develop your backup plan: What consequence will you apply the next time your kid lies? Write down the day and time you will meet with your kid to explain the consequence and attain your kid's agreement to stop this behavior.

5. If this behavior continues despite your efforts, seek outside guidance from a trained professional. *Don't wait.*

➡ See also *Anger, Cynicism, Impulsivity, Negative Peer Pressure, Stealing.*

MAKEOVER PLEDGE

How will you use the seven tips and the Behavior Makeover Plan to help your kid achieve long-term change? On the lines below, write exactly what you agree to do within the next twenty-four hours to begin your kid's behavior makeover.

_____

_____

_____

MAKEOVER RESULTS

All behavior makeovers take hard work, constant practice, and parental reinforcement. Each step your kid takes toward change may be a small one, so be sure to acknowledge and congratulate every one of them along the way. It takes a minimum of twenty-one days to see real results, so don't give up too soon. Remember that if one strategy doesn't work, another will. Write your child's weekly progress on the lines below. Keep track of daily progress in your Makeover Journal.

Week 1

_____

_____

_____

Week 2

_____

_____

_____

Week 3

RESOURCES

Golden Rules, by Wayne Dosick (San Francisco: HarperSanFrancisco, 1995). A readable parent guide featuring ten key values that parents should teach their kids.

Teaching Your Children Values, by Linda and Richard Eyre (New York: Simon & Schuster, 1993). A highly usable guide of practical ways to help children develop honesty, trustworthiness, and self-discipline, and other important values.

Why Johnny Can't Tell Right from Wrong, by William Kilpatrick (New York: Simon & Schuster, 1993). Shows how to correct weak conscience development by providing youngsters with the stories, models, and inspiration they need in order to lead good lives.

A Big Fat Enormous Lie, by Marjorie Sharmat Weinman (New York: Dutton, 1978). A little boy learns that lies turns into monsters and telling the truth is the only way to make them disappear. Ages 3 to 8.

Liar Liar Pants on Fire! by Miriam Cohen (New York: Greenwillow, 1985). Great book about a first grader, new to school, who lies to impress his classmates. Ages 4 to 7.

Don't Tell a Whopper on Fridays! The Children's Truth-Control Book, by Adolph Moser (Kansas City, Mo.: Landmark Editions, 1999). A kid-friendly book that discusses the problems of lying and the importance of telling the truth. Ages 7 to 11.

20

Materialistic

Our twelve-year-old daughter brings something home from the mall every single day whether she needs it or not. It's as though her whole existence is based on how much she owns and what she's going to buy next. When a new product is advertised, she has to own it. Her friends are the same. Is there a way to turn her materialistic streak around, or do I have to get a third job?

—Sun-lee, a mother of two from Miami, Florida

"That's so uncool. I have the latest model."
"Mom, I'll just die if I don't get one."
"But everyone else has two!"

BEHAVIOR TIP

We have to convince our kids that their identity isn't based on what they have but who they are. Make sure you provide a good example, and set very clear limits.

Advertising aimed at kids has become big business. Consider this: media surveys find that the average American child sees fifty to one hundred TV commercials every day. What's more, $3 billion is spent annually on advertising directed at them. Those marketing efforts appear to be succeeding. Not only are kids spending more—a whopping $3 billion annually—but they're becoming consumer driven. A study by Penn State's Smeal College of Business concluded that today's kids are not only more materialistic, but are also becoming so at much younger ages. The survey found no difference between the level of materialism of nine and fourteen year olds. It's our job as parents to instill in our children the understanding that their moral character, contribution to society, and quality of their relationships have far more value than anything material they could possibly acquire.

SEVEN TIPS TO
SQUELCH MATERIALISM

Here are a few tips to guide you in squelching materialism and greediness in your kid:

1. *Say no, and don't feel guilty.* Always giving your kid what he wants doesn't do him any favors. After all, *you* don't always get what you want in life. So add *no* more often to your vocabulary, and say it to your kid without guilt. Parenting isn't a popularity contest, and there will be lots of times your decision won't be appreciated. So be it. Your role is to raise a decent kid, and always giving in to his whims won't help you succeed in your quest.

2. *Teach prioritizing.* Use your kid's spending decisions as opportunities to teach financial planning as well as how to control urges. For instances, on holidays, birthdays, or back-to-school shopping, require your kid to make a list of desired gifts and then prioritize his requests in order of

preference. Young kids can draw pictures and put their choices in order. Establish clear limits as to how many gifts your kid will receive for holidays and birthdays.

3. *Limit TV.* Research has shown that the fewer commercials our kids see, the less materialistic they become. So help your kid become aware of advertisers' marketing aims. Better yet, cut down on your kids' TV time altogether. A study found that when kids' TV viewing was cut by one-third, they were 70 percent less likely than their peers to ask parents for a toy the previous week.

4. *Require giving.* One of the ways to zap kids' voracious consumer appetites is by requiring that they give to others. Begin by having your family choose a favorite cause. For example, collect blankets from neighbors for shelters; give part of a weekly allowance to needy kids; adopt an orphan through Save the Children; deliver used toys (in good condition) to the fire department. Once your family decides on a cause, commit to carrying it out. Or give your kids their allowance and require that a portion go to a charity of their choice.

5. *Encourage "no purchase" gifts.* Start a family tradition for birthdays or holidays that at least one present from each member must be handmade, *not purchased.* The gesture helps kids recognize that the best gifts are those that come straight from the heart. Possibilities are endless: a letter, poem, collage, painting, drawing, poster that depicts the child's appreciation and love for the recipient, or a pledge to do something that the recipient would enjoy, for example, sweeping out the garage, fixing breakfast in bed, taking out the trash, washing the car, pulling weeds, or getting up early to bring in the newspaper.

6. *Share your own values.* Show your kids how you value loving relationships and how moral character, service to the community, and other values transcend the materialistic world.

7. *Praise their good qualities.* Don't forget to acknowledge your kid whenever she is generous, selfless, compromis-

DID YOU KNOW?

A recent survey by *Time* found that nearly two out of three parents felt their children measure their self-worth more by possessions than they themselves did at the same age.

ing, loving, and compassionate. Doing so helps diminish materialism.

BEHAVIOR MAKEOVER PLAN

Many studies find kids are more materialistic today than in the past. Do you agree? What might be contributing to this surge of materialism? How are things different today than when you grew up? What can parents do to help kids be less materialistic?

A recent study found that parents who are more materialistic tend to have kids who are more materialistic. Think about the kind of example you are setting for your kid. For instance, do you model fiscal prudence or buy things impulsively? Make a plan to change your behavior if need be.

Now it's time to take action to begin making over your kid's behavior:

1. What might be contributing to your kid's materialistic streak? Among the many possibilities are an excessive allowance, overgenerous relatives, and easy parental monetary handouts. List possible sources, and then put a halt to them.
2. One of our biggest jobs is to help our kids learn to live independently, and that means they'll need to learn how to manage their own money without our financial contributions.

Seriously reflect on this question: "Am I raising my child to be fiscally capable?" If you have any doubts, then what will you do to help so he does? Does he need an allowance, a checking account, a budget, a savings program? Create a plan so he succeeds.

3. Reread the first five tips, and choose the ones you want to experiment with. Jot down your thoughts; then develop a plan.

4. Peers play a big part of kids' buying urges. If you see that peer pressure is contributing to your child's materialistic streak, teach her assertive skills to say no and counter the pressure.

5. Review Tips Six and Seven. How do you plan to encourage specific qualities and activities in yourself and your children that nurture strong character and spirituality and discourage materialism? Think of specific family activities that you can do together that provide service and instill identity through character and behavior. Write a plan.

➡ See also *Negative Peer Pressure, Rudeness, Selfishness.*

MAKEOVER PLEDGE

How will you use the seven tips and the Behavior Makeover Plan to help your kid achieve long-term change? On the lines below, write exactly what you agree to do within the next twenty-four hours to begin your kid's behavior makeover.

_____

_____

_____

MAKEOVER RESULTS

All behavior makeovers take hard work, constant practice, and parental reinforcement. Each step your kid takes toward change may be a small one, so be sure to acknowledge and congratulate every one of them along the way. It takes a minimum of twenty-one days to see real results, so don't give up too soon. Remember that if one strategy doesn't work, another will. Write your child's weekly progress on the lines below. Keep track of daily progress in your Makeover Journal.

Week 1

_____

_____

_____

Week 2

_____

_____

_____

Week 3

_____

_____

_____

RESOURCES

A Penny Saved, by Neale Godfrey, with Ted Richards (New York: Simon & Schuster, 1995). A resource for ideas about chores, allowance, and financial planning.

Kid's Allowances—How Much, How Often and How Come. A Guide for Parents, by David Mccurrach (Franklin, Tenn.: Kids Money Press, 2000). A practical approach to teaching kids to manage their money responsibly. Also used as a tool to encourage saving, sharing, and appropriate gift giving.

The Berenstain Bears Get the Gimmies, by Stan and Jan Berenstain (New York: Random House, 1988). Gran and Gramps come up with a plan when the cubs get greedy. Ages 4 to 7.

Alexander Who Used to Be Rich Last Sunday, by Judith Viorst (Glenville, Ill.: Scott Foresman, 1980). A perfect introduction to money management for kids aged 4 to 9. Alexander, like most other kids, has a problem saving his money.

Neale S. Godfrey's Ultimate Kids' Money Book (New York: Simon & Schuster, 1998). Playful photo collages and colorful drawings make up this fact-filled compendium of everything kids 8 to 13 could possibly need to know about money.

The Kid's Guide to Money: Earning It, Saving It, Spending It, Growing It, Sharing It, by Steve Otfinoski (New York: Scholastic, 1996). A guide for kids ages 9 to 12 that explains the fundamentals of how to thrive in the American economy.

21

Meanness

At our family reunion yesterday, I saw a side of my nine-year-old son that I don't like one bit. We were sitting around the pool, and all the kids were swimming except my five-year-old nephew. The kids kept urging him to jump in, but my nephew said he couldn't swim. And that's when my son hopped out, pushed his little cousin in, and held his head under. I immediately dove in the water and pulled him off. What really bothered me was that he didn't seem to realize how upset his cousin was—the poor boy in tears!

—Maria, mother of two from Phoenix, Arizona

BEHAVIOR TIP

No one is born mean. Kids are hard-wired for empathy and compassion, but unless we nurture those traits, they will lie dormant, and more selfish, angry, and insensitive behaviors can emerge.

"Don't sit next to me: you smell."

"Hey, fatty! You're going to break the chair."

"Don't even both coming to our try-outs Jimmy. You'll never be able to afford the equipment."

If we want our kids to be kind, it is imperative that they recognize that mean words and deeds are hurtful. Parents can play an important role in helping their kids recognize that unkind actions do have consequences. Research by Nancy Eisenberg from the University of Arizona finds that parents who give clear messages about the impact that hurtful behaviors can have on others tend to raise kinder and more empathic children. So turn your kids' unkind behaviors into teachable moments by talking things through to ensure that they understand the hurt that unkindness can cause. Although it may take a few minutes, the time will be very well spent because the process is one of the best ways to raise warmhearted kids.

FOUR STEPS TO REDUCE MEAN BEHAVIOR

Here are four discipline steps to use to correct your kid's unkind behaviors and boost empathy.

Step 1. Target the Mean Behavior, Not Your Kid

When you see your kid being mean, immediately call her attention to the behavior. Don't fall into the trap of giving a lengthy sermon on the Golden Rule (our lectures generally turn kids off anyway). Instead, take time to name and briefly describe the child's unkind actions. Your message should focus *only* on your child's unkind behavior, not on the child. You want to make sure she clearly understands what unkind behavior you object to and why you disapprove. Here are a few examples of how to target unkind behavior:

No More Misbehavin'

"Calling your cousin 'Four Eyes' was unkind. Name-calling is not nice because it puts someone down. That's something I just can't allow."

"Telling your sister fat jokes and calling her 'fatty' is not kind. You're laughing at her, not with her. You may not tease if it hurts the person's feelings."

"Not asking your friend which show he wanted to watch was uncaring. You're watching only what you want and not considering what he'd like. I expect you to be a more thoughtful host."

Step 2. Help Your Child Empathize with Her Victim's Feelings

The critical part of disciplining a child who has acted unkindly is helping her understand how her actions affected the other person. Here are a few questions that help kids reflect on the impact their unkind actions had on their victim's feeling:

"Can you see how upset your brother is? How did your behavior make him feel?"

"You made her cry. How do you think she feels?"

"Did you notice how your unkindness made her feel? How would you feel if somebody did that to you?"

Step 3. Teach a New Behavior to Replace the Mean Action

Now ask your kid one critical question: "Next time, what will you do instead?" Too often, we overlook this step because we assume that the child knows a new way to behave. Don't make that assumption! I've seen many kids become repeat offenders because no one took the time to talk them through what their replacement behavior should be. After all, the most effective discipline teaches children how to act right. So teach your kid a kind, new behavior to replace the mean action— for example, encourage a friend, apologize, share, or give a compliment. Then help your child practice the new behavior so it becomes a habit.

Step 4. Give Your Child the Opportunity to Make Amends

A final part of your discipline is to help the child learn to take responsibility for her meanness by making amends. Martin Hoffman's research found that parents who call attention to the harm done by the child and encourage her to make reparations can increase their children's consideration and helpfulness. It's very important for the child to learn that once she has been mean, the action can't be taken back, but that she can ease the other person's discomfort or hurt she caused by apologizing, replacing damaged property, or going out of her way to do something positive for the injured party. Insist that she be involved in making her own plan. And above all, make sure in no uncertain terms that your kid knows that you will never tolerate cruel, mean behavior.

BEHAVIOR MAKEOVER PLAN

Studies show that mean-acting kids are on the rise. What do you think is contributing to this trend? Experts say kids aren't born mean; they learn to behave in this way. Where are kids

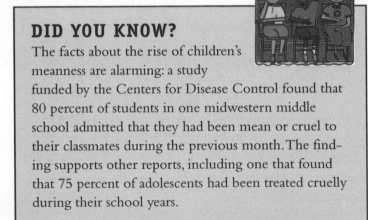

DID YOU KNOW?
The facts about the rise of children's meanness are alarming: a study funded by the Centers for Disease Control found that 80 percent of students in one midwestern middle school admitted that they had been mean or cruel to their classmates during the previous month. The finding supports other reports, including one that found that 75 percent of adolescents had been treated cruelly during their school years.

learning cruelty? Have you ever been mean to your kids? Have your kids ever seen you being mean to your spouse, family, or friends? What can parents do to reduce factors that might be escalating mean behaviors? What might you do to nurture compassion in your child? Make a list of ideas, and then choose one to act on.

Now it's time to take action to begin making over your kid's behavior. Use your Makeover Journal to write down your thoughts and develop your plan.

1. Reflect on what might be triggering your child's mean streak. When were you first concerned about his unkind behaviors? What concerned you? Now identify people he displays the behavior toward—for instance, you, your partner, siblings, friends, adults, younger kids, pets, neighborhood kids. Talk to other caregivers who know your child well and can observe his behavior in different social settings. Jot down notes.
2. Review the list of common reasons kids are mean. Could any of these be causing your kid to act unkindly? Once you determine the underlying cause of your kid's mean behavior, make a plan to remedy it.

Common Reasons Kids Are Mean

_____ *Lack of empathy.* He may not fully grasp how someone else feels because of his unkindness.
_____ *Lack of self-esteem.* She feels unworthy, so she brings the other person down.
_____ *Need to retaliate.* He has been picked on and teased, and wants to "get back."
_____ *Desire to be included.* As a way of fitting into a particular group, she puts outsiders down.
_____ *Lack of problem-solving skills.* Not knowing how to solve conflicts, he resorts to insults or name-calling.
_____ *Jealousy.* She envies the other kid, so she brings him down to feel better about herself.

_____ *How he's treated.* He is treated unkindly, so he mimics the same unkind behaviors.

_____ *Desire for power over someone else.* Teasing makes her feel superior.

_____ *No expectations for kindness.* No one tells him that unkindness is not allowed.

_____ *Poor social skills.* She doesn't know the skills for getting along—cooperating, negotiating, compromising, encouraging, listening—so she resorts to bringing the other child down.

4. Review the four steps to correcting mean behavior. Reflect on the most recent unkind behavior your kid displayed. How would you have applied the steps to correct your kid's behavior?

5. Think through what you will do and say the next time your child is unkind. How will you apply the steps to turn your kid's behavior around? Write a few notes to help you remember how you will discipline more effectively to squelch the behavior.

➡ See also *Anger, Bullying, Cynicism, Intolerance, Lack of Friends, Put-Downs, Rudeness, Selfishness.*

MAKEOVER PLEDGE

How will you use the four discipline steps to correct unkindness and the Behavior Makeover Plan to help your kid achieve long-term change? On the lines below, write exactly what you agree to do within the next twenty-four hours to begin your kid's behavior makeover.

_____

_____

_____

MAKEOVER RESULTS

All behavior makeovers take hard work, constant practice, and parental reinforcement. Each step your kid takes toward change may be a small one, so be sure to acknowledge and congratulate every one of them along the way. It takes a minimum of twenty-one days to see real results, so don't give up too soon. Remember that if one strategy doesn't work, another will. Write your child's weekly progress on the lines below. Keep track of daily progress in your Makeover Journal.

Week 1

_____

_____

_____

Week 2

_____

_____

_____

Week 3

_____

_____

_____

RESOURCES

The Brighter Side of Human Nature, by Alfie Kohn (New York: Basic Books, 1990). Drawing from hundreds of studies in half a dozen fields, Kohn makes a powerful case that caring and generosity are just as natural as selfishness and aggression.

The Caring Child, by Nancy Eisenberg (Cambridge, Mass.: Harvard University Press, 1992). A wonderful classic on understanding how caring develops.

A Special Trade, by Sally Wittman (New York: HarperCollins, 1978). When she was young, the little girl's grandfather pushed her in her stroller. When she's five, Grandfather has a stroke and she pushes Grandfather in the wheelchair. Wonderful for kids 4 to 7.

Somebody Loves You, Mr. Hatch, by Eileen Spinelli (New York: Bradbury, 1991). A year-round Valentine to read to children on the impact they have on others. Ages 6 to 10.

The Great Gilly Hopkins, by Katherine Paterson (New York: HarperCollins, 1987). A heart-wrenching tale of a foster child who is beseeched with unkindness and becomes hardened to rejection. Ages 11 to 13.

Of Mice and Men, by John Steinbeck (New York: Penguin, 1993). The friendship between a mentally disabled and warm-hearted Lenny and his protector, George, depicts a world that can sometimes be cruel and selfish. The 1992 movie version is highly recommended. For advanced readers.

Negative
Peer Pressure

M y eleven-year-old daughter was caught stealing candy out of a teacher's cabinet with two other girls. My concern is that she is so easily led by others and goes along with whatever they do. When she's older, the temptations will no longer be candy, but sex, alcohol, and drugs. How can I help her stand up for what she knows is right and not buckle in to peer pressure?
—Ruth a mother of three daughters from
Savannah, Georgia

Shoplifting.
Cheating.
Drugs and alcohol.

BEHAVIOR TIP

Resisting peer pressure becomes harder and harder as kids get older. We must give our kids strong values and personal identity from an early age so they can weather the storm of negative peer influence.

Sexual promiscuity.

Violence.

Peer pressures facing today's kids are enormous. Of course, we always hope that our kids will be able to say no to such negative influences, but it's often difficult because such choices are not always popular with their peers. The truth is that it takes real moral strength not to be influenced by others. We must help our kids develop the inner strength of character needed to buffer negative pressures and then teach them specific assertiveness skills. Only then will they be able to stand up to their peers.

SIX STRATEGIES TO RESIST NEGATIVE PEER PRESSURE

Here are six strategies you can teach your kid to stand up to peer pressure. I use the acronym ASSERT to help kids recall six ways they can stick up for their beliefs:

1. A—*Assert yourself with physical confidence.* Teach your kid to stand up for his beliefs and not back down by using confident posture: stand tall with feet slightly apart, head high, and look the person straight in the eye. Emphasize that the posture he uses to deliver his lines is usually more important than the words he says.
2. S—*Say no firmly.* Once your kid decides not to do what is being asked, stress that he must say no to the person using a friendly but firm and determined voice and *then not give in.* Remind your child that his job is not to try changing the other person's mind, but to keep himself out of trouble and follow his beliefs.
3. S—*Say goodbye and leave.* Emphasize that standing up to a friend isn't easy. Stress that he may face intimidation, teasing, or rejection for his choice, but that's what courage is all about. Sometimes the best option is to walk away from the

situation. Set up a policy with your kid that whenever he feels unsafe in a situation, he should phone, and you agree pick them up with no questions asked.

4. E—*Give a reasonable excuse.* Your child could give the peer an excuse: "I told Dad I'd be home," "I have homework," or "I promised my friend I'd come by." Tell your kids it's okay to use you as an excuse: "My mom will ground me for life if I did that!"

5. R—*Repeat your decision.* Tell your child it's sometimes helpful to repeat his decision several times like a broken record: "No, it's not right," "No, it's not right." It makes him sound assertive and helps him not back down from his stand.

6. T—*Tell reasons.* Thinking about the possible consequences of the choice helps strengthen kids' convictions not to proceed with what they're asked to do. So tell your kid to give the person the reason he's saying no: "It's illegal," "I'll be grounded," or "I could get hurt."

BEHAVIOR MAKEOVER PLAN

Think about when you grew up. What kinds of peer pressure did you face when you were a child? When you were a

DID YOU KNOW?
A survey of 991 kids ages nine to fourteen revealed troubling facts about peer pressure: 36 percent of the middle schoolers surveyed feel pressure from peers to smoke marijuana, 40 percent feel pressure to have sex, 36 percent feel pressure to shoplift, and four out of ten sixth graders feel pressure to drink.

teen? How did your parents deal with it? How did you deal with it? Was that a successful response? Would you have responded any differently now? Did you ever pressure friends to do something they didn't want to do? What was their response?

Now reflect on kids growing up today. How is it different from when you grew up? Do you think pressure today is more difficult, the same, or less tough? Why? What kinds of pressure do you think your kid faces from friends? Which kinds worry you the most? And remember that peer pressure can be positive—for instance, healthy competition, inspiring role models, stimulating new ideas.

Talk to other parents, and find out the kinds of pressures they are concerned about. Do you share any of the same concerns? Are they doing anything to help their kids resist peer pressure?

Now it's time to take action to begin making over your kid's behavior. Use your Makeover Journal to write down your thoughts and develop your plan.

1. The best way kids learn to resist negative peer pressure is by watching how we stick up for ourselves. Reflect on the kind of assertive example you are setting for your child. For example, what do you do when your business colleague asks you at a family dinner to tell your boss tomorrow that she is ill so she can take the day to shop? Or what do you do if a neighbor comes around with a half-filled petition to prevent a black couple from buying the house next door? How can you tune up your daily behavior so your kid sees how to be assertive and respectful at the same time? Write it.

2. Talk with your child about peer pressure. You might begin, "Have you ever been urged by a friend to do something you didn't want to do? How did you handle it? Did it work?" Explain that there will be lots of times when

friends ask her to do things that she doesn't want to do. Emphasize that though it's sometimes hard, she shouldn't be afraid to stand up for what she believes. Do make sure to talk often with your child about values so she has a firmly planted inner conscience and knows what she and her family stand for.

3. Identify an issue your kid may have to deal with now or in the near future. Here are a few: cheating on a test, shoplifting, giving homework answers, using drugs, looking at pornographic materials, drinking, sneaking out at night, smoking, or taking unsafe risks.

4. Review the six assertive strategies with your child. Plan to teach them over the next few days.

5. Practice each strategy together using peer pressure issues that your kid might have to deal with. Here are a few examples to role-play:

   A friend wants you to go to the store and shoplift with her. If you don't do it, she says you won't be her friend.

   You're taking a test, and a classmate wants you to give her the answers.

   You're at a slumber party. The group wants to sneak out to drink at the park.

   Role-play the parts, switching between who's the friend and who's receiving the pressure so your child can watch how you use the strategy and assert yourself.

➡ See also *Bossiness, Cynicism, Lying and Cheating, Materialistic, Shyness, Stealing.*

MAKEOVER PLEDGE

How will you use the six assertive strategies and the Behavior Makeover Plan to help your child achieve long-term change to combat peer pressure? On the following lines, write exactly what you agree to do within the next twenty-four hours to begin your kid's behavior makeover.

_____

_____

_____

MAKEOVER RESULTS

All behavior makeovers take hard work, constant practice, and parental reinforcement. Each step your kid takes toward change may be a small one, so be sure to acknowledge and congratulate every one of them along the way. It takes a minimum of twenty-one days to see real results, so don't give up too soon. Remember that if one strategy doesn't work, another will. Write your child's weekly progress on the lines below. Keep track of daily progress in your Makeover Journal.

Week 1

_____

_____

_____

Week 2

_____

_____

_____

Week 3

_____

_____

_____

RESOURCES

Stick Up for Yourself: Every Kid's Guide to Personal Power and Positive Self-Esteem, by Pamela Espeland, Gershen Kaufman, and Lev Raphael (Minneapolis, Minn.: Free Spirit Press, 1999). Realistic, how-to advice for kids on being assertive, building relationships, solving problems, and boosting self-esteem. A teacher's guide is also available. Ages 8 to 12.

What Do You Stand For? A Kid's Guide to Building Character, by Barbara Lewis (Minneapolis, Minn.: Free Spirit Publishing, 1999). An inspiring book that invites kids to build strong positive character traits such as honesty, empathy, and tolerance. Ages 11 and up.

Cliques, Phonies, and Other Baloney, by Trevor Romain (Minneapolis, Minn.: Free Spirit Publishing, 1998). Written for every kid who has ever felt excluded or trapped by a clique, this book blends humor with practical advice as it tackles a serious subject. Ages 8 to 13.

Teen Esteem, by Pat Palmer (San Luis Obispo, Calif.: Impact Publishers, 1989). A guide for developing the skills and self-esteem necessary to cope with such adolescent challenges as peer pressure and substance abuse. Ages 13 to 17.

Joshua T. Bates Takes Charge, by Susan Richards Shreve (New York: Knopf, 1993). Joshua remembers how a group of bullies used to tease him for being held back a grade and sees the same boys teasing a new student. He must make a choice. Ages 9 to 12.

What Would You Do? A Kid's Guide to Tricky and Sticky Situations, by Linda Schwartz (Santa Barbara, Calif.: Learning Works, 1990). A commonsense guide that helps kids think through how they would handle more than seventy unexpected or frightening situations. Ages 8 to 12.

BEHAVIOR 23

Overperfectionism

I *don't quite know how to describe my daughter's problem. The best term I can come up with is* failure paralyzed. *She's twelve years old and overly concerned about making sure everything she does is perfect. If she doesn't answer every test question correctly and makes a mistake (and they're rare), she sees herself as a failure. I can only imagine what will happen when she gets her first A– on her report card.*

—Greg, a dad with two kids from Boise, Idaho

BEHAVIOR TIP
It should be okay to make mistakes in your household, and this message may need to be emphasized again and again: "Everyone makes mistakes. Don't worry about your mistakes. Think about what you'll do differently the next time."

"I can't believe I could be so stupid!"

"I'll never be as good as she is at science."

"Since I made that mistake at the last student recital, I'll never play the piano in public again."

Making mistakes is how we learn, and especially how young children learn. Unfortunately, far too many kids (and grownups!) have never learned the value of making mistakes. It's important that we all learn to bounce back and learn from our big and little defeats. Successful people don't let setbacks derail them; they just find new routes to success. Kids must realize that mistakes don't need to mean failure but instead can be learning opportunities in disguise.

SIX STRATEGIES TO REDUCE OVERPERFECTIONISM

Use the following as a guide to help your kid bounce back from setbacks:

1. *Give permission to make errors.* We need to give our kids permission to fail and help them recognize that mistakes can be positive learning experiences. So make mistakes be okay in your household. Say again and again, "It's okay to make a mistake."
2. *Show acceptance.* Whenever your kid makes a mistake, show your support with both your words and your nonverbal reactions. The quickest way our kids will learn to erase the idea that mistakes are fatal is feeling our accepting response to their errors.
3. *Don't yell, shame, criticize, judge, blame, or ridicule.* Nobody (especially children!) likes to make mistakes, and they hate to be reminded that they made them.
4. *Don't call it a mistake!* A common behavior of kids who bounce back is that they are not thrown by errors. In fact, they

often call mistakes by other names *(glitch, bug, a temporary)* so they won't discourage themselves in the middle of their learning. Help your kid come up with a word to say inside his head whenever he encounters a mistake. Any word will do; just make sure to help him practice saying it over and over so he'll remember to use it when he really makes a mistake.

5. *Model how to cope.* Turn your own mistakes into success lessons for your child by modeling how you cope with your error. First, say to your child what your mistake was. Then say what you learned. Here's the formula: "My mistake was . . . " "I learned . . . from my mistake." Example: "I really blew that recipe for the cheesecake. Next time I'll read the whole recipe first, so I'll remember to add the eggs." "I had to redo a whole report at work today because I forgot to save the document on my hard drive. Next time, I'll be sure to save as I go along."

6. *Teach an affirmation.* Help your kid learn a statement to say to himself to bounce back from defeat—for example, "It doesn't have to be perfect." "It's okay to make a mistake." "I can turn it around." "Everybody makes mistakes." Once your child selects one, help him practice saying the same affirmation out loud several times for a few days. The more he hears it, the greater is the chance he'll remember it and use it.

BEHAVIOR MAKEOVER PLAN

How did you handle defeat and failure when you were growing up? Do you see any of those same behaviors in your child? Kids love to hear that their parents made mistakes when they were growing up. Have you shared your pain of failure with your child? Consider doing so. Did you learn any coping strategies that helped you bounce back? What were they? Where did you learn them? Have you modeled any of those strategies to your child? If not, think about how you might teach them to your child. Write down your reflections and plan.

DID YOU KNOW?

Harold Stevenson, a professor of psychology at the University of Michigan, sought to answer a question many Americans ask: "Why do Asian students usually do better academically than U.S. students?" After spending hundreds of hours observing students and interviewing their teachers in the United States and Asia, the researchers reached a conclusion: a critical key lies in what parents emphasize about learning. Asian parents strongly stress the value of perseverance and not letting mistakes derail efforts. And on the whole, Asian kids worked longer and harder than their U.S. counterparts because they understood that success is based on effort. They also recognized that mistakes are inevitable and used them as a way to improve their performance. American parents put their emphasis instead on the end product: the grade or score their kids achieved. The result was that the researchers found kids in the United States had shorter attention spans, gave up more quickly, and often were overperfectionists who never realized the value learning from mistakes.

Now it's time to take action to begin making over your kid's behavior. Use your Makeover Journal to write down your thoughts and develop your plan.

1. Think about your kid's behavior. Has your kid *always* shown overperfectionist behaviors? If not, when did you first notice them? Why do you think they emerged just then? What factors might have triggered the trait? Write your thoughts.

2. Reflect on which issues exacerbate your kid's perfectionism tendencies. Be specific. For instance, don't say "school" if not *every* school subject concerns her; maybe it's only math or spelling tests that bother her. Make a list of areas that tend to trigger your kid's fear of mistakes. Now reread the list to see if there is a pattern. You may discover that your child is concerned about being the best only in front of a group or always getting a perfect score on every class test. Is there anything you can do to alleviate her concerns by helping her learn to perform just for the fun of performing or help her realize that even the most intelligent people always learn from their inevitable slips and mistakes? Write your thoughts.
3. Review the strategies. Choose two to try with your kid. Write down your plans.
4. How do you typically react to your kid's errors? These reactions are especially deadly: yelling, shaming, criticizing, judging, ridiculing, or saying "I told you so." Now reflect on how your kid responds to your reaction. What might you do to change your reaction so it is more affirming and noncritical? Write what you'll say the next time your kid makes an error or fears failure. Here are three possibilities:

> Focus on what she's trying to achieve: "How did you want this to turn out?"
>
> Affirm your belief in her: "I know you can do it. Hang in there."
>
> Support trying again: "Just because it isn't easy doesn't mean you're not good at it."

➡ See also *Anxiety, Giving Up Easily, Hooked on Rewards, Poor Sportsmanship.*

MAKEOVER PLEDGE

How will you use the six strategies and the Behavior Makeover Plan to help your kid achieve long-term change? On the lines below, write exactly what you agree to do within the next twenty-four hours to begin your kid's behavior makeover.

_____

_____

_____

MAKEOVER RESULTS

All behavior makeovers take hard work, constant practice, and parental reinforcement. Each step your kid takes toward change may be a small one, so be sure to acknowledge and congratulate every one of them along the way. It takes a minimum of twenty-one days to see real results, so don't give up too soon. Remember that if one strategy doesn't work, another will. Write your child's weekly progress on the lines below. Keep track of daily progress in your Makeover Journal.

Week 1

_____

_____

_____

Week 2

_____

_____

_____

Week 3

_____

_____

_____

RESOURCES

"I Think I Can, I Know I Can!" by Susan Isaacs and Wendy Ritchey (New York: St. Martin's Press, 1989). A wonderful guide to help raise confident, secure kids who can overcome fears and bounce back from mistakes.

Fortunately, by Remy Charlip (New York: Macmillan, 1987). An absolute must for young readers. It's a model on turning your "unfortunates" into "fortunates." Ages 5 to 9.

Nobody Is Perfick, by Bernard Waber (Boston: Houghton Mifflin, 1971). A young boy finally realizes through much trial and error that nobody is "perfick," including himself! Ages 5 to 8.

Nobody's Perfect, Not Even My Mother, by Norma Simon (New York: Albert Whitman & Co., 1981). The message comes through loud and clear in this story: it's okay not to be perfect because no one is. Ages 5 to 8.

Be a Perfect Person in Just Three Days! by Stephen Manes (New York: Bantam-Skylark, 1991). Milo finds a book at the library on "how to be the perfect person!" He follows the directions carefully and finally learns the message in the end: "Being perfect is boring! Besides you're already perfect just being yourself!" Ages 8 to 12.

Mistakes That Worked, by Charlotte Foltz Jones (New York: Doubleday, 1991). A series of short stories describing over forty inventions that were all discovered by accident, including Silly Putty, ice cream cones, pizza, chocolate chip cookies, Velcro, aspirin, Frisbees, and even X-rays. Ages 9 to 12.

Perfectionism: What's Bad About Being Too Good? by Miriam Adderholdt-Elliott (Minneapolis, Minn.: Free Spirit Publishing, 1987). Discusses the dangers of being a perfectionist and has wonderful tips on easing up on oneself, gaining control over life, and getting professional help when needed. Ages 11 to 13.

No More Misbehavin'

24

Poor Sportsmanship

I watched my stepson's Little League game and was appalled with his behavior. He's a great player, but during the game, I saw him argue the rules, make excuses for his strikeouts, and blame everyone for his team's loss. At this rate, nobody's going to want him on their team regardless of how well he can play. How can I turn this behavior around?

— Tony, a stepdad of five kids from Evanston, Illinois

BEHAVIOR TIP

Any competitive situation requires honesty, fair play, compromise, cooperation, and empathy. As parents, we must model and help our kids develop those traits.

"The referee sucks."

"The coach never gave me another chance."

"I'm better than Amy. Why does she always get a better score?"

One of the most humiliating parenting moments is watching your kid act like a poor sport. Oh, he may be the best player on the field, the best singer in the chorus, or the smartest kid in the class, but as soon as he starts arguing, cheating, changing the rules to suit him, or booing, his abilities are no longer the issue. Now his character is at stake. Some of us aren't doing such a great job of modeling good sportsmanlike behavior ourselves. Besides poor modeling, the emphasis in kids' lives these days—from getting into the right preschool to getting into a highly competitive college—is often all about winning, winning, winning—and winning at any cost. It's all the more reason to nurture good sportsmanship. And make sure we tune it up in our own behavior as well.

FIVE STEPS TO SQUASH POOR SPORTSMANSHIP

Use the following steps as a guide to help your kid become a better sport.

Step 1. Identify Good Sportsmanship

The first step to improving your kid's sportsmanship is to evaluate which sports manners need a tune-up. A list of principles of good sportsmanship follows to help in your assessment:

Principles of Good Sportsmanship

_____ Takes the game seriously; no clowning

_____ Shares materials; doesn't hoard

_____ Waits his turn

_____ Accepts criticism

_____ Encourages peers; doesn't criticize their errors or abilities

_____ Is humble: doesn't brag or show off

_____ Stays positive: doesn't cheer others' mistakes or boo

_____ Avoids arguments with referee, music director, teacher, other adults, or peers

_____ Congratulates opponents

_____ Sticks to the rules; doesn't change midstream or cheat

_____ Doesn't quit midstream or leave when bored or tired

_____ Accepts defeat gracefully; doesn't cry, complain, or make excuses

_____ Works to improve performance

Step 2. Teach the Principles of Good Sportsmanship

Choose one of the principles of good sportsmanship from the list above. Begin by asking your kid to explain how he would use it. Rehearse the principle a few times at home, and then find opportunities for your kid to use it at a play rehearsal, classroom competition, or scheduled sport activity. Later that day, review how things went: "How did the other kids react? What will you do next time?" Continue teaching new principles as instances come up.

Step 3. Teach How to Encourage Peers

Good sports support and encourage each other. One way to help your kid be more encouraging is to teach the Two Praise Rule: you must praise your peers at least twice before the event ends. Discuss a few encouraging comments or actions so he has a beginning repertoire—such as "great song," "super," "great shot," and giving high fives. Continue to expand the list as opportunities materialize. Then suggest he practice the rule at any group activity— a team game, a scout meeting, a friend's house, or school— as well as at home.

Step 4. Correct Poor Sportsmanship Immediately

When your kid displays poor sportsmanship, take her aside to correct the action right away. "I heard you blaming others for your mistake." "You're fighting with the referee." "You're not letting anyone else take a turn." Then make sure she understands how to correct her behavior. If your kid displays any aggressive or uncivil behavior such as booing, hitting, or cheating, remove her immediately from the activity. Explain that she must be considerate of other people's feelings; if she is not, she may not participate.

Step 5. Play with Your Kids

One of the best ways to help your kid learn good sportsmanship is to play games together. Start by reviewing the rules, and then remind your kid he must stick by them: "Good sports don't argue about the rules. They agree to them at the beginning and don't change them unless everyone agrees to. They also take the game seriously and don't quit." Then have your kid shake hands and pledge to abide by the rules. Toss a coin into the air, and have your kid call out a side to see who goes first. As you play, deliberately make a few mistakes. Instead of making excuses, model how to handle errors: "Wow, I wasn't thinking that time," or "You got me there!" And when there is a doubt as to whose turn it was, suggest another coin toss to make things fair. You might even lose the game—on purpose, of course—but be subtle enough not to let your kid know. Show him how to lose gracefully: "Good game. Let's play again tomorrow." Then shake hands.

DID YOU KNOW?

The National Association of Sports Officials told the Associated Press recently that it receives two to three calls a week from an umpire or referee who has been assaulted by a parent or spectator. The complaints range from verbal abuse to the official's having his car run off the road by an irate parent. Youth sports programs in at least 163 cities are so concerned about the trend of poor parent sportsmanship that they now require parents to sign a pledge of proper conduct while attending their kids' games. How do adults display sportsmanship around your kid?

BEHAVIOR MAKEOVER PLAN

Think about where your kid might be learning poor sportsmanship. How well are you and your partner modeling good sportsmanship? Do you yell at the coach or referee? Do you complain to your child about her teachers? Do you cheer when your kid's opponent gets hurt? Might the example of the adults or other kids be influencing his behavior? If so, what can you do to create better examples of good sportsmanship for your kid? Write a plan.

Now it's time to take action to begin making over your kid's behavior. Use your Makeover Journal to write down your thoughts and develop your plan.

1. Take a serious look at why your kid might be demonstrating poor sportsmanship. For instance, is it that he hasn't

learned good sports behaviors, or are there other contributing factors? I've listed possibilities to help you reflect on reasons. Once you determine the contributors, think through what you'll do to remedy it.

Reasons for Poor Sportsmanship

_____	Short attention span; impulsive
_____	Doesn't enjoy the game; it's something you want him to do
_____	Poor athletic skills or ability
_____	Coach is too negative, competitive, or plays favorites
_____	Doesn't understand the rules of the game
_____	Doesn't enjoy being with the kids
_____	Low self-esteem
_____	Afraid of losing or making a mistake
_____	Overemphasis on winning (from parents, kid, or coach)

2. Review Step One. Observe your kid's sports behavior at a sporting event, park, playground, or neighborhood. HINT: Do this without his knowing you're watching. Jot down the behaviors you notice need improving. Use it as your ongoing lesson plan.
3. Review Step Two. Jot down which sports principles you'll tune up first. Think how you will teach the rule and when you will begin.
4. Review Step Three. How will you help your kid learn the Two Praise Rule? What are ways you might use the rule with your family?
5. Review Step Four. The next time your kid displays poor sportsmanship, how will you respond?
6. Review Step Five. Pick an activity to do together that your kid will really enjoy.

➡ See also *Anger, Bossiness, Lack of Friends, Lying and Cheating, Overperfectionism, Rudeness, Selfishness.*

MAKEOVER PLEDGE

How will you use the five steps and the Behavior Makeover Plan to help your kid achieve long-term change? On the lines below, write exactly what you agree to do within the next twenty-four hours to begin your kid's behavior makeover.

_____

_____

_____

MAKEOVER RESULTS

All behavior makeovers take hard work, constant practice, and parental reinforcement. Each step your kid takes toward change may be a small one, so be sure to acknowledge and congratulate every one of them along the way. It takes a minimum of twenty-one days to see real results, so don't give up too soon. Remember that if one strategy doesn't work, another will. Write your child's weekly progress on the lines below. Keep track of daily progress in your Makeover Journal.

Week 1

_____

_____

_____

Week 2

_____

_____

_____

Week 3

_____

_____

_____

RESOURCES

How to Win at Sports Parenting: Maximizing the Sports Experience for You and Your Child, by Jim Sundberg and Janet Sundberg (Colorado Springs, Colo.: Waterbrook Press, 2000). How to help your kids enjoy the sports they play, deal with game-day emotions in a healthy manner, and learn valuable sports-to-life lessons.

Learning to Play, Playing to Learn: Games and Activities to Teach Sharing, Caring, and Compromise, by Charlie Steffens and Spencer Gorin (Los Angeles: Lowell House, 1997). Over sixty entertaining kid activities that will help to manage aggressive behaviors, foster cooperation, and nurture positive conduct.

The Cheers and the Tears: A Healthy Alternative to the Dark Side of Youth Sports Today, by Shane Murphy (San Francisco: Jossey-Bass, 1999). Offers parents and coaches sensible advice and healthy alternative approaches to the competitive and stressful world of youth sports.

The Total Sports Experience for Kids: A Parents' Guide to Success in Youth Sports, by Aubrey Fine and Michael Sachs (South Bend, Ind.: Diamond Communications, 1997). An excellent book for those interested in how to put together great youth sports programs.

Way to Go, Coach! by Ron Smith and Frank Smoll (Portola Valley, Calif.: Warde Publishers, 1996). A terrific book for coaches that stresses how to nurture sportsmanship in kids.

Put-Downs

O ur nine year old just started calling her younger sisters hurtful names and making derogatory comments about them like, "You're stupid" and "Dummy." Obviously, the girls are hurt. But now the younger girls are saying the comments too. I've told them not to name-call, but they're still doing it. How do I stop it?

—Cheryl, a mom of three from Syracuse, New York

"Hey, nerd!"
"You suck!"
"You're so out of it."
"Can't you *ever* do anything right?"

BEHAVIOR TIP

Put-downs are learned. To nip them in the bud, check yourself and anyone else around your kid to see where she is picking up this bad habit.

Nothing can be further from the truth than the old nursery adage, "Sticks and stones may break my bones, but names will never hurt me." One of the quickest ways to erode family harmony and self-esteem is saying put-downs—those derogatory, negative, sarcastic comments kids zap each other with. And they are clearly on the rise. Studies reveal that kids from average families receive 460 negative statements as opposed to 75 positive acknowledgments daily. That means a child is hearing more than six times as many negative as positive comments. As the old song goes, "You have to accentuate the positive to eliminate the negative." Make sure you're surrounding a negative kid with positive examples so he has an appropriate model to copy.

FIVE STRATEGIES TO SQUELCH PUT-DOWNS

Use these activities to help your kid recognize the destructiveness of put-downs:

1. *Establish zero tolerance.* Gather your family together and say, "In this family, put-downs are not allowed. They tear people down on the inside, and our job in this family is to build people up." Now take a vow as a family to squelch them by creating a Family Care Covenant that clearly spells out in writing that put-downs are not permissible in your family. After all members sign it, post it in a visible place as a concrete reminder.

2. *Bury put-downs.* Chick Moorman, a national educational consultant, told me that one of the most powerful activities he has ever observed was a classroom "put-down funeral." The teacher began the ceremony by asking students to write as many put-downs as they could think of on slips of paper. The put-downs were placed in a shoe box, and the students then marched solemnly to the play-

ground, where they buried the box. The symbolic gesture clearly conveyed to the class that those put-downs were buried and were never to be used again. They were dead. Consider holding a put-down funeral in your backyard.

3. *Enforce turnarounds.* Establish a family rule: "Any put-down must be turned into put-up." This means that whenever a family member says a negative comment, she must turn it around and say a put-up—a positive, caring statement—to the recipient. A word of caution: the turnaround rule is wonderful, but it works only if it is consistently enforced. For some kids, putting the put-up in writing is far more comfortable than saying it. That's okay: it's a first step to making over behavior.

4. *Teach appropriate alternatives.* Explain to your child that one of the easiest ways to make the world a kinder place is by saying caring words. Ask her, "What are the words you say that make other people smile and feel good?" Then make a poster of ideas and display it. In my classroom, we always called caring words "heart stretchers," and the name always stuck. Here are a few to get you started: "Tell me what I can do." "I enjoyed that." "Hope you feel better." "Do you need anything?" "Are you all right?"

5. *Set a consequence for put-downs.* If you've tried all the approaches and still don't see an attitude change, it's time to set a consequence. See a list of consequences on pages 299–300. One possibility that's often effective is that the negative offender must do reparation for the recipient, such as doing her chore that day. Wow, does that one work!

BEHAVIOR MAKEOVER PLAN

Experts suggest that one of the best ways to stop physical confrontations is by eliminating put-downs. That's because fights usually start with one person insulting another, who then sends an insult back. Soon it spirals into a war. Have you seen this

DID YOU KNOW?

A national survey conducted by the National Parent-Teacher Organization found that the average parent makes eighteen critical, negative comments to his child for every one positive comment. Could you be serving as a negative role model to your kids?

conflict spiral with your kids? Friends? Spouse? Colleagues? National leaders? How do *you* react when someone insults you? What reaction would escalate a conflict? Reduce the chances of a conflict? How will you teach your family about the conflict spiral?

Next, think about your interaction with your family. Do you ever use insults? Sarcastic put-downs? Disrespectful nicknames? Could your behavior (or your partner's) be giving your kid permission to use put-downs? If so, what will you do to change your behavior? Write a plan.

Now it's time to take action to begin making over your kid's behavior. Use your Makeover Journal to write down your thoughts and develop your plan.

1. Where else might your kid be learning this behavior? Keep in mind that television shows are rampant with dialogue that includes sarcasm, put-downs, and name-calling. Are you monitoring what your kid is watching? If not, you might consider doing so.
2. Are there particular individuals your kid is more prone to use put-downs toward? If so, who? Now ask why this is so. For instance, is he being teased, jealous, needing attention, impulsive, being bullied, thinks it's "cool"? List possibilities

so you can get at the root of the problem and thereby develop an effective plan.

3. One reason kids name-call is that they don't know a more appropriate way to express their frustrations to their offenders. If this might be true of your kid, what will you do to help him learn how to assert himself without being insulting? Write your plan.

4. Review the five strategies. Which ones will you teach your kid? The rest of your family? Think through your teaching steps so you can ensure that your kid learns a new behavior.

➡ See also *Bullying, Cynicism, Meanness, Rudeness, Sibling Battles, Talking Back.*

MAKEOVER PLEDGE

How will you use the five strategies and the Behavior Makeover Plan to help your kid achieve long-term change in eliminating name-calling and put-downs from his behavior? On the lines below, write exactly what you agree to do within the next twenty-four hours to begin your kid's behavior makeover.

_____

_____

_____

MAKEOVER RESULTS

All behavior makeovers take hard work, constant practice, and parental reinforcement. Each step your kid takes toward change may be a small one, so be sure to acknowledge and congratulate every one of them along the way. It takes a minimum of twenty-one days to see real results, so don't give up too soon. Remember that if one strategy doesn't work, another will. Write your child's weekly progress on the lines below. Keep track of daily progress in your Makeover Journal.

Week 1

_____

_____

_____

Week 2

_____

_____

_____

Week 3

_____

_____

_____

RESOURCES

Mom, They're Teasing Me: Helping Your Child Solve Social Problems, by Michael Thompson and Lawrence Cohen, with Catherine O'Neill Grace (New York: Ballantine Books, 2002). Practical, reassuring advice to help parents deal with some of the most painful moments of childhood.

Chrysanthemum, by Kevin Henkes (New York: Mulberry Books, 1996). Chrysanthemum always thought her name was perfect—until she started kindergarten and the kids made fun of it. A perfect book for young kids about name-calling and put-downs. Ages 4 to 8.

The Meanest Thing to Say: Little Bill Books for Beginning Readers, by Bill Cosby (New York: Scholastic, 1997). A wonderful way to help

No More Misbehavin'

kids learn a lesson of a prosocial way to combat meanness and name-calling. Ages 4 to 9.

Simon's Hook: A Story About Teases and Put-Downs, by Karen Gedig Burnett (Roseville, Calif.: GR Publishing, 1999). A wonderful picture book that helps kids learn great strategies for handling put-downs. Ages 6 to 10.

Stick Up for Yourself: Every Kid's Guide to Personal Power and Positive Self-Esteem, by Gershen Kaulman, Lev Raphael, and Pamela Espeland (Minneapolis, Minn.: Free Spirit Publishing, 1999). Discusses problems facing young people such as making choices, sticking up for yourself, and solving problems. Great for any age, but especially ages 9 to 12.

Lord of the Flies, by William Golding (Upper Saddle River, N.J.: Prentice Hall, 1959). The classic novel about a group of English schoolboys stuck on a deserted island and the destructiveness of put-downs. Mature middle schoolers.

26

Rudeness

O ur polite eleven year old (or so we thought) seems to have forgotten every manner we thought we'd taught him. We were on the subway last week, and he didn't even think to offer his seat to an elderly woman who was standing next to him. Even common courtesies like "please" and "thank you" that were so etched in his behavior have evaporated. We're hoping it's only temporary. Meanwhile, we're afraid to send the kid out in public. Is it too late???
—Roger, a dad from Victoria, British Columbia, Canada

BEHAVIOR TIP

The way to teach manners is to work on one or two at a time, and then have your kids practice them enough so they can use them *without* your etiquette reminders.

Cutting in at the front of a line.

Interrupting his teacher in class.

Slamming the door in someone's face.

Leaving your cell phone on in church (or any other public place, for that matter).

Scores of studies find that ill-mannered children are less popular and don't do as well in school. You just can't help but react negatively to people who are impolite. Courteous kids, however, have an edge now and later in life: on job interviews, applicants displaying good social graces have a leg up. Therefore, it's critical that we make sure our children are "manner wise" so that they can reap those benefits. And in a world that too often emphasizes incivility, discourtesy, and sometimes just plain crudeness, it's especially important that parents tune up their kids' manners.

FOUR STEPS TO ELIMINATE RUDENESS

Here are four steps to tune up courteous behaviors and squelch rudeness in kids.

Step 1. Replace Rudeness with New Manners

The place to start helping your kid eliminate rudeness is by identifying your kid's rude behaviors and replacing each with a new manner. Choose one or two manners to teach at a time. That way your child is more likely to incorporate them into his daily life and (most important) use them *without your etiquette reminders.* There's a whole gamut of manners to choose from, including how to meet others, how to be a good host or guest, proper eating etiquette, phone etiquette, Internet etiquette, as well as an array of polite words.

Step 2. Explain the New Manner

It's always a mistake to assume kids know how to do a new behavior. Don't make that assumption: take a minute to demonstrate the new manner to your child. Here's how you might explain phone manners: "It's important that you answer with a polite and clear voice. Let's pretend someone is calling. Listen to what I say: 'Hello, this is the Sweeney residence. Who's calling, please? Oh, hello, Mr. Jones. Just a minute please, I'll get my dad.'"

Step 3. Provide Manner Practice Opportunities

New behaviors are learned best through repetition, so give your kid lots of opportunities to practice the manner you're working on. Some families target a manner or two each week. Keep in mind that one of the easiest ways to teach kids manners is to eat together regularly. What better time to practice conversation skills and table manners, chewing with your mouth closed, and learning which fork to use with each course?

Step 4. Correct Rudeness Immediately

When an inevitable slip does happen, correct the rude behavior. You could say, "Begin again, please." It's just a nicer way of saying, "It's not right, so do it over." One critical point: always try to offer corrections privately, *never* in front of other kids or adults. It's also helpful if you correct your child's impolite behavior by specifically telling him *what* he did wrong and *how* to make it right. Here's an example: "Starting to eat without waiting first for Grandma to sit down was impolite. Being polite means always waiting until everyone is seated. Next time, please wait." Manners take time and practice to learn, so encourage your kid's etiquette efforts as he practices the new behaviors. If the rude behaviors persist, you might try requiring him to repeat the correct polite behavior ten times in a row when the two of you are alone.

No More Misbehavin'

BEHAVIOR MAKEOVER PLAN

How did you learn manners when you grew up? What were your parents' etiquette standards? How did they correct you if you were rude? Was it effective? Now think about your parenting: What kind of manners do you expect from your kids? How different are your standards from your parents' expectations for courtesy? Do you consistently enforce your expectations to your kids? How do you react to your kid's discourteous behavior? Is it working?

There's great truth to the saying, "Manners are caught, not taught." Reflect on what your kids are catching from your example. Ask yourself, "Do I consistently treat my kids with courtesy and respect?" "How do I treat my spouse, neighbors, work colleagues, friends, and strangers?"

Now it's time to take action to begin making over your kid's behavior. Use your Makeover Journal to write down your thoughts and develop your plan.

1. Read over Step One. Then take a good look at your child's manners and think about what especially bothers you. You might need to tune into his behavior for a few days. Make a list of rude behaviors that need to be replaced.

2. Select one or two manners to work on this week. To help remind you of your weekly makeover goal, write the chosen manners on a calendar, your journal, or daily organizer, or even post it on your refrigerator so all family members remember.

3. Demonstrate the new behavior. Tell your child that you expect him to use the behavior both at home and in public. He may not feel confident at first using the new manners. Provide opportunities for him to practice the behavior in the safety of home.

4. Because your kid needs opportunities to try the new behavior out in the real world, look for possibilities: dinner at a restaurant, a visit to someone's home, inviting a child (or teacher!) over, spending the night at a friend's house, going to a birthday party, playing on the baseball team, taking a walk to the park, or hosting a party.

5. Your goal is to make sure your child can use the newly learned skills without your structured guidance. When she does, you'll know your efforts paid off, and it's time to begin teaching a new manner. Refer to your manner list, and choose one or two more.

6. Expect backsliding and a few slip-ups, but *don't allow rudeness* from your child. Think through what consequence you'll use if he acts rudely. It's best not to reprimand kids publicly: their reaction can become an even bigger disturbance. A more effective technique is creating a private signal that you both agree on *before* he leaves the house. It could be as simple as pulling on your ear or touching your nose. Whenever you use it, your kid knows he's acting inappropriately and needs to stop immediately. He also knows that if his rudeness continues, you will remove him from the setting or take him home.

7. Whatever corrective action you decide on, have a heart-to-heart talk with your child about your expectations *before*

No More Misbehavin'

you're in public. Then make sure you consistently enforce your plan every time your child acts discourteously.

➡ See also *Bossiness, Lack of Friends, Meanness, Poor Sportsmanship, Put-Downs, Selfishness, Talking Back.*

MAKEOVER PLEDGE

How will you use the four steps and the Behavior Makeover Plan to help your kid achieve long-term change in courtesy? On the lines below, write exactly what you agree to do within the next twenty-four hours to begin your kid's behavior makeover.

_____

_____

_____

MAKEOVER RESULTS

All behavior makeovers take hard work, constant practice, and parental reinforcement. Each step your kid takes toward change may be a small one, so be sure to acknowledge and congratulate every one of them along the way. It takes a minimum of twenty-one days to see real results, so don't give up too soon. Remember that if one strategy doesn't work, another will. Write your child's weekly progress on the lines below. Keep track of daily progress in your Makeover Journal.

Week 1

_____

_____

_____

Week 2

_____

_____

_____

Week 3

_____

_____

_____

RESOURCES

More Than Manners! Raising Today's Kids to Have Kind Manners and Good Hearts, by Letitia Baldrige (New York: Rawson Associates, 1997). A road map for guiding kids to succeed in life by enhancing decency, kind hearts, and great manners.

Perfect Pigs: An Introduction to Manners, by Marc Brown and Stephen Krensky (New York: Little, Brown, 1983). A picture book that introduces basic manners to young tykes.

Manners, by Aliki (New York: Greenwillow Books, 1990). An assortment of manners cleverly illustrated. Ages 4 to 9.

Social Smarts: Modern Manners for Today's Kids, by Elizabeth James (New York: Clarion Books, 1996). Offers advice to kids on how to handle all types of social situations. Ages 8 to 11.

How Rude! The Teenagers' Guide to Good Manners, Proper Behavior, and Not Grossing People Out, by Alex J. Packer (Minneapolis, Minn.: Free Spirit, 1997). Sound advice for teens about the world of manners conveyed in a humorous way. Ages 12 to 15.

Netiquette, by Virginia Shea (New York: Albion Publishing, 1994). Do's and don'ts guide for on-line manners. Highly recommended. Ages 12 to 15.

Selfishness

I am the stepmom of a six-year-old girl. The problem is we're already noticing that she thinks only of herself. It's all about me, me, me, and the world has been constructed to satisfy her every need. She doesn't care what other people feel or think. She's never grateful for anything we do, and she keeps expecting more. We obviously did something wrong, so how do we turn things around?
— Judy, a stepmom of three from Butte, Montana

"I don't care what he wants, I'm doing it my way."
"I don't see why I have to share this."
"I want it, and I want it now!"

BEHAVIOR TIP

If you want your kid to be less self-centered, *expect* it. And don't expect anything else. It's one of the most effective, as well as least used, makeover techniques.

If you're at all concerned that your kid is spoiled, know you're in the same shoes as most other parents these days. Polls show that the majority of parents feel they're raising selfish, self-centered kids. But children aren't born this way. They arrive in this world already wired with the miraculous capacity to be concerned about others. Of course, young kids are more egocentric by nature, but most move into the "other-centered" stages with age, experience, and good parental guidance. The problem is that unless empathy—the foundation for generosity and selflessness—is nurtured, it lies dormant in our kids' character. The result is selfish, unappreciative kids stuck in the "me stage," and they are clearly on the rise. Although this obnoxious behavior is learned, it *can* be unlearned. Let's get started!

SIX STRATEGIES TO CURB SELFISHNESS

Use the following six strategies to help make over your kid's selfish streak:

1. *Fight the tendency to overindulge.* Simply commit to raising an unspoiled kid. Don't give in to his every little whim. Don't overindulge him with material possessions. And don't think you're damaging his self-esteem by telling him no. Instead, fight the tendency to spoil him. You'll be much happier with your end product: a more appreciative, giving kid.
2. *Establish limits.* Set clear behavioral limits, and stick to them. That's hard if you think your primary goal is to be your kid's best friend, so reset your thinking. See yourself as the parent, and recognize that hundreds of child development studies conclude that kids whose parents set clear behavioral expectations turned out less selfish and had higher self-esteem.

No More Misbehavin'

3. *Reinforce generosity.* Learning to share is essential for squelching selfishness. An easy way to increase it is by catching your kid being generous and describing what she did so she'll be more likely to repeat the same behavior: "I saw how you divided your toys with your friend. That was good sharing." "Thanks for sharing your video games. Your brother really appreciated it."

4. *Ask often, "How does the other person feel?"* One way to shift kids from thinking only about themselves is to ask them to ponder how other people feel. As occasions arise, pose the question often, using situations in books, news, TV, and movies as well as real life. "The tornado destroyed most of the town in Georgia. How do you think the people feel?" "Daddy's mom is so sick. How do you think Daddy feels?" Each question forces your kid to think about other people's concerns besides his own and moves him another step from self-centeredness.

5. *Expect gratitude.* One of the biggest mistakes parents make is assuming kids will turn out to be appreciative and giving. Don't make that mistake. If you want your kid to be generous, unselfish, and giving, then nurture, model, prioritize, reinforce, and expect those behaviors. Make gratitude a priority in your home—and the sooner you start, the better.

6. *Squelch selfish behaviors immediately.* Anytime your kids say or do anything selfish or without empathy, call them on it. Tell them why their behavior was wrong, and if the selfish behavior continues, consider applying consequences. (See pp. 299–300.)

BEHAVIOR MAKEOVER PLAN

An overwhelming number of studies report that this is the most selfish generation of kids ever. Do you agree? What might be contributing to this rise of self-centeredness and greed? Think about when you grew up. What was so different then to make

DID YOU KNOW?

A 2001 poll conducted by TIME/CNN found that 80 percent of people think kids today are more spoiled than kids of ten or fifteen years ago. What's more, two-thirds of parents admit that their kids are spoiled. What are your thoughts? Do they match how you are raising your kids?

kids less selfish? Think about parenting methods. Which ones can cause the increase in selfishness? Also, examine your own parenting. Is there anything you might be doing to exacerbate your kid's self-centeredness? Write down your ideas and concerns that might help you develop an effective makeover.

Now it's time to take action to begin making over your kid's behavior. Use your Makeover Journal to write down your thoughts and develop your plan.

1. Review the first two strategies, which urge you to fight the tendency to overindulge your kid. Could this be part of what is inciting her self-centeredness? If so, what will you do to reduce your indulgences to your kid? Talk to your partner and relatives and see if you can agree on a sensible strategy. Write down your plans, and then commit to them. Periodically reread them to remind yourself of your pledge.

2. Reread Strategy Two, and consider the limits in your own home. Jot down the rules you feel are most important, and then ask yourself if they are clear to your kid. For instance, if you asked your kid what your main rules are, would he be able to recite them? When your kid breaks a rule, what happens? For example, does he get away with it, or is he

disciplined? And are you respectfully treated "as the boss"? Note any concerns, and then plan how to address them.
3. Unspoiled kids have learned not to put themselves first always, but instead to consider the needs of others. Review Strategies Three through Five. What can you do to prioritize generosity and stretch your child to be aware of the feelings and needs of others?

Spoiled, self-centered behaviors are tough to change. The key to success is *not* to focus just on changing your kid's behavior, but also to alter parenting responses and home conditions that may be contributing to this behavior. Don't give up on your plan if you don't see rapid change. In fact, chances are that you won't. Instead, be steadfast with your efforts, and the makeover will happen.

➡ See also *Materialistic.*

MAKEOVER PLEDGE

How will you use the six strategies and the Behavior Makeover Plan to help your kid achieve long-term change? On the lines below, write exactly what you agree to do within the next twenty-four hours to begin your kid's behavior makeover.

_____

_____

_____

MAKEOVER RESULTS

All behavior makeovers take hard work, constant practice, and parental reinforcement. Each step your kid takes toward change may be a small one, so be sure to acknowledge and congratulate every one of them along the way. It takes a minimum of twenty-one days to see real results, so don't give up too soon. Remember that if one strategy doesn't work, another will. Write your child's weekly progress on the lines below. Keep track of daily progress in your Makeover Journal.

Week 1

_____

_____

_____

Week 2

_____

_____

_____

Week 3

_____

_____

_____

RESOURCES

Wimpy Parents: From Toddler to Teen: How Not to Raise a Brat, by Kenneth N. Condrell (New York: Warner Brothers, 1998). Expounds on the dangers of overly permissive parenting.

Spoiled Rotten: Today's Children and How to Change Them, by Fred G. Gosman (New York: Warner Books, 1993). A convincing statement of how spoiling kids is hurtful and specific advice on how to undo the harm.

Too Much of a Good Thing: Raising Children of Character in an Indulgent Age, by Dan Kindlon (New York: Hyperion, 2001). A solid testament of the dangers of overprotecting and overindulging our kids.

Me First, by Helen Lester (Boston: Houghton Mifflin, 1995). Pinkerton Pig is pushy and greedy but overcomes his selfishness when he learns that being first isn't always the best. Ages 3 to 5.

The Selfish Giant, by Oscar Wilde (New York: Putnam, 1995). A wonderful tale about a once-selfish giant whose heart finally melts when he helps a small boy. Ages 5 to 8.

Whipping Boy, by Sid Fleischman (New York: Harcourt, 1993). Young self-centered Prince Brat runs away with his whipping boy in this briskly told tale of high adventure that won the Newbery Medal. Ages 10 to 13.

BEHAVIOR 28

Short Attention Span

My husband and I are so upset. Our nine year old came home from school today with a note from the school nurse recommending he begin taking daily doses of some drug called Ritalin next week. Seems like his teacher has been complaining that he can't stay in his seat, doesn't pay attention, fidgets all the time, and gets distracted while trying to finish his work. He's always been a lively, spontaneous, impulsive kid and seems normal to us. But they say he has disease called attention deficit disorder. What's going on here?

—David and Sarah, parents of three,
from Norfolk, Virginia

BEHAVIOR TIP

A lot of kids have short attention spans; far fewer have something that could be described as an attention deficit disorder. As parents, we have to be very careful to understand the difference, recognize where our kids fall on the spectrum, and handle it accordingly.

"Karla's always jumping up to look out the window."
"Joshua has such trouble finishing his history reports."
"Why can't your child ever sit still?"

There's a controversy across the country today: one in thirty American youngsters between the ages of five and nineteen has a prescription for the drug Ritalin, and in some U.S. schools as much as 30 to 40 percent of a class may be taking prescribed stimulants in order to control their classroom behavior. Diagnosis of attention deficit disorder and attention deficit hyperactivity disorder is clearly on the rise. Some experts say there is an epidemic or plague of pathological children who can't hold still, concentrate, or pay attention. Other experts say these are just normal kids who aren't getting the teaching or parenting attention they deserve. Still others feel these are regular kids who just don't want to hold still and need to move around. Our job as parents is to protect our children from overmedication, but at the same time to deal to the best of our ability with any problems they have paying attention or getting their work done at school or elsewhere. And if you and your child's physician determine that medication would be helpful, it must not prevent you from dealing with the underlying issue: your child needs to know how to focus on and finish his work and become a successful lifelong learner. There are techniques that can be learned to help him do that.

SIX STRATEGIES TO IMPROVE A SHORT ATTENTION SPAN

Here are a few strategies to help your kid stay focused and succeed in learning:

1. *Keep him at the right level.* Make sure your child's schoolwork is geared to his appropriate stage of academic development. For instance, if he tests at a 1.5 reading level, don't expect him to

read a book for kids at a 4.2. The best assignments are always geared one step higher than what children are capable of.

2. *Set up a special place for homework.* Be sure that your kid has a quiet spot to do his work where there are no distractions like TV or other family members. Make sure he has a desk, good lighting, a sturdy chair, and all necessary school supplies so he doesn't have to get up to hunt around for anything.

3. *Shorten work sessions.* Clock how long your kid can generally stay in his seat. If he can hold still for only five minutes, don't make him stay there for ten. Take that time as his normal work session, and plan breaks at necessary intervals so he can finish his work in appropriate segments. It sometimes helps to use an oven timer for him to keep track of when his next break is due. Gradually increase the length of sessions as his concentration improves.

4. *Chunk tasks.* Now that you know how long your kid can work without having to take a break, divide his assignments into reasonable segments that fit his current attention span. Try to increase the length of these segments and the length of time he can do them without stopping little by little.

5. *Keep to a schedule.* Kids need a routine. Set a homework time every day that works best for him, and then stick to it.

6. *Help him remember.* There are many techniques you can teach your child to help him recall and retain information. Suppose his homework is to read about dinosaurs:

- With a young child, have him listen to you read, and then stop every minute or so and ask, "What's one thing you heard?"
- Give your kid a big sheet of paper and colored markers. After you've read for a minute or so, stop and have him quickly draw an image based on what you just said.
- When your child is reading, show him how to write one main idea on a three- by five-inch note card after finishing each paragraph or page. These cards can be used later to review the material.

- At school, taking notes can be an invaluable way to remember important points the teacher has said or list future assignments. Show your child how to sequence and organize notes so he can use them on his own.
- Teach paraphrasing, which is how to repeat back a short version of what someone has just said. Being able to restate and understand a speaker's message is a crucial skill for lifelong learning. Have him practice this at home during family meals or other teachable moments during the day.
- Encourage his efforts. Give your kid a lot of praise for trying every step of the way. Don't compare his work to that of siblings or friends. And celebrate every small improvement in his attention or productivity.

BEHAVIOR MAKEOVER PLAN

Were you a restless, fidgeting, restless kid who loved to run around rather than sit in your chair? Did you enjoy daydreaming? Were your parents concerned? How did you do in

---

DID YOU KNOW?
The International Narcotics Control Board reports that the United States "accounts for approximately 90 percent of the total world manufacture of and consumption of Ritalin," and children are the primary users. The Federal Drug Administration categorizes Ritalin as a class 2 controlled substance in the same category as amphetamines, methamphetamine, Dexedrine, and other recreational stimulants known on the street as "speed."

---

school? How are you doing now? Are you on any medication to help you attend?

Now think about your kid. How would you describe his ability to focus and stay on task? How does he compare to his siblings and other kids his age? What concerns you most? Write your biggest concern.

Now it's time to take action to begin making over your kid's behavior. Use your Makeover Journal to write down your thoughts and develop your plan.

1. Get in your kid's shoes. Pretend you're in his classroom and you're doing a tough assignment that you really have to concentrate on. How are you feeling? What can you do to make your kid feel more comfortable and competent? Write a plan.
2. Think about your kid when he's having a hard time focusing on a task at hand. How do you respond when he has trouble concentrating? Does it help him get the job done and feel okay about himself? What's one thing you can do to make the process go better? Write your thoughts.
3. Review Strategy One. Talk to your kid's teacher to make sure your child's work is geared to his age and ability.
4. Review Strategy Two. If you haven't done so, set up a special work place for your child.
5. Review Strategies Three though Five. Discretely assess your kid's attention span, and then help him organize his work accordingly. Keep stretching work time gradually as his focus and productivity increase.
6. Review Strategy Six. Choose two or three appropriate techniques to apply to your kid's situation. If you don't see any improvement after a few weeks, consult a professional.

➡ See also *Anxiety, Giving Up Easily, Homework Battles, Impulsivity, Overperfectionism.*

MAKEOVER PLEDGE

How will you use the six strategies and the Behavior Makeover Plan to help your kid achieve long-term change? On the lines below, write exactly what you agree to do within the next twenty-four hours to begin your kid's behavior makeover.

_____

_____

_____

MAKEOVER RESULTS

All behavior makeovers take hard work, constant practice, and parental reinforcement. Each step your kid takes toward change may be a small one, so be sure to acknowledge and congratulate every one of them along the way. It takes a minimum of twenty-one days to see real results, so don't give up too soon. Remember that if one strategy doesn't work, another will. Write your child's weekly progress on the lines below. Keep track of daily progress in your Makeover Journal.

Week 1

_____

_____

_____

Week 2

_____

_____

_____

Week 3

RESOURCES

Although a few of the following resources are written for children diagnosed with attention deficit disorders, they are included because they offer excellent strategies for increasing attention spans.

MegaSkills, by Dorothy Rich (Boston: Houghton Mifflin, 1992). A wonderful guide that shows parents specific ways to teach the values that matter most in school success: responsibility, effort, initiative, and more.

Ritalin Is Not *the Answer,* by David B. Stein (San Francisco: Jossey-Bass, 1999). A drug-free program for children diagnosed with attention deficit disorder or attention deficit–hyperactivity disorder.

The Wildest Colts Make the Best Horses, by J. Breeding (Austin, Tex.: Bright Books, 1996). A fresh perspective about "spirited" kids.

Talking Back to Ritalin: What Doctors Aren't Telling You About Stimulants for Children, by P. R. Breggin (Monroe, Me.: Common Courage Press, 1998). Must reading for any parents considering the use of medication for their kid.

The Myth of the A.D.D. Child, by Thomas Armstrong (New York: Dutton, 1995). A wealth of information and practical strategies for helping kids with short attention spans.

Treating Huckleberry Finn: A New Narrative Approach to Working with Kids Diagnosed ADD/ADHD, by David Nylund (San Francisco: Jossey Bass, 2000). A drug-free strategy for treating playful, adventuresome, restless, and rebellious kids.

Shyness

We have an eleven-year-old son who is extremely shy. Whenever we introduce him to new people, he barely acknowledges their existence and looks so uncomfortable. If another kid tries to have a simple conversation with him, he becomes almost mute. What can we do to help him feel more confident with people, especially those his own age?

> —Marsha, a mother of three from Baton Rouge, Louisiana

"You go ahead without me."
"I'm afraid to raise my hand."
"I'd rather be by myself."

BEHAVIOR TIP

One of the biggest reasons kids act shy is that they are labeled shy. *Never* let anyone—teacher, friend, relative, sibling, stranger, you—categorize your child as *shy*.

Kids who hang back and are shy are not experiencing life to its fullest. Shy kids curtail their experiences, don't take the necessary social risks, and as a result don't gain confidence in social situations. Not being able to join a group and make new friends will haunt them the rest of their lives. Finally, the pain of social rejection will set in. Shyness is by no means a "bad behavior," but because it can handicap kids in social success, it is included among the "38 bad behaviors." The good news is that we can help kids feel more comfortable in groups by teaching them the skills of social competence.

FIVE TIPS TO HELP KIDS OVERCOME SHYNESS

Use the following five tips to help your kid gain confidence in social settings:

1. *Encourage eye contact.* As you're talking with your child, say, "Look at me," "Put your eyes on my eyes," or "I want to see your eyes." By consciously reinforcing the skill and modeling it regularly, your child will soon be using eye contact. If your kid is uncomfortable about using eye contact, tell her to look at the bridge of the speaker's nose. With some practice, she usually no longer needs the technique and will look more confidently into the speaker's eyes.

2. *Teach conversational openers and closers.* Make a list with your kid of easy conversation openers to use with different groups of people—for example, what he could say to someone he already knows, an adult he hasn't met previously, a friend he hasn't seen in a while, a new student in his class, or a child he'd like to play with on the playground. Then take turns rehearsing the conversation together until your child feels comfortable trying them on his own. HINT: Practicing conversation skills on the tele-

phone with a supportive listener on the other end is always less threatening for shyer kids than doing so face-to-face.

3. *Rehearse social situations.* Prepare your kid for an upcoming social event by describing the setting and expectations and who else will be there. Then help him practice how to meet others, table manners, basic conversational skills, and even how to say good-bye gracefully.

4. *Practice skills with younger peers.* Philip Zimbardo, a renowned shyness expert and coauthor of *The Shy Child,* recommends pairing older shy kids with younger children for brief play periods, so create opportunities for your kid to play with one other child who is younger: a younger sibling, cousin, neighbor, or one of your friend's younger kids. For teens, baby-sitting is a great way for a shy kid to earn money as well as practice social skills—starting a conversation, using eye contact—that she was reticent about trying with kids her age.

5. *Arrange one-on-one play opportunities.* Fred Frankel, a psychologist and developer of the world-famous UCLA Social Skills Training Program, suggests one-on-one play dates as the best way for kids to build social confidence. This is a time when your kid invites only one child over for a couple of private play hours to get to know one another and practice friendship-making skills. Provide snacks, and try to keep interruptions to a minimum: siblings should not be included, and television viewing should not be a play option.

DID YOU KNOW?

Philip Zimbardo tells us that two out of every five people consider themselves shy. Has this become a self-fulfilling prophecy for your child?

BEHAVIOR MAKEOVER

Start by thinking about your own personality temperament. Do you consider yourself shy? What about when you were growing up? Were you labeled shy? Were any of your siblings, relatives, or parents shy? Were any of them labeled shy? Are there certain situations that make you more uncomfortable? What helps you feel more comfortable in group settings?

Now it's time to take action to begin making over your kid's behavior. Use your Makeover Journal to write down your thoughts and develop your plan.

1. Consider your parental expectations. Are they in line with your child's abilities, strengths, and comfort level, or might they be contributing to your kid's lack of confidence? For instance, here are a few parenting behaviors to seriously consider. Check any that you might need to change.

   _____ Do you ever force your kid to perform in public?

   _____ Are you overly concerned if he doesn't accomplish a particular task?

   _____ Are you in the habit of doing things for your kid?

   _____ Do you typically speak for your child and fight his battles?

   _____ Do you discourage her from trying new things?

   _____ Do you push him to do things that might be important to you but not to him?

   _____ Do you compare her performance and personality to that of her siblings?

2. Reflect on your behavior. How do you typically react to your child's shyness? If someone comments to you about your kid's shyness, especially in front of your kid, how do you

No More Misbehavin'

respond? Is there any behavior you could change in yourself that might help your kid feel more self-confident? Write a plan, and then commit to using it.

3. Reread the five strategies for gaining confidence in social settings. Choose one that you think would work best for your kid. Then write out how you plan to use the tip.

➡ See also *Anxiety, Cynicism, Lack of Friends, Negative Peer Pressure.*

MAKEOVER PLEDGE

How will you use the five tips and the Behavior Makeover Plan to help your kid achieve long-term change? On the lines below, write exactly what you agree to do within the next twenty-four hours to begin your kid's behavior makeover.

_____

_____

_____

MAKEOVER RESULTS

All behavior makeovers take hard work, constant practice, and parental reinforcement. Each step your kid takes toward change may be a small one, so be sure to acknowledge and congratulate every one of them along the way. It takes a minimum of twenty-one days to see real results, so don't give up too soon. Remember that if one strategy doesn't work, another will. Write your child's weekly progress on the following lines. Keep track of daily progress in your Makeover Journal.

Week 1

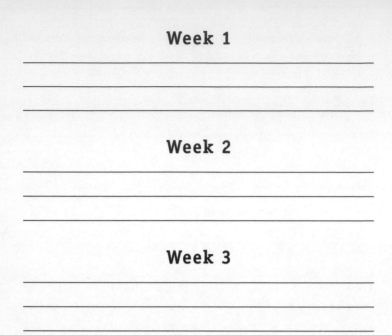

Week 2

Week 3

RESOURCES

The Shy Child: Helping Children Triumph over Shyness, by Ward Kent Swallow with Laurie Halse Anderson (New York: Time Warner, 2000). A parenting manual that offers pragmatic step-by-step solutions to help shy kids lead more confident lives.

The Shy Child: A Parent's Guide to Preventing and Overcoming Shyness from Infancy to Adulthood, by Philip G. Zimbardo and Shirley Radl (New York: Doubleday, 1982). A must-read for parents of shy kids of any age. Invaluable!

Painfully Shy: How to Overcome Social Anxiety and Reclaim Your Life, by Barbara G. Markway and Gregory P. Markway (New York: St. Martin's Press, 2001). Written by two clinical psychologists for adults, the book offers techniques to help shy individuals master social anxiety. A parent could offer several of these ideas to an anxious preteen.

Shy Charles, by Rosemary Wells (New York: Penguin Putnam Books for Young Readers, 2001). Charles is as quiet as a mouse, and it doesn't bother him one bit. His parents try, but Charles resists all of their efforts to make him become more outgoing. Ages 4 to 7.

Little Miss Shy, by Roger Hargreaves (New York: Putnam, 1998). Part of the delightful Little Miss Bossy, Little Miss Chatterbox series, the simple text and illustrations are perfect for kids 3 to 7.

I Don't Know Why . . . I Guess I'm Shy: A Story About Taming Imaginary Fears, by Barbara S. Cain (Washington, D.C.: American Psychological Association, 1999). Shows children that shy feelings don't have to get in the way of having fun and making friends. Ages 5 to 8.

30

Sibling Battles

I 'm at my wit's end. It seems all my kids do is fight, and I spend most of my time acting like a referee. My husband says that when I step in, I'm just making it worse. Then my son always tells me that I let his younger brother "get away with murder." Well, if I don't intervene, the two spend the day locked in mortal combat. Any ideas????

—Leticia, mother of two from Grand Rapids, Michigan

"Jenna hit me!"
"Give me back my CD!"
"You broke my favorite Barbie!"

BEHAVIOR TIP

Don't take sides. During conflicts between siblings, stay neutral and make suggestions only when your kids seem stuck. Taking sides builds resentment and feelings of favoritism.

Sibling quarrels are among the most exasperating home front issues. Put any two kids together for a length of time, and the three little words you're most likely to hear are, "It's not fair!" Don't go crazy trying to make things equal; it's impossible! Although battles are inevitable, world war doesn't have to be the outcome. There are a few things you can do that will alleviate the bickering *and* in the process help your kids learn to treat each other more peacefully. Besides, if they don't learn how to get along at home, where else will they learn?

FIVE STRATEGIES TO EASE SIBLING WARS

Use the following strategies as a guide in boosting family harmony and stopping sibling battles:

1. *Calm everyone down.* Intervene when emotions are high but *before* an argument escalates. Use what works best to calm everyone down: running a quick lap outside, doing five jumping jacks, taking three slow deep breaths, lying down for a few minutes, cuddling a teddy bear. If needed, separate the two kids until they can calm themselves and work things through: "I see two angry kids who need to cool down. You go to your room and you to your room until you can talk calmly."
2. *Clarify feelings.* Sometimes all that is needed is for someone to acknowledge the hurt kid's feelings. Try it: "You're hurt because you think your brother is being treated more fairly than you are." "You're frustrated because you're not getting a turn at Nintendo."
3. *Let each kid tell the story.* To help kids feel that they're really being heard, ask each one to take a turn explaining what happened. Ask everyone to focus on the child who is speaking and really listen. No interrupting is allowed, and everyone gets a turn. If you think you don't understand, ask

for clarification: "Could you explain that to me again?" When the sibling is finished, briefly restate her view to show that you do understand. You might then ask, "What can you do to solve this problem?"

4. *Make the kids part of the solution.* Ask those involved what they plan to do to solve "their" problem. Making kids part of the solution often causes them to stop, think, and quiet down. Do set guidelines for talking it out: no interrupting, no put-downs, and only calm voices are allowed. By taking turns, kids can learn to make their points with words, not blows. One dad sets an oven timer and says, "Let's see if you can work this through calmly for three minutes. Then I'll return." Another mom sits her preschoolers on the couch and tells them they can't get up until they talk it out.

5. *See it from the other side.* Kids often get so caught up in feeling they're being treated unfairly that they don't stop to

DID YOU KNOW?

Have you taught your kids how to solve their own problems? Data show doing so will help minimize those sibling battles. George Spivack and Myrna Shure, Philadelphia-based psychologists who conducted over twenty-five years of research, found children as young as three and four years old can be taught to think through their problems. They also discovered that children skilled in problem solving were less likely to be impulsive and aggressive when things didn't go their way, tended to be more caring and less insensitive, were better able to make friends, tended to achieve more academically, and were more likely to solve problems peacefully.

think how the other person might be feeling. So ask, "See it from the other side now. How does your sister feel?" This also builds empathy.

BEHAVIOR MAKEOVER PLAN

Start your kid's behavior makeover by thinking about your childhood. Did you fight with your siblings (or childhood friends)? What did you fight about? Did your parents intervene? Was that helpful? Did you ever learn to get along? What skills did you use to help reduce your conflicts? How did you learn them? Talk to other parents to find out how they're dealing with sibling battles. What works for them?

Now it's time to take action to begin making over your kid's behavior. Use your Makeover Journal to write down your thoughts and develop your plan.

1. Identify what's triggering the conflicts. Is the other child getting more attention, being manipulative, or bullying? Does he have more toys? Do you take sides? Is the hurt child feeling she is not being listened to or is being taken advantage of?
2. Try to witness—without their awareness—a conflict. Tune into the behaviors of your kids before the fighting starts. How do your kids typically respond to each other in a heated moment? What behavior does one kid (or both of them) use that escalates the situation, such as insulting, hitting, swearing, or biting? Is there a skill you could teach that might defuse the conflict before it becomes full-blown?
3. How do you typically respond to sibling conflicts? Do both kids think your actions are fair? How do your kids react? Does your response escalate, reduce, or neutralize the conflict?
4. Read the strategies, and select the two that you think would work best for your kids. Experiment to see how effective they are in reducing sibling conflicts with your kids.

Sibling battles are inevitable, so completely terminating them is unrealistic. Nevertheless, you can minimize them. Once you try a strategy, be consistent with it until you see change.

➡ See also *Anger, Chore Wars, Fighting, Hitting, Put-Downs, Yelling.*

MAKEOVER PLEDGE

How will you use the five strategies and the Behavior Makeover Plan to help your kids achieve long-term change? On the lines below, write exactly what you agree to do within the next twenty-four hours to begin your kid's behavior makeover.

_____

_____

_____

MAKEOVER RESULTS

All behavior makeovers take hard work, constant practice, and parental reinforcement. Each step your kid takes toward change may be a small one, so be sure to acknowledge and congratulate every one of them along the way. It takes a minimum of twenty-one days to see real results, so don't give up too soon. Remember that if one strategy doesn't work, another will. Write your child's weekly progress on the lines below. Keep track of daily progress in your Makeover Journal.

Week 1

_____

_____

_____

No More Misbehavin'

Week 2

_____

_____

_____

Week 3

_____

_____

_____

RESOURCES

Kids, Parents, and Power Struggles: Winning for a Lifetime, by Mary Sheedy Kurcinka (New York: HarperCollins, 1999). Creative techniques for using power struggles as pathways to better understanding within any family. Useful for any age. Addresses the cause of power struggles rather than just the symptoms.

Siblings Without Rivalry: How to Help Your Children Live Together So You Can Live Too, by Adele Faber and Elaine Mazlish (New York: Avon, 1998). A classic in helping parents reduce sibling rivalry.

Positive Discipline A–Z: 1001 Solutions to Everyday Parenting Problems, by Jane Nelsen, Lynn Lott, and H. Stephen Glenn (Roseville, Calif.: Prima Publishing, 1999). An excellent parenting resource. Particularly helpful sections include "fighting friends," "sibling rivalry," and "fighting siblings."

The Berenstain Bears Get in a Fight, by Stan and Jan Berenstain (New York: Random House, 1995). Brother and Sister Bear get into a major sibling battle, and Mama Bear helps them work things out. Ages 4 to 8.

Bang, Bang, You're Dead, by Louise Fitzhugh (New York: HarperCollins, 1969). Two kids battle for command of a hill, then work out their disagreement. Ages 5 to 8.

Superfudge, by Judy Blume (New York: Bantam Doubleday Dell, 1994). A favorite among kids 8 to 12 about an older brother who must deal with his very annoying younger brother.

BEHAVIOR 31

Stealing

I found a video game in my twelve-year-old son's closet, and I know it doesn't belong to him. I'm positive he stole it from the store. He has everything he wants, so why would he steal? I'd hate to think I have the makings of a kleptomaniac on my hands. Now what do I do?

—Karen, a mother of two from Louisville, Kentucky

"Come on, put it in your backpack. Nobody's watching."
"I could never have paid for this myself."
"Let's take all of them. It'll be so cool!"

BEHAVIOR TIP

How parents react to their kids' stealing can be either destructive or productive in helping them learn right from wrong. The best reaction is to make sure the child understands not only your expectation for honesty but also why it's important.

The one behavior that's guaranteed to shake up even the calmest parents is discovering that their kid has stolen something. Be assured that stealing is far more common than you might realize, especially among the younger set with still a flimsy grasp of ownership. Around age five to seven is when kids usually understand the hurtful effects of stealing. Once they realize that stealing violates someone's rights and can result in serious legal action against them, they view stealing much more seriously. One thing is certain: kids of all ages must learn that taking things without permission isn't right and can have serious consequences.

FOUR STEPS TO STOP STEALING

Whether your child is young or older, the same basic parenting rules about eliminating stealing apply. These four steps will guide you in creating long-lasting behavior change.

Step 1. Calmly Confront and Assess Your Child's Intention

The first step is to try and determine answers to the five essential "W" questions: *What* happened? *Where* and *when* did the incident take place? *Who* was your child with? *Why* did your child steal? Unfortunately, asking straight out, "Why did you steal?" usually gets nowhere. The best approach is to begin with a direct response that describes what you believe happened and how you feel about it. Here is an example: "Tim, I was upset to find a video game that doesn't belong to you in your closet. How did it get there?" If that gets no response, you may have to flat-out ask, "Did you take it?"

Two parenting don'ts are important to remember. First, *don't overreact*. Certainly, you will be angry and frustrated, but try to stay calm. Second, *don't accuse* your child of stealing or label her a thief. Accusations never solve anything, and your child may lie to avoid punishment or your disapproval.

Instead, take it for granted you have a problem, and deal with it together.

Step 2. Review Why Stealing Is Wrong

Spell out your expectations about honesty. This is the time to make sure your child understands the reason stealing is not right and why it defies your family's moral standards. Be brief and stick to why stealing is wrong: "Taking something that doesn't belong to you without asking is very wrong. We do not take things that don't belong to us. We need to be able to trust each other. I expect you to respect other people's property and always ask permission before you borrow something that is not yours." Keep in mind that young kids often have difficulty grasping the difference between borrowing and taking, so you might need to explain the concepts of ownership and respect for property.

If your child is older, you might discuss possible consequences of stealing, such as losing friends, developing a bad reputation, losing people's trust, and getting into trouble with the law. Remind him that some stores have a zero tolerance policy. They will not forgive a first offense if you return the item and will automatically call the police. Do remember that your one-time honesty talk will never be enough to create long-lasting behavior change. Plan to review honesty frequently over the next few weeks with your child, so he not only understands your expectations but also incorporates the virtue into his daily actions.

Step 3. Reprimand and Reflect on the Impact

Kids often don't stop to think about the hurtful effects of stealing. Try to get your child into his victim's shoes, and realize how upsetting it is to have your personal possessions or retail assets taken away. If your child is younger, try play-acting using one of his favorite toys. After "stealing" the toy, ask, "How would you feel if somebody stole your toy? Would it be fair?" With an older kid you might ask, "Pretend you're the victim, and you found out all the money in your wallet has been stolen. How would you feel? What would you want to say to the person?"

Step 4. Require Restitution to Right the Wrong

The final step is to make sure that your child realizes *why* stealing is wrong and *what to do to make it right*. The best punishment is requiring her to apologize to the victim and return the stolen item. (It's usually best if you accompany her.) If the theft occurred at a store, brief the store owners, so a sympathetic clerk doesn't excuse your kid from the deed. If the item is now damaged or no longer returnable, your child should pay the cost. You may have to cover her expenses at the time, but then make her responsible for paying you back through her allowance or additional assigned chores. BEWARE: Find out if the store requires police intervention for any theft before you go in. Then use your best judgment as to how best to proceed.

BEHAVIOR MAKEOVER PLAN

If we want our kids to be honest, we must model honesty so they know how we expect them to behave. Start by assessing your daily honesty example. For instance, do you

DID YOU KNOW?

A survey of over twenty thousand middle school and high school students found that 47 percent of all respondents admitted they had stolen something from a store in the previous twelve months. More than a quarter of high school students said they had committed store theft at least two times.

ever eat a small sample from the grocery store's candy or fruit bins without paying, take a small "souvenir" from a restaurant or hotel (an ashtray, soap dish, or the like) that was not meant to be taken, or bring a few office supplies home from your workplace? If so, think about the message it's sending to your kid. Then commit yourself to improving your example.

Now it's time to take action to begin making over your kid's behavior. Use your Makeover Journal to write down your thoughts and develop your plan.

1. Reread Step One because the most important part of changing your child's behavior is to determine what might be prompting her to steal. You might talk with adults who know your child well and whose opinions you trust for insight. Although kids often steal just to see if they can get away with it, the behavior may be signaling a more deep-seated need that is not being met. There certainly are many possibilities to consider—for example:

   _____ Is there a change in your family such as a divorce, a new baby, or a new job that is making your child crave attention?

   _____ Does she exhibit impulsivity and always want things right away?

   _____ Is he insensitive and not realize the hurt he's causing the victim?

   _____ Does she fail to grasp the concept of honesty, ownership, or asking permission?

   _____ Are rules about ownership in your home lax?

   _____ Might he be feeling peer pressure and the need to fit in and gain group access?

   _____ Could she be angry or jealous and be trying to get back at someone?

   Once you discover why your kid is stealing, ask yourself what you'll do to remedy the problem. For instance, if you think your kid is shoplifting as a means to gain favor with peers, you'll need to help him find friends who will nurture his character as well as learn to stand up to his peers. Write out the steps you'll take to remedy the problem; then commit to doing them with your kid.

3. Reread Step Two, and plan how you will help your child learn to respect other people's property. For instance, will you role-play the concept of ownership, read stories or fables about honesty, or boost the concept through daily teachable moments? Don't assume your child has internalized the value of honesty; this virtue must be taught and reviewed often.

4. Decide on what action you'll take to make sure your kid understands the consequences of stealing. Steps Three and Four will guide you in developing your plan. The most important part is making sure your child understands not only that stealing is wrong, but also that he is ultimately responsible for his actions.

5. If stealing has become a frequently repeated behavior, consider getting outside help by talking to a trained counselor. This behavior must be squelched quickly.

➡ See also *Defiance, Impulsivity, Lying and Cheating, Materialistic, Negative Peer Pressure.*

MAKEOVER PLEDGE

How will you use the four steps and the Behavior Makeover Plan to help your kid achieve long-term change in honesty? On the lines below, write exactly what you agree to do within the next twenty-four hours to begin your kid's behavior makeover.

_____

_____

_____

MAKEOVER RESULTS

All behavior makeovers take hard work, constant practice, and parental reinforcement. Each step your kid takes toward change may be a small one, so be sure to acknowledge and congratulate every one of them along the way. It takes a minimum of twenty-one days to see real results, so don't give up too soon. Remember that if one strategy doesn't work, another will. Write your child's weekly progress on the lines below. Keep track of daily progress in your Makeover Journal.

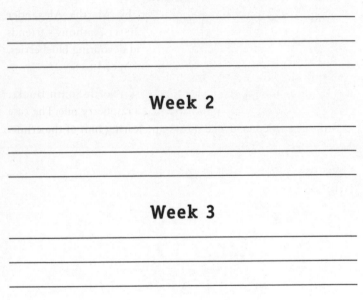

Week 1

_____

_____

_____

Week 2

_____

_____

_____

Week 3

_____

_____

_____

RESOURCES

Raising Good Children: From Birth Through the Teenage Years, by Thomas Lickona (New York: Bantam Books, 1985). An absolute must for parents on how to help kids develop a lifelong sense of honesty, decency, respect for others, and more.

Dealing with Your Kids' Seven Biggest Troubles: Lying, Cheating, Stealing, Sexual Acting Out, Drugs and Alcohol, Suicide, Violence, by Val J. Peter (Omaha, Neb.: Boys Town Press, 2000). A renowned organization offers solid advice on dealing with troubling teen problems.

When Good Kids Do Bad Things: A Survival Guide for Parents of Teenagers, by Katherine Cordy Levine (New York: Pocket Books, 1991). An expert adolescent counselor and foster mom to nearly four hundred kids tells how to preserve your sanity and keep your good kid good—even when he or she is doing something bad.

Gold Coin, by Alma Flor Ada (New York: Atheneum, 1991). A thief goes to extreme lengths to rob a traveling healer woman of a gold coin and is reformed during his attempts to follow her. Ages 5 to 10.

We're in Big Trouble, Blackboard Bear, by Martha Alexander (Cambridge, Mass.: Candlewick Press, 2001). Anthony's friends accuse Bear of stealing goldfish, honey, and devouring blueberries. He admits his guilt and replaces the losses. Ages 4 to 8.

It Wasn't Me! by Udo Weigelt (New York: North South Books, 2001). Raven is accused of taking Ferret's raspberry pile. The case seems sealed when evidence shows up clearing him of the crime. Ages 6 to 9.

32

Swearing

*M*y twelve year old started using obscene words every day. I
don't know where he gets this kind of foul language; he
certainly doesn't hear it at home. I'm so afraid he will forget where he is and do this at school or, even worse, around his grandparents. They'd have a stroke! So do I buy everyone earplugs, wash his
mouth out with soap, or do something else instead to stop him?

—Deborah, single mom of three, Edina, Minnesota

"Don't you dare use those words again!"
"If you talk like that in school, they'd suspend you!"
"Where did you learn to talk like that?"

BEHAVIOR TIP

There are two secrets to curing a foul-mouthed kid:
first, define what's unacceptable; second, censor anything out of his mouth that exceeds your civility clause
and *don't back down.*

There's nothing new about kids' swearing. It's typical and almost a rite of initiation for many preteens and teens. It's a behavior you should also expect preschoolers to try. Usually when they've finished experimenting with their "poopoo head" stage, a foul word or two will creep into their vocabulary. But you're never quite prepared when "Oh, shit!" "Damn!" or an explicit four-letter word slips out of your angelic kid's mouth, especially in public. Older kids' language can reach extremes of vulgarity and ugliness that are impossible to ignore. *ABC Nightly News* reported that 80 percent of Americans polled in a national survey feel vulgarity is only getting worse and has become part of our culture. It's just another reason that you need to work on this behavior makeover so swearing will not become ingrained in your kid.

FOUR STEPS TO CURING FOUL-MOUTHED KIDS

You can use the following four steps to guide you in ridding your kid of swearing and using foul language.

Step 1. Define Your Boundaries

Determine which words, gestures, religious profanities, and jokes you consider offensive. Then spell them out so they're clear to your kid. Mention any swear words you've heard your kid or friend say. The rule is, "If in doubt, don't say it." Other expletives can be added to your list as you and your kid hear them in movies, on musical lyrics, or even uttered by people.

Step 2. Explain Why Swearing Is Unacceptable

If you want your kid to change his behavior, he needs to understand why you consider this language wrong and offensive. Here are a few talking points to get your discussion started:

"Swearing can become a habit that's tough to break."

"Once you start, it's easy for swear words to slip out of your mouth. And you never know who might hear them: your grandparents, for example, or your teacher."

"People may think poorly of you as a person with no manners."

"Nice people don't swear, and I want people to think of you as nice."

"Swearing is offensive to many people. Most people don't want to hear it, so it's being rude."

"They may think poorly of our family. That means every member's reputation suffers because of your behavior."

"Certain words border on sexual harassment and racial insult. Saying them not only causes hurt to the recipient, but can also get you into serious legal trouble."

Be sure to add your own beliefs and values to the talk.

Step 3. Teach Acceptable Substitutes

Usually swearing is expressed over our frustrations, shock, or anger. Kids get locked into using a few choice cuss words because they don't know any appropriate alternatives. Help your kid discover some. First, have fun brainstorming alternative words that aren't offensive and won't get him into trouble: *fudge, shucks, holy cow, bugger! darn.* Or have him invent his own word: *hooley-booley* or *shooberger.* Then tell him to select one or two favorite choices, and encourage him to say them instead of his current offensive repertoire. Do remember on occasion to acknowledge your kid's efforts in using proper language.

Step 4. Set a Consequence for Cursing, Then Calmly and Consistently Use It

You may be shocked or embarrassed, but try not to overreact whenever your child swears. Kids often experiment with new behaviors because they want to see our reactions. So just deal with it matter-of-factly. For a young first offender, get down

No More Misbehavin'

eye-to-eye and firmly say, "In this family, we don't use that word" or "Polite people don't talk like that." The behavior usually disappears quickly in young kids. With an older kid, state a reminder: "You know the rule. I don't want to hear that word again."

If you see that swearing has become a habit, then it's time to set a consequence. See pages 299–300 for a list of options. Remember, there's no negotiation.

BEHAVIOR MAKEOVER PLAN

Reports show that we are far more casual about using vulgar-ities in our society today than we were half a century ago. Do you agree? How different is the prevalence of swearing today than when you were growing up? Did you ever swear in front of your parents? How did they handle it? Was it effective?

Next, reflect on the language that you and your partner use. If you're guilty of swearing in front of your kid, then make a pledge to stop it. Besides, telling your kid swearing is off-limits and then hearing you do it sends a very wrong message.

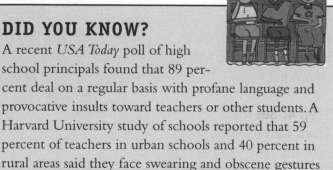

DID YOU KNOW?

A recent *USA Today* poll of high school principals found that 89 per-cent deal on a regular basis with profane language and provocative insults toward teachers or other students. A Harvard University study of schools reported that 59 percent of teachers in urban schools and 40 percent in rural areas said they face swearing and obscene gestures from students.

Now it's time to take action to begin making over your kid's behavior. Use your Makeover Journal to write down your thoughts and develop your plan.

1. Monitor his culture a bit more closely: TV, Internet, movies, video games, and CDs. Could they be influencing his new vocabulary choices? Do you need to set stricter standards on his entertainment choices? If so, what will you do? And what about his peer group? Do they all think cursing is cool? Set your kid straight about that.

2. Consider why your kid is swearing. Might he want to appear tough or more mature, provoke an emotional reaction, get attention, or gain status with peers? Also, is he angrier or more frustrated lately and needs ways to respond to his strong feelings? If you recognize there's another cause that's triggering his swearing, think it through, and then make a specific plan to cure it.

3. Review Step One. What words, gestures, and jokes do you consider offensive? List them; then share them with your kid so he's clear on your guidelines.

4. Review Step Two, and then jot down a few talking points that express your views best. Discuss them with your kid.

5. Review Step Three. Help your kid brainstorm alternative words to replace his swear words.

6. If swearing continues, review Step Four, and decide what consequence you will set for future infractions. Ignoring foul language will not give your kid guidelines for his behavior, so be consistent with your consequences.

➡ See also *Anger, Intolerance, Meanness, Negative Peer Pressure, Put-Downs, Rudeness.*

MAKEOVER PLEDGE

How will you use the four steps and the Behavior Makeover Plan to help your kid achieve long-term change in ending swearing and using bad words? On the lines below, write exactly what you agree to do within the next twenty-four hours to begin your kid's behavior makeover.

_____

_____

_____

MAKEOVER RESULTS

All behavior makeovers take hard work, constant practice, and parental reinforcement. Each step your kid takes toward change may be a small one, so be sure to acknowledge and congratulate every one of them along the way. It takes a minimum of twenty-one days to see real results, so don't give up too soon. Remember that if one strategy doesn't work, another will. Write your child's weekly progress on the lines below. Keep track of daily progress in your Makeover Journal.

_____

_____

_____

Week 1

_____

_____

_____

Week 2

_____

_____

_____

Week 3

RESOURCES

Cuss Control: The Complete Book on How to Curb Your Cursing, by James O'Connor (New York: Three River Press, 2000). Adult advice on how to break a habit that the author feels is greatly contributing to the decline of civility and good manners.

When Your Kids Talk Dirty, by Jay Timothy (San Jose, Calif.: Resources Publications, 1996). In addition to helping parents deal with swearing, the easy-reading text offers older kids a perspective as to why they talk dirty—a key step toward behavior change.

Yes, Your Teen Is Crazy! Loving Your Kid Without Losing Your Mind, by Michael J. Bradley and Carroll O'Connor (Gig Harbor, Wash.: Harbor Press, 2001). How parents can help their kids through the tumultuous teen years.

Elbert's Bad Word, by Audrey Wood and Don Wood (New York: Harcourt, 1988). Young Elbert, after shocking his parents and guests by using a bad word, learns some acceptable substitutes from a helpful wizard. Ages 4 to 8.

The Berenstain Bears and the Big Blooper, by Stan Berenstain and Jan Berenstain (New York: Random House, 2000). The cubs hear a certain word they've never heard before. Mama Bear explains it is the kind of word that *nobody,* not even adults and certainly not cubs, should use at *any time.* Ages 4 to 8.

Little Daisy and the Swearing Class, by Ralph Bouma (Sand Springs, Okla.: Triangle Press, 1998). Try using this one to expound on the negative affects of swearing for kids aged 9 to 12.

33

Talking Back

G enerally, our eight year old is kind-hearted and cooperative. Lately, he has become mouthy and defiant. He says those little smart comments that kids usually reserve for each other to my husband and me, like "You aren't my boss," "You are so stupid," and "You don't know anything." The talking back is driving us nuts! HELP!

—Nancy, a mother of two from Tulsa, Oklahoma

You politely say to your child, "Jane, I want you home by three." And your sweet little darling in a sassy tone retorts, "Yeah, right."

BEHAVIOR TIP
There are two secrets to ending back talk. First, catch it early before it becomes a habit. Second, once you decide to squelch it, be consistent *and don't back down.*

You calmly ask your kid, "Can you please take out the garbage?" And your prized offspring snarls, "Take it out yourself!"

Back talk and sass are on the rise, and these behaviors seem to bug every adult. The behavior usually starts at about five years of age. If you allow back talk to continue, negative results can spread like wildfire. Believe me, no teacher, coach, scout leader, or other child's parent appreciates a disrespectful kid. Luckily, disrespectful behaviors such as whining, back talk, and sassiness are some of the easiest inappropriate behaviors to get rid of.

FOUR STEPS TO ELIMINATE BACK TALK

You can use the following four steps to guide you in squelching your kid's back talk and rudeness.

Step 1. Call Out the Back Talk on the Spot

Determine which behaviors you consider disrespectful so that your child is clear on what you expect. All kids slip every once in a while, but is there a disrespectful word, phrase, or body gesture your child is using fairly frequently? That's the behavior you can target. And whenever your child does display this behavior, name it on the spot. Here are a few examples of how other parents have done this. Notice how their message addresses only the disrespectful behavior and *not* the child's character:

"When I talk to you, you roll your eyes. It looks disrespectful, and you need to stop."
"Telling me to 'chill out' when I talk to you is unacceptable. You may not talk that way."
"You use a complaining voice whenever you want something. You need to use a more respectful tone."

Step 2. Refuse to Engage When Your Kid Talks Back

Studies in child development reveal that kids are much more likely to stop talking back if they see it's ineffective in getting attention. So stay neutral and don't respond. Don't sigh, shrug your shoulders, or look exasperated. Also do not coax, bribe, or scold; such tactics almost never work and will probably just escalate the behavior. If you must, look at something else or, if all else fails, go lock yourself in the bathroom. *Just refuse to continue the conversation until your child stops talking back—and be sure to respond in this way every time.* Usually when kids see you are not going to give in, they will stop. Here are a few examples:

"Stop. Telling me I don't know anything is disrespectful. We'll talk when you talk right."
"I don't listen to sass. If you want to talk to me, talk respectfully. I'll be in the other room."
"We'll talk when you can listen respectfully without rolling your eyes and smirking."

Step 3. If Back Talk Continues, Set a Consequence

Suppose that you've been clear with your expectations, yet the sass and back talk continue. Now it's time to set a consequence for the rudeness. Effective consequences are clear to the child, have a specific duration, relate directly to the disrespectful deed, *and* fit the kid. Once you set it, consistently enforce it, *and don't back down!* For repeat offenders, it's best to develop a written plan that is signed by all involved and readily accessible. One more thought: do consider letting your child participate in creating her own consequences; they often are much harsher than ones you'd set. Refer to pages 299–300 for a list of consequences. Many moms have told me they've had success in eliminating back talk by having their child repeat a phrase more respectfully at least ten times. For example, "Yeah, right" would be repeated using the correct tone that says, "Yes, I will, Mom."

Step 4. Encourage Respectful Behavior

One of the simplest ways to increase the frequency of a behavior is to reinforce it when we see our child doing it right. Studies have shown, however, that the majority of the time we do the opposite: instead of catching our kids being respectful, we point out when they are acting incorrectly. So any time you see or hear your child practicing respectful behaviors, acknowledge them and express your pleasure. Here are a few examples:

"Danny, I like that respectful tone."

"Jenny, thank you for listening so politely when I was talking."

"That's a nice voice, Kelly. Good for you for remembering how to say your words right."

"I know that you were frustrated, Tyler, but you didn't swear that time. It's hard changing a bad habit, but you're really trying."

BEHAVIOR MAKEOVER PLAN

Start by asking yourself if you remember talking back to your parents or other authority figures as a kid. Did your siblings? What was your parents' response? Did it work? Now think

DID YOU KNOW?

In a survey quoted in *Child* magazine, only 12 percent of the two thousand adults polled felt that kids commonly treat others with respect; most described them as "rude," "irresponsible," and "lacking in discipline."

No More Misbehavin'

about kids today. Reports say disrespectful, sassy kids who defy authority are on the rise. What might be causing the escalation? Where do kids learn to talk back?

Now it's time to take action to begin making over your kid's behavior. Use your Makeover Journal to write down your thoughts and develop your plan.

1. Take a good look at your child's behavior and think about what especially bugs you. What are the types of disrespect, and when are they happening?
2. Determine what happened right before this bad behavior that provoked the disrespect in the first place.
3. Identify how you typically respond to your kid. Ask yourself why it isn't working.
4. Reread the four steps to squelching talking back. If possible, discuss them with your partner or another parent.
5. Recognize that in most cases, Steps One and Two are mandatory for behavior makeovers. If those steps eliminate your kid's back talk, then skip to Step Four. If not, try Step Three, and set consequences that are appropriate for your child.

➡ See also *Defiance, Put-Downs, Swearing, Whining.*

MAKEOVER PLEDGE

How will you use the four steps and the Behavior Makeover Plan to help your kid achieve long-term change? On the lines below, write exactly what you agree to do within the next twenty-four hours to begin your kid's behavior makeover.

_____

_____

_____

MAKEOVER RESULTS

All behavior makeovers take hard work, constant practice, and parental reinforcement. Each step your kid takes toward change may be a small one, so be sure to acknowledge and congratulate every one of them along the way. It takes a minimum of twenty-one days to see real results, so don't give up too soon. Remember that if one strategy doesn't work, another will. Write your child's weekly progress on the lines below. Keep track of daily progress in your Makeover Journal.

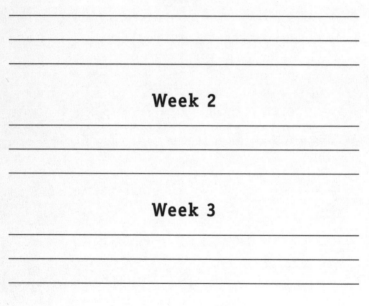

Week 1

_____

_____

_____

Week 2

_____

_____

_____

Week 3

_____

_____

_____

RESOURCES

1–2–3–Magic: Effective Discipline for Children 2–12, by Thomas W. Phelan (Child Management, 1996). A simple, effective child management program conducted by instituting a system of counting and time-outs, delivered in a straightforward and unemotional manner.

Backtalk: Four Steps to Ending Rude Behavior in Your Kids, by Audrey Ricker and Carolyn Crowder (New York: Fireside, 1998). A commonsense guide to stopping disrespectful behavior.

Discipline Without Shouting or Spanking: Practical Solutions to the Most Common Preschool Behavior Problems, by Jerry Wychoff and Barbara Unell (New York: Simon & Schuster, 1985). Nonviolent options for correcting the most common behavior problems for preschoolers, including tantrums, whining, negativity, back talk, and aggression.

Raising Your Spirited Child, by Mary Sheedy Kurcinka (New York: HarperCollins, 1991). An excellent resource for parents of difficult kids with loads of practical advice for handling aggression, acting out, and tantrums.

Setting Limits with Your Strong-Willed Child: Eliminating Conflict by Establishing Clear, Firm, and Respectful Boundaries, by Robert J. MacKenzie (Roseville, Calif.: Prima Publishing, 2001). If your kid constantly misbehaves and ignores your requests for proper behavior, this book is worth exploring.

The Manipulative Child: How to Regain Control and Raise Resilient, Resourceful, and Independent Kids, by Patrick Cotter and E. W. Swihart (New York: Bantam, 1998). How to say no without guilt and get your kids back on track.

BEHAVIOR 34

Tattling

O ur six-year-old son continually tattles on his younger brother, Sam, who is four. It's as though he just waits to find something Sam's done wrong to tell me. I thought this behavior would go away, but I'm afraid it's turning into a full-time hobby. How do I get him to stop before Sam decides to take up residence elsewhere?

—Martin, a foster dad of seven kids from
Charleston, South Carolina

"I'm going to tell."

"Mom, Jimmy pushed me."

"Sally didn't make her bed."

> ## BEHAVIOR TIP
> The best way to extinguish tattling is to lay down one law: unless the report is intended to keep the accused out of trouble or harm, you won't listen.

Tattling is a learned behavior that usually starts when kids are preschoolers. It's really the first step on the road to that other annoying "any age" behavior called malicious gossiping. Usually, the tattler's intent is to get the other person in trouble or to get our attention but in a socially unacceptable way. Another reason kids tattle is for control. (Think about it: it's pretty powerful knowing you can get a sibling or friend in trouble.) Tattling has no redeeming qualities; it only causes bad feelings between the tattletale and the accused and often leads to sibling wars on the home front. Besides, the information is rarely useful.

THREE STEPS TO
ELIMINATE TATTLING

Here are three steps you can use as a guide to help you squelch tattling and malicious gossip.

Step 1. Explain the Difference Between Tattling and Reporting

Telling an adult that someone is hurt or could get in trouble is not the same as tattling: it's acting responsibly. In these times especially, it is important that kids tell adults if someone might be in danger, threatened, scared, or hurt. In these cases, reporting is not to get people in trouble but to help them stay out of trouble or harm. This is a good time to discuss the names of adults your child can feel safe reporting troubling issues that might arise. Explain also the difference between gossiping and reporting. Praising a friend for some achievement or announcing an important event is not the same as spreading a hurtful rumor that might not be true.

Step 2. Set a "No Tattling" Rule; Then Enforce It

Once your child knows the difference between tattling and reporting, establish a firm no-tattling rule. The best rules are simple and clear: "I'm not listening unless someone's in trouble" or "Is this helpful or unhelpful news?" These responses are often enough to help young kids realize you're interested only in hearing helpful information. The secret to eliminating snitching is to be consistent with your policy every time your kid tattles.

Step 3. Teach How to Solve Problems

One reason kids tattle is they may not know how to solve problems, so they turn to us to do it for them. Rescuing your kid won't develop his self-reliance, so teach him how to work through a problem so he can learn to rely on himself. STOP is a simple four-part problem-solving method you can teach to kids:

1. Stop and ask yourself, "Is this really my problem?"
2. Think: "What's the problem?"
3. Options: Name ways to solve it.
4. Plan: Choose the best option and make a plan to use it.

Here's how the conversation might go with your kid:

KID: Guess what Billy's doing?

MOM: Use STOP. Ask yourself: Is that your problem or his?

KID: Well, Billy could get hurt.

MOM: Okay, now do Think: What's the problem?

KID: Billy is climbing on the counter to get a cup. He could fall.

MOM: What are your options so he doesn't fall?

KID: Climb up and get a cup for him, or give him a paper cup.

MOM: So what's your plan? Which is the better choice?

KID: I'll give him a paper cup.

MOM: I knew you could figure it out. Next time you won't need my help. Go do it!

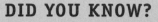

DID YOU KNOW?

A recent survey found that 81 percent of American teens said they are
more willing, following a wave of horrific shootings on
school campuses, to report students who pose a threat
to school safety. Make sure your kid understands that
reporting threats is not tattling or malicious gossip.
When it comes to school safety, kids may well be the
best metal detectors: two-thirds of adolescents who
commit homicide or suicide share their intentions with
a peer. Impress on your kids the importance of telling
an adult legitimate concerns with the guarantee that
their report will be taken seriously.

BEHAVIOR MAKEOVER PLAN

Start by asking yourself what might be provoking your child
to tattle. Here are a few possibilities: Could he be craving your
attention? Does she really know how to solve problems? Does
he think he's being your helper by reporting everything? Is she
jealous of a sibling or trying to get back at another kid? Talk
to other adults who know your kid well. Does he exhibit the
same behavior around them? Once you decide why your child
is tattling, you can develop a plan to remedy the problem.

Next, take a good look at your own behavior. How do
you typically react to your child's tattling? You may be unin-
tentionally encouraging her tattling by giving attention to it
and responding to her every little complaint. If so, plan how
you will change your response. The best response is usually
neutral: "Hmm" or "Ohh." Downplay your reaction, and
refuse to play into it.

Now it's time to take action to begin making over your kid's behavior. Use your Makeover Journal to write down your thoughts and develop your plan.

1. Reread Step One. If you haven't explained the difference between tattling and reporting to your child, think through what you will say and when you will say it. You might want to role-play situations to help your child recognize the distinction.
2. Talk to other parents and teachers to find out if they have rules about snitching. Then develop your family no-tattling rule. Make it simple and clear. Then announce it to your child.
3. Reread Step Three, and reflect on whether your child really knows how to solve problems by herself. If not, plan to teach her the STOP method of solving problems.

Remember to tell your child that whenever she feels unsafe or thinks someone might be hurt, she should report her concerns to an adult she trusts. Encourage your kid to always use her gut instincts to be safe.

➡ See also *Lack of Friends, Lying and Cheating, Sibling Battles, Whining.*

MAKEOVER PLEDGE

How will you use the three steps to eliminate tattling and the Behavior Makeover Plan to help your kid achieve long-term change? On the lines below, write exactly what you agree to do within the next twenty-four hours to begin your kid's behavior makeover.

_____

_____

_____

MAKEOVER RESULTS

All behavior makeovers take hard work, constant practice, and parental reinforcement. Each step your kid takes toward change may be a small one, so be sure to acknowledge and congratulate every one of them along the way. It takes a minimum of twenty-one days to see real results, so don't give up too soon. Remember that if one strategy doesn't work, another will. Write your child's weekly progress on the lines below. Keep track of daily progress in your Makeover Journal.

Week 1

_____

_____

_____

Week 2

_____

_____

_____

Week 3

_____

_____

_____

RESOURCES

Dealing with Tattling: The Conflict Resolution Library, by Don Middleton (New York: Rosen Publishing Group, 1999). Explains what tattling is, why people do it, and what the consequences might be; then suggests alternatives to this behavior and ways to resolve problems created by tale bearing.

Armadillo Tattletale, by Helen Ketteman (New York: Scholastic, 2000). Minding your own business can be tough sometimes, especially if your oversize ears are just the right size for eavesdropping and telling distorted tales. The text conveys a great message: it's important to respect the privacy of others and understand that gossip can hurt. Ages 3 to 7.

Telling Isn't Tattling, by Kathryn M. Hammerseng (Seattle, Wash.: Parenting Press, 1996). Many kids have trouble knowing the difference between telling and tattling. This book for young kids helps them learn when to tell an adult they need help and when to deal with problems themselves. Ages 4 to 7.

The Way It Happened, by Deborah Zemke (Boston: Houghton Mifflin, 1988). Here is the classic event of how rumors can start and blow way out of proportion if no one listens. Ages 6 to 9.

Teased

H elp! I just moved to a new neighborhood with my eight-year-old son. The girl next door, who is twelve, has been teasing him ever since he arrived. First, she invited him over, then left him alone. This week she's been calling him on the phone and makes fun of his height; she calls him Short-Cakes. Last week, she left him a really nasty note about his new haircut. I tried to speak to her mother, but it was like trying to reason with a guest on the Jerry Springer Show. My son hates school now and wants to move back to where we came from.

—Melanie, a single mother from Jackson, Mississippi

BEHAVIOR TIP

Being a victim can become a learned behavior. It's not the only way to respond to malicious teasing. That's why we must teach our kids skills to stick up for themselves from an early age.

"Mom, she called me a wimpy punk."

"He's always making mean faces at me."

"Why does she make fun of my weight in front of the other kids?"

Some of the toughest problems parents must deal with happen in the neighborhood or right on the school playground, where mean kids abound. Although we can't prevent the pain that teasing, racial slurs, and insults can cause, we can lessen our kids' chances of becoming victims. The best thing to do is teach our kids how to deal with their tormentors.

SIX STRATEGIES TO DEAL WITH TEASING

Here are a few strategies that are highly effective in helping kids deal with teasers:

1. *Assert yourself.* Teach your child to face his teaser by using a confident posture: head high, standing tall, and looking the person straight in the eye. Your child should name the unfair behavior and tell the aggressor in a firm, calm voice to stop: "That's teasing. Stop it," or "Go away." Sometimes the best response is just to say, "Cut it out!" Keep in mind that how kids deliver their lines is usually far more important than what they say, so help your child practice using assertive posture.

2. *Ignore it.* Tormentors love to know that their teasing has upset their victims, so help your child find a way not to let it get to her. I asked a group of eleven year olds how they handle unfair teasing, and they unanimously said the worst thing a kid can do is let the teaser know the teasing hurts, even if it does. Here are their suggestions on how to ignore teasers:

- Pretend they're invisible.
- Walk away without looking at them.
- Look at something else and laugh.
- Look as if it doesn't bother you.
- Stay quiet.
- Look completely uninterested.

Ignoring a teaser isn't easy. It takes lots of practice and encouragement from parents for kids to learn this skill.

3. *Question the insult.* Ann Bishop, who teaches violence prevention programs, tells her students to respond to an insult with a nondefensive question: "Why would you say that?" or "Why would you want to tell me I am dumb or fat or whatever and hurt my feelings?"

4. *Use "I want."* Communication experts suggest teaching your child to address the tormentor, beginning with "I want" and saying firmly what she wants changed: "I want you to leave me alone" or "I want you to stop teasing me." The trick is to say the message firmly and forcefully so that it doesn't sound wimpy.

5. *Agree with the teaser.* Consider helping your child create a statement agreeing with her teaser—for example:

TEASER: You're dumb.
CHILD: Yeah, but I'm good at it.

TEASER: Hey, Raghead.
CHILD: You're right. I'm an Arab and proud of it.

6. *Make fun of the teasing.* Fred Frankel, author of *Good Friends Are Hard to Find,* suggests that victims answer every tease with a reply *but not tease back.* The teasing often stops, Frankel says, because the child lets the tormentor know he's not going to let the teasing get to him (even if it does). Suppose the teaser says, "You're stupid." The child says a rehearsed comeback, such as, "So?" "You don't say," "And

your point is?" or "Thanks for telling me." Frankel says the delivery is crucial: it must be rehearsed and said with as minimum of emotional heat as possible.

BEHAVIOR MAKEOVER PLAN

Think about your childhood. Were you ever teased? How did you deal with it? Was that a successful response? Did you tell anyone about it? If so, how did that person respond? What would you do differently today? And what about since then? Have you experienced any spiteful teasing in your workplace or home lately? Have you ever teased someone yourself? Can you remember why you did that and what you think about it now? Talk to other parents to find out if their kids are experiencing hurtful teasing. If so, what are they doing to help them deal with it?

Now it's time to take action to begin making over your kid's behavior. Use your Makeover Journal to write down your thoughts and develop your plan.

1. Review the strategies with your child, and pick the top two with which to experiment.
2. Rehearse and practice the strategy with your child. Role-play the parts, switching between who's the teaser and who's the one being teased.

3. When he feels comfortable enough with the new skill, encourage him to try it the next time he's teased.
4. Remind him that it may not work the first time, but the more he uses it, the easier it will get.
5. If it really doesn't work, begin again. Pick another technique, rehearse and role-play, and try again.

Consider This

I'm convinced that when our kids are around the age of four or five, we as parents and teachers are doing something very wrong by allowing them to learn the role of victim and victimizer. For example, when preschool kids get into conflicts or problems, we're often asking them to solve it by themselves. "Let them work it out," we say, wanting a quick or simple fix. But that's too easy an out. What we should be doing instead is this:

1. Stop the behavior right away.
2. Send a clear message that hurtful teasing is not to be tolerated.
3. Show both kids what to do instead. The teaser needs to learn empathy, social skills, and anger control. The child who is being teased needs to learn assertiveness and how to stick up for himself.

➡ See also *Bullied, Lack of Friends, Negative Peer Pressure.*

MAKEOVER PLEDGE

How will you use the six strategies and the Behavior Makeover Plan to help your kid achieve long-term change? On the lines below, write exactly what you agree to do within the next twenty-four hours to begin your kid's behavior makeover.

_____

_____

_____

MAKEOVER RESULTS

All behavior makeovers take hard work, constant practice, and parental reinforcement. Each step your kid takes toward change may be a small one, so be sure to acknowledge and congratulate every one of them along the way. It takes a minimum of twenty-one days to see real results, so don't give up too soon. Remember that if one strategy doesn't work, another will. Write your child's weekly progress on the lines below. Keep track of daily progress in your Makeover Journal.

Week 1

_____

_____

_____

Week 2

_____

_____

_____

Week 3

_____

_____

_____

RESOURCES

Sticks and Stones: Seven Ways Your Child Can Deal with Teasing, Conflict, and Other Hard Times, by Scott Cooper (New York: Random House, 2000). A wonderful compilation of strategies to help kids stand up to mean-spirited kids.

Your Child: Bully or Victim? Understanding and Ending School Yard Tyranny, by Peter Sheras (New York: Fireside, 2002). A rich parent resource of suggestions for empowering the victim as well as civilizing the bully.

"Why Doesn't Anybody Like Me?" A Guide to Raising Socially Confident Kids, by Hara Estroff Marano (New York: Morrow, 1998). Practical ways based on solid research to help kids be well liked by peers.

What to Do . . . When Kids Are Mean to Your Child, by Elin McCoy (Pleasantville, N.Y.: Reader's Digest, 1997). Helpful advice from experts, parents, and kids on handling teasing and meanness.

Loudmouth George and the Sixth Grade Bully, by Nancy L. Carlson (Minneapolis, Minn.: Carolrhoda Books, 1987). Loudmouth George has his lunch repeatedly stolen by a large bully. He and his friend teach the bully a lesson he'll never forget. Ages 4 to 7.

Stick Boy, by Joan T. Zeier (New York: Atheneum, 1993). Skinny Eric grows seven inches during the sixth grade and becomes the victim of a class harasser. Ages 10 to 12.

36

Temper Tantrums

I'm beginning to think our three year old is possessed. When she doesn't get her way, she has a tantrum: wailing, falling to the ground, and flailing around. It's quite a sight. Yesterday, she had one on our lawn in full view of our neighbors over a candy bar. I was mortified! Should I locate a witch doctor, or is there another approach?
—Kelly, mother of four, Edmonton, Alberta, Canada

"You won't believe what our angelic daughter did at the store! She looked like she trying out for a part in *The Exorcist!*"

BEHAVIOR TIP

A tantrum is a device kids use to get what they want because they've learned it works. The secret to stopping them is *never* to give in to the outburst.

"He kicked and screamed and yelled because I wouldn't give him what he wanted. The stares I got from other parents were so embarrassing!"

Tantrums are sure to be in the top of parents' list of "obnoxious kid behaviors." These are really Oscar-winning performances at their best: ear-piercing screaming, thrashing, and out-of-control behavior. When your kid uses his routine at school or the park, it's just plain humiliating. So why do kids go through these exhausting dramatics? Simply because they've learned that tantrums are a successful—though highly uncivilized—attention-getting antic. You should expect your one to three year old to try this behavior on you, and it's equally as common in girls as in boys. Older kids sometimes resort back to the tantrum stage, especially if there's been a recent stress or change in their lives. We can name an adult or two who has yelled, slammed doors, and broken something. Whether your kid continues using outbursts to get her way depends on how you react the first times she tries it. Once she learns that it succeeds—that is, she gets her way—she's likely to try it again (and again and again).

FIVE STEPS TO SQUELCHING TANTRUMS

Use these five steps to guide you in eliminating tantrums in your kid.

Step 1. Anticipate the Tantrum to Prevent the Outburst

The biggest mistake we make is waiting until our kids are in full meltdown to deal with their out-of-control behavior. Your best bet is to anticipate its onset *before the explosion*. Watch for your kid's unique signs that a tantrum is on its way—tension, antsy, a whimper—and immediately redirect his behavior:

"Look at that little boy over there." "Want to get out of the stroller and push it with Mommy?" Sometimes it helps pointing out your kid's frustration signs: "Looks like you're getting tired. Let's take a walk."

Little tykes don't yet have the maturity to gauge their emotions, so you'll need to be their self-regulator at first. If you see your youngster getting frustrated, that's the time to try calming techniques to help him stay in control. Get eye to eye and talk soothingly to him: rub his back, hold him gently, or hum a relaxing song. Sometimes putting what your child feels into words can stop an explosion: "Waiting is hard, especially when you want to go home right this minute." He might not have the language to express his frustrations, so hearing you say them can be reassuring. Once you figure out what works best for your child's temperament, use it quickly. Kids' behavior can turn into a full-blown tornado in record time.

Step 2. Set a Zero Tolerance Policy for Tantrums

Once your kid explodes, absolutely refuse to interact with your kid until the tantrum subsides. He needs to know this behavior will not be tolerated. Don't coax, yell, spank, or try to reason with your kid; none of them usually works. Besides, he won't hear you above his screams. If you must, use earplugs or put a set of headphones on, but do not respond in any way. Don't even make eye contact. It's sometimes necessary to gently hold a really out-of-control kid to keep him from hurting himself or others, but once he's at a safer point, go about your business.

Step 3. Use Time-Out for Persistent Tantrums

The best consequence for persistent tantrums is time-out. Handle the tantrum the minute it occurs; don't wait to deal with it later. Calmly move your kid to a secluded spot or selected time-out area. Make sure no TV, toys, or other kids are around. Your child must know he doesn't deserve to play or receive any attention from anyone when he uses inappropriate behavior.

The length of time is different for each kid, but your kid should remain in time-out—or the "angry place" or "cool-down chair"—until he's calm for at least two minutes. If he begins screaming and flailing again, he returns to time-out. Usually, the hardest part of this whole ordeal is for you remain calm. Tantrums are scary, and your calmness will help your kid get back in control. BEWARE: Don't let your kid use a tantrum to get out of a responsibility (such as doing a chore or homework). He must know that when he's in control, he's expected to finish the task.

Step 4. Consistently Use the No-Tantrum Policy Everywhere

Once your establish your behavior policy, it's critical that you use the same response *every time* he acts out so he knows you mean business. That means when you're in public too. Remove your kid from the scene: find a private area, go to the car until he acts right, or leave altogether. Sure, it's awkward and inconvenient. Yep, you will get stares, but you can't tolerate his inappropriate behavior.

If your kid's using tantrums with other caregivers—such as your partner, teachers, relatives, baby-sitters, or day care workers—establish a plan together for handling the behavior. Consistency is critical in squelching out-of-control behavior. Establish a time-out area at the away-from-home site, and emphasize that the adult must pay absolutely no attention to your kid until he's in control. Your child should be allowed to participate with others only when his behavior is appropriate. Make sure you stay in touch with other caregivers to assess your kid's makeover progress.

Step 5. Teach Positive Alternatives to Losing Control

It's essential that your child realize that it's okay to get upset, but that it's not okay to display it in such an uncivilized manner. So when you're both calm, talk about appropriate ways to handle frustrations. Many times kids continue using incorrect behaviors simply because they don't know a more acceptable way to behave. Show him how to express feelings using words instead of tantrums. Teach him a few feeling words—such as *angry, mad, sad, grumpy, tired,* or *frustrated*—and then encourage him to label how he feels: "I'm mad" or "I feel really cranky." Do praise him when he tells you his frustrations: "You asked for help when you were upset. Good for you!" You could also role-play ways to help him communicate his needs appropriately: "Instead of grabbing the game, tell your brother that you'd like a turn. Now you try." Although tantrums are never pleasant, you can use them to teach important lessons on communicating needs and handling frustrations appropriately.

BEHAVIOR MAKEOVER PLAN

Start your child's behavior makeover by talking to other parents about tantrums. It will help you recognize that tantrums are more common than you might suspect. How often do

DID YOU KNOW?

One of the best ways to extinguish tantrums is to ignore them. T. Berry Brazelton, the renowned pediatrician and author, shares this essential rule: the more involved you are in trying to lessen the tantrum, the longer the tantrum will last. So pay no attention to your wailing kid, and try to go about your business so you don't reinforce his inappropriate behavior.

their kids have them? What sets off their behavior? How are they responding? What seems to work?

Now it's time to take action to begin making over your kid's behavior. Use your Makeover Journal to write down your thoughts and develop your plan.

1. Reread Step One, and then determine what sets your kid off. Watch your child for the next few days. Write down the pattern you notice that happens *right before* his explosion. When you're aware of what provokes the tantrum, remedy it. Then you can prevent or minimize the outburst.
2. How are you responding to your kid's tantrums? If possible, talk to another adult witness. What part of your response isn't effective? Also, see if there are any adults your kid is *not* displaying this behavior with, and try to figure out why he isn't having tantrums with them.
3. Reread the remaining four steps. Recognize that in most cases, Steps One, Two, and Four are mandatory for tantrum makeovers. If these steps don't successfully squelch your kid's inappropriate behavior, then add Step Three and administer time-out.
4. If your kid is exhibiting tantrums with other caregivers, then reread Step Four and set up a meeting and create a behavior plan. Remember that you'll be more successful if you work consistently together.
5. Review the positive alternatives in Step Five, and pick one to help your child handle frustrations more appropriately. Practice the strategy with your child until he's comfortable using it on his own, and then reinforce his efforts.
6. If you notice this behavior is continuing (particularly if your kid is school age) or if your child has noticeable difficulties calming down, it's time to seek professional help.

➡ See also *Anger, Anxiety, Hitting, Impulsivity, Yelling.*

MAKEOVER PLEDGE

How will you use the five steps and the Behavior Makeover Plan to help your kid achieve long-term change and end tantrums? On the lines below, write exactly what you agree to do within the next twenty-four hours to begin your kid's behavior makeover.

_____

_____

_____

MAKEOVER RESULTS

All behavior makeovers take hard work, constant practice, and parental reinforcement. Each step your kid takes toward change may be a small one, so be sure to acknowledge and congratulate every one of them along the way. It takes a minimum of twenty-one days to see real results, so don't give up too soon. Remember that if one strategy doesn't work, another will. Write your child's weekly progress on the lines below. Keep track of daily progress in your Makeover Journal.

Week 1

_____

_____

Week 2

_____

_____

Week 3

RESOURCES

Tears and Tantrums: What to Do When Babies and Children Cry, by Aletha J. Solter (Goleta, Calif.: Shining Star Press, 1997). Psychological and physical benefits to tears and tantrums are offered, as well as causes, implications, and empathetic solutions.

Tantrums: Secrets to Calming the Storm, by Ann E. Laforge (New York: Pocket Books, 1996). Helps parents cope effectively with public outbursts, diagnose pretantrum conditions, control anger, and teach kids positive alternatives to losing control.

No More Tantrums: A Parent's Guide to Taming Your Toddler and Keeping Your Cool, by Diane Mason (New York: McGraw-Hill, 1997). An essential guide that offers parent-tested solutions to the frustrations of raising a toddler.

The Chocolate-Covered-Cookie Tantrum, by Deborah Blumenthal (New York: Clarion Books, 1999). Sophie sees a girl eating a delicious-looking chocolate-covered cookie, and when her mother does not have one to give to her, she throws a temper tantrum. Great for little tykes.

Tiger and the Temper Tantrum, by Vivian French (Boston: Larousse Kingfisher Chambers, 1999). Young Tiger is used to throwing temper tantrums. Mother puts her paw down, and Tiger learns there are more acceptable ways to get your needs met. Ages 4 to 8.

Tristan's Temper Tantrum, by Caroline Form (Child's Play International, 1996). The story of Tristan the volcano who awakens from a thousand-year slumber and finds that nobody wants to play with a bad-tempered volcano. Ages 4 to 8.

Don't Rant and Rave on Wednesdays! The Children's Anger-Control Book, by Adolph Moser (Kansas City, Mo.: Landmark Editions, 1964). Uses cartoon-like illustrations and offers straightforward text suggesting ways to control anger and express feelings healthfully. Ages 8 to 12.

BEHAVIOR 37

Whining

O ur four year old has developed this horrible new habit that's driving my husband and me crazy. Anytime she wants to get her way, she uses a whiny voice that is so grating it reminds me of a dentist's drill. It's so embarrassing that we're afraid to take her out in public. Please tell us what we can do so she stops whining. We're becoming hermits!

—Sue, a mother of three from Pittsburgh, Pennsylvania

"I can't stand his tone. It's worse than nails scraping on a chalkboard."

"Once she starts, I know she'll keep it up until I give in."

"She's only four, but her begging is driving me crazy!"

BEHAVIOR TIP

The top reason kids whine is to get our attention. They will continue to use this irritating behavior if we give in because they've learned it works! *So don't give in!*

Whining—that pitiful, loud, grating sound—is one of the most irritating of kid behaviors. The pitch is an exasperating blend of crying and nagging that's as annoying as a dentist's drill. If that's not enough, whiners have an amazing ability to stretch syllables so they almost slap you back in your face: "Pleeeeeeease" or "Daaaaad!" What's more, whining can quickly turn into a full-blown, ugly tantrum. Although whining usually peaks at around four years of age, it can continue well into the school years. There's some good news though: whining is learned, so the behavior can be unlearned. And the sooner you start your kid's behavior makeover, the less likely it will become an annoying, troublesome habit.

FOUR STEPS TO SQUELCH WHINING

You can use the following four steps to guide you in eliminating whining and making over your kids' behavior.

Step 1. Establish a Zero Tolerance for Whining

Rest assured, all kids whine occasionally, but the surest way to turn this grating attention-getter into a full-fledged habit is to give in and let your little nagger win. Take heed: once you back down and surrender, kids usually continue using the technique as a way to get what they want. Worse yet, if not stopped, whining often escalates to back talk, arguing, and tantrums. *So the bottom line is, don't let your kid think it works.*

The best way to stop the behavior is to flat-out refuse to listen to nagging requests unless they're spoken with a polite tone. At the first whimper of a whine, firmly say, "Stop! I don't listen to whining voices. Tell me what you want with a nice tone." Then walk away or turn around and ignore your kid. Turn back when the whining stops (even for a few seconds) and say, "I do listen to a nice voice. Can I help you now?" The trick is to not to look irritated or to react.

Step 2. Demonstrate Appropriate Voice Tone

Choose a calm time to talk with your kid about why whining is unacceptable. A key point is to make sure he knows the difference between a whining voice and a normal speaking tone. You might say: "The tone of voice you used to try to get my attention is whining. I will only listen to polite voices."

Next, show your child what a more acceptable voice sounds like. Don't assume he knows the correct way to get your attention. Whining may have become such a habit that he simply isn't aware of his irritating tone. Take a moment to ensure that your child knows what kind of a voice you expect—for example, "Here's my whining voice: 'I don't wanna do this.' Here's my polite one: 'Can you please help me?' When you want something, make your voice sound like my polite voice. Now you try." Be careful not to mimic your child. Your goal is to be instructional so he understands your expectations without feeling ridiculed.

Step 3. Lay Down Your Rules

Announce from now on that he should expect an automatic no *any* time he whines. Then refuse to listen to even the first note of a whine uttered from your kid's lips. Usually whining stops when kids realize it's getting them nowhere, so your child has to realize that your rule is nonnegotiable.

Step 4. Set a Consequence If Whining Continues

You may be wondering, "What happens if my kid still whines?" The answer is simple: you *must* set an immediate consequence so your kid knows you won't tolerate it. And it's the same for back talk, hitting, spitting, or arguing. Don't make the mistake of thinking you can wait until you're home to correct your kid's misbehavior. Wherever the whining occurs is where the consequence must be administered. That may mean the huge inconvenience of changing plans when your kid starts up his whining routine during a shopping outing. But if you really want to end the behavior, you'll calmly say on the spot: "That's whining, and you know the rule. We're leaving now."

Consequences stop bad behaviors only if they're used *every time the behavior occurs.* Take heed: if you don't follow through, the whining usually increases. That's because your child has learned you just might give in. You must also stay unemotional when administering consequences: no lecturing, displaying anger, or appearing irritated. Also, remember to praise your kid when he uses the right voice tone. Breaking a habit takes time, so always encourage his good efforts. Above all, *don't give in.*

BEHAVIOR MAKEOVER PLAN

Start by thinking about whining kids. Why do you think they use this behavior? Whining is learned, so where do you think kids learn it? How do other parents you know respond to whining? How did your parents respond? Which parenting

DID YOU KNOW?

Audrey Ricker and Carolyn Crowder, authors of *Whining: Three Steps to Stopping It Before the Tears and Tantrums Start,* say whining almost never stops without parental intervention. The few kids who do stop whining on their own usually do so because they've found more efficient, but usually not more constructive, ways of getting their needs met. Those ways may include lying, stealing, or sneaking out after hours or even more destructive behaviors like drug and alcohol abuse.

responses do you think are most successful in stopping whining behavior? Why?

Now it's time to take action to begin making over your kid's behavior. Use your Makeover Journal to write down your thoughts and develop your plan.

1. Think about how you typically respond to your kid's whining. If possible, discuss this with your partner or another parent who knows you and your child well. Why hasn't your response succeeded in stopping the behavior? Does your child use this behavior with other adults? If so, who? Who doesn't he use this behavior around? Why not?

2. Reread Steps One, Two, and Three, and commit to no longer tolerating your kid's whining. Think through what you will say to explain your new behavior expectation. Most important is to plan how you will respond the next time your kid whines. Recognize that in most cases, Steps One and Two are mandatory for behavior makeovers.

3. Usually there's a predictable pattern to kids' behavior in which certain situations are more likely to provoke bad conduct. Think about your kid, and identify the kinds of circumstances that might incite her to whine. For instance, is there a time of the day she is more likely to sulk: When she's hungry or tired? When you're on the phone and she wants your attention? When you're tired? Once you're aware of the pattern, you can anticipate when your child is more likely to resort to using the behavior and head it off before it starts. For example, you might distract her attention before she starts whining: "Look, there's a gorgeous butterfly!" Kids often whine to get attention, so responding promptly to your child can fend it off. "I'll be off the phone in two minutes. As soon as I'm done, let's read a book."

4. If it's not nipped in the bud, whining rarely stops by itself. If the whining continues, try Step Four and set consequences that are appropriate for your child. Remember

that the best consequences fit the situation and are administered immediately. Make a list of what you could do when your kid whines in a public setting and at home. At the first whimper, you'll be ready. Here are a few consequence ideas suitable for whining:

For a young whiner, create a "whining chair" at home, and use it when necessary: "That's whining. Go sit in the whiner's chair for two minutes so you remember to use your nice voice when you want something."

When driving, pull to the side of the road (when safe), and wait until your kid talks correctly. Feel free to listen to the radio or even read as you wait. He'll get the point.

In a public setting, such as a restaurant, a mall, a movie theater, or a park, immediately leave the scene with your kid. You and your spouse may have to resort to driving in two cars, with your whiner leaving the scene of the crime with one of you.

The best news is that it usually takes only one or two times before your kid gets the message that you mean business. Just don't back down!

➡ See also *Anger, Impulsivity, Rudeness, Talking Back, Yelling.*

MAKEOVER PLEDGE

How will you use the four steps and the Behavior Makeover Plan to help your kid achieve long-term change and stop whining? On the lines below, write exactly what you agree to do within the next twenty-four hours to begin your kid's behavior makeover.

_____

_____

_____

MAKEOVER RESULTS

All behavior makeovers take hard work, constant practice, and parental reinforcement. Each step your kid takes toward change may be a small one, so be sure to acknowledge and congratulate every one of them along the way. It takes a minimum of twenty-one days to see real results, so don't give up too soon. Remember that if one strategy doesn't work, another will. Write your child's weekly progress on the lines below. Keep track of daily progress in your Makeover Journal.

Week 1

_____

_____

_____

Week 2

_____

_____

_____

Week 3

_____

_____

_____

RESOURCES

Taming the Dragon in Your Child, by Meg Eastman and Sydney Craft Rozen (New York: Wiley, 1994). An excellent parenting resource to reduce back talk and whining.

No More Misbehavin'

Whining: Three Steps to Stopping It Before the Tears and Tantrums Start, by Audrey Ricker and Carolyn Crowder (New York: Fireside, 1998). A commonsense guide for parents to stopping whining behavior.

Winning the Whining Wars, by Cynthia Whitham (Los Angeles: Perspective Publishing, 1991). Another good parent guide to limit whining and back talk.

How to Lose All Your Friends, by Nancy Carlson (New York: Viking Press, 1994). A great picture book that looks at all the negative friendship consequences to displaying behaviors such as whining, not sharing, and never smiling. Ages 3 to 8.

How Rude! The Teenagers' Guide to Good Manners, Proper Behavior, and Not Grossing People Out, by Alex J. Packer (Minneapolis, Minn.: Free Spirit, 1997). Sound advice for teens about the world of manners conveyed in a humorous way. Ages 12 to 15.

38

Yelling

I'm hoping there's something—anything—you can suggest. It seems the only way our twelve year old communicates is by yelling. He starts out in a normal tone but quickly escalates to a sonic-boom pitch. Now our other kid is yelling too. He doesn't do this with his friends, so why is it my kids only yell at each other? How can we make things better?

—John, a dad of two kids from Orlando, Florida

"MMOOOOMMMM, WHERE'RE MY SNEAKERS?"
"I DID IT ALREADY!"
"I HATE YOU, JIMMY!"

BEHAVIOR TIP

The primary reason kids yell is that they hear the people they're living with yell. So don't yell at anyone in or out of your family, and whenever your kid yells, *never* yell back.

Yelling in any household is a sure way to shatter not only patience but also family harmony. Besides, no one likes to be around screamers. Tolerating a yelling kid just teaches him that the way to get what he wants is by upping the volume. Worse yet, the more frequent the yelling is, the more it has to be used to be effective. Family members get used to the screaming, the pitch gets louder, the frequency gets longer, and soon everyone starts using it so they can be heard. Unless your child has a hearing problem—and please don't make any assumptions—yelling is learned. Eliminating this behavior will do absolute wonders in creating a calmer and more peaceful family. So don't wait!

FOUR STEPS TO ELIMINATE YELLING AND BOOST FAMILY HARMONY

Here are four steps to guide you in squelching yelling and help your kid learn to communicate using a more appropriate voice tone.

Step 1. Firmly Convey and Calmly, "No Yelling!"

Begin by firmly conveying your behavior standard that yelling will no longer be tolerated. Tell your screamer that while it's okay to be angry, he may not use a yelling voice to express his feelings. Then convey your "no yelling" expectations to all family members. Consider asking them to take a "no yelling" vow. The pledge is written on a piece of paper, signed by all members, and posted as a concrete reminder.

Step 2. Absolutely Refuse to Engage with a Screamer

Consider creating a signal—such as pulling your ear or a time-out hand gesture—agreed on by you and the screamer signifying an inappropriate voice tone. Then as soon as his voice goes one scale above a normal range, give the signal. It means he needs to lower his voice immediately, or you won't listen. If he continues using a loud, yelling tone, absolutely refuse to listen. Firmly (and calmly) explain, "That's yelling. I listen only when you use a calm voice." Walk away, and go about your business until he talks respectfully. As long as he yells, keep walking. If you have to lock yourself in the bathroom, do so. He needs to know you mean business, so be consistent.

Step 3. Teach Alternative Ways to Express Needs

Many kids yell and scream because they don't know how to express their frustrations any other way. So teach a new way.

One way is to practice the new tone. Don't assume your kid knows what an acceptable voice tone sounds like; show him: "That voice is yelling and unacceptable. Listen to how a calm voice sounds when I want something. Then you make your voice sound like mine." Or "Your voice is too loud. Are you angry? Tell Susan why you're angry using a regular voice."

Another way is to use "I" messages. Explain that instead of starting messages with *you,* begin with *I.* It helps your kid stay focused on the person's troublesome behavior without putting the person down so the chances for emotional outbursts (and yelling) are lessened. The child then tells the offender what the person did that upset him. He may also state how he'd like the problem resolved—for example, "I get really upset when you take my stuff. I want you to ask me for permission first," or "I don't like to be teased. Please stop."

Step 4. Set a Consequence for Persistent Yelling

If you've tried all the methods and yelling continues, it's time to set a consequence. Make sure you explain the consequence at a relaxed time, not during a screaming match. Tell a younger kid that each time he yells, he will be sent to time-out or the "thinking chair" for a few minutes to help him remember how to talk right. At the end of the time-out, help him express his concerns using an appropriate voice tone. An appropriate consequence for older kids is losing telephone privileges for a set length (an hour or the evening, depending on the circumstances): "If you can't talk nicely to your family, then you won't be able to talk to your friends." Once you set the consequence, consistency is crucial! Use the same consequence every time he yells.

BEHAVIOR MAKEOVER PLAN

Think about your childhood. How did your parents usually communicate their feelings to each other? Did you hear them do much yelling? How about among your siblings? How did your parents typically respond to your yelling? How about in your workplace? Identify a few individuals whom you'd describe as screamers. What sets them off? What responses from others typically cause their screaming to escalate? Have you noticed what types of responses usually calm them down?

Next, how do you typically respond to your kid's screaming? Does your reaction calm him down or set him off? HINT: The fastest way to escalate a behavior issue with your kid is to yell back. If your behavior needs tuning up, write down the steps you'll take to change.

Now it's time to take action to begin making over your kid's behavior. Use your Makeover Journal to write down your thoughts and develop your plan.

1. Tune into your kid's behavior. Why is your kid yelling? What circumstances cause him to yell? Is there a certain time of day he is more likely to yell? Who does he yell at? Is there someone he does not scream at? For instance, does he yell at his friends, siblings, teacher, you, your partner? Write down your thoughts to help discover any behavior patterns.
2. Yelling is usually a learned behavior style that can also be a way to vent frustrations. Could this be an issue with your kid? Is he angry, frustrated, picked on, overwhelmed, needing attention, physically tired, or sick? Does he feel he isn't being listened to? Might he be feeling powerless? Think about what's causing your kid to yell. Write how you will fix the problem.
3. Review the four steps to eliminating yelling. What are you willing to do? If you want to boost family harmony and reduce yelling, then something needs to be altered in your kid's environment. What will you change? Think through your plan, and then commit to following through.

➡ See also *Anger, Fighting, Sibling Battles, Temper Tantrums.*

MAKEOVER PLEDGE

How will you use the four steps and the Behavior Makeover Plan to help your kid achieve long-term change? On the lines below, write exactly what you agree to do within the next twenty-four hours to begin your kid's behavior makeover.

_____

_____

_____

MAKEOVER RESULTS

All behavior makeovers take hard work, constant practice, and parental reinforcement. Each step your kid takes toward change may be a small one, so be sure to acknowledge and congratulate every one of them along the way. It takes a minimum of twenty-one days to see real results, so don't give up too soon. Remember that if one strategy doesn't work, another will. Write your child's weekly progress on the lines below. Keep track of daily progress in your Makeover Journal.

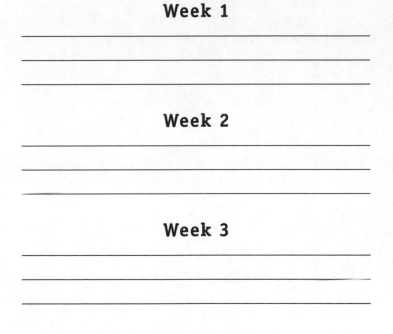

Week 1

_____

_____

_____

Week 2

_____

_____

_____

Week 3

_____

_____

_____

RESOURCES

Peaceful Parents, Peaceful Kids: Practical Ways to Create a Calm and Happy Home, by Naomi Drew (New York: Kensington Books, 2000). A must-have parenting book for raising kids who are more cooperative, peaceful, and less stressful.

The Mad Family Gets Their Mads Out: Fifty Things Your Family Can Say and Do to Express Anger Constructively, by Lynne Namka (Charleston, Ill.: Talk, Trust and Feel Press, 1995). Useful ways to help kids who are struggling to express anger constructively and help families learn how to deal with anger in nonviolent ways and relate to each member positively.

Tired of Yelling: Teaching Our Children to Resolve Conflict, by Lyndon D. Waugh (Atlanta, Ga.: Longstreet, 1999). A psychiatrist offers parenting solutions for defusing family tension and helping toddlers through teens learn skills of peacemaking.

Harriet, You'll Drive Me Wild! by Mem Fox (New York: Harcourt, 2000). Harriet doesn't mean to be troublesome. She's always very sorry for her behavior afterward. Her mother doesn't like to yell and usually gently reprimands her. But as her shenanigans escalate, so does her mom's blood pressure. When that edge is finally reached, Harriet's mom yells and yells. Ages 4 to 8.

When Sophie Gets Angry—Really, Really Angry (New York: Scholastic, 1999). A little girl who has trouble managing her anger learns how to take time to cool off and regain her composure. Ages 3 to 7.

Anger Management Workbook for Kids and Teens, by Anita Bohensky (Growth Publications, 2001). A workbook that teaches anger control techniques, coping methods, and problem-solving ideas for preadolescents and teens.

PART 4

How to Use Consequences

*Success is a ladder that cannot be climbed
with your hands in your pockets.*
—American proverb

"How many times do I have to tell you?"
"Didn't you know I really meant it?"
"That's the third time this week!"
"When are you ever going to learn?"

There's a guarantee that comes with parenting: kids are bound to do what you don't expect. It's just one of those things about being a kid. That's why you must be prepared with a contingency plan if your kid keeps misbehaving—and that's despite your great lecture, posted house rules, and stern looks. Obviously, you can't let your kid get away with bad behavior. He has to learn to take responsibility for his poor choices, so that's when consequences become part of the makeover. It's one of the most important discipline secrets as well as an essential sanity saver.

As you've probably noticed, there are references to consequences throughout this book. You don't usually need to use punishment for effective discipline, *and you never should resort to spanking or other corporal punishment*. Nevertheless, there are definitely occasions when consequences become necessary. Every situation is different, but here is a list of general guidelines for the use of any kind of consequence that you can apply to your situation and your child.

Whenever you apply a consequence, you should:

1. *Announce the consequence.* Prepare your kid by letting him know well ahead that there will be a consequence if the same misbehavior is repeated. You might even put the consequence in writing so it's absolutely clear that any hitting will result in disciplinary action. Have your kid sign the agreement so there's no doubt that your intentions are serious. HINT: Consider asking your kid to think of an appropriate consequence for his misbehavior. It's a great way to involve your kid in taking responsibility for his poor choices. Kid-created consequences are usually tougher than those parents set. You don't have to agree to his suggestions; it's just a way to involve him in the process.

2. *Fit the consequence to the crime.* An appropriate consequence for rudeness would be to have to do a chore for the kid to whom he has been rude; for stealing, it might be to return the stolen property and pay for any damages.

3. *Fit the consequence to your kid's development level.* For example, don't require a five-year old to write, "I will not fib," one hundred times.

4. *Don't negotiate.* Once you set a consequence, stick to it, and be consistent.

5. *Don't wait.* Set and carry out the consequence as immediately as convenient at the scene of the crime. For example, if your kid has a tantrum in a restaurant, remove him immediately, and enforce the consequence that has been previously agreed to.

6. *Get everybody on board.* Tell your spouse, teacher, baby-sitter, grandparents, and anyone else who needs to know that you and your kid have agreed to the behavior makeover.

7. *Preserve your kid's dignity.* Always discipline in private, and treat your kid respectfully. Stay calm and remain neutral. Be an example to your kid of how to behave under pressure.

CONSEQUENCES TO STOP PROBLEM BEHAVIORS

Now that we've reviewed the general guidelines, here's a list of potential consequences that you might try depending on the age of your child and the circumstances of the bad behavior:

• *Monetary penalty.* Establish a family jar with a lid that stays in one place in your home—perhaps the kitchen counter or the family room table. Then set an agreed monetary fine for designated misbehaviors. Each time any kid demonstrates the misbehavior, he is fined and must put the set amount of money in the jar. When the jar is filled, donate the money to a charity of the family's choosing. For kids short on money, make and post a list of chores that can be done to work off the fine.

- *Extra chores.* Make a list of extra work chores—those beyond any of the regular responsibilities the kid might have already, such as vacuuming, dusting, raking leaves, or sweeping the patio. Any misbehavior means the kid must do one of the jobs. If your kid's behavior has affected another family member, he or she may be required to do a chore for the offended party, which relieves that person of a duty, or helps this person in some other way.

- *Apologies.* Saying "I'm sorry" (in a voice that truly conveys the child is sorry) is always a way of responding to a misbehavior that affects other people. In some cases, a special apology may be required. Writing a note, having a face-to-face session, or delivering a small handmade gift can be a valuable consequence for some behaviors. An apology can also be required in addition to another consequence.

- *Grounding.* Other than at school or church time, your kid must stay in the house for a specified length of time—generally one to three days—and lose all social privileges. For a much younger child, the length is usually no more than an hour or two. If the offense is particularly egregious, many parents also pull some or all home entertainment privileges—TV, video games, and phone.

- *Loss of privileges.* Any continued display of the targeted misbehavior can result in your kid's losing certain specified privileges. Make sure it's something you have control over—for example, watching TV, playing video games, using the phone, listening to music, or use of a common family area.

USING TIME-OUT

Time-out is appropriate when a child is immediately removed from an activity for inappropriate behavior and asked to sit alone quietly for a specified time to think about his actions. It can be a very effective way to help an aggressive kid calm down. In fact, many parents call the time-out location "the

No More Misbehavin'

thinking chair" or "cool-down corner." Time-out is the kind of consequence that should be customized depending on the age of your child, his temperament and personality, and the severity of the misbehavior. For some kids, it's an unendurable cruelty, and for others it's no fun but not a big deal either.

Here are a few general tips for using time-out:

- Find a quiet, safe, well-lit, and isolated part of the house, and set it aside for time-out.
- Be sure to set aside an appropriate chair (no beanbag or recliner).
- Be sure there's no access to games, toys, music, pets, food, TV, friends, phone, or other distractions.
- Make sure the area is one where she may not receive attention and is out of the general household traffic.
- Set an appropriate time. The simplest rule for determining the time length for kids seven and under is one minute for each year of the child's age (three years equals three minutes, six years equals six minutes, and so on). Remember that these are the minimum times. Do *not* let your kid out earlier. The length of the extinction depends on the severity of the infraction and your child's age.
- Always tell your child exactly how long he is required to remain in time-out. Set a timer with a bell so you know exactly when the time is up. Then keep the timer near you so you maintain control of it.
- Don't shave time off the time-out period. Once it's set, stick to it and be consistent.
- The clock starts as soon as your kid stops resisting and begins the time-out properly.
- Once time-out is established as a consequence, it must be enforced. The child is not allowed to leave time-out until he behaves appropriately: sitting quietly without talking and remaining for the stipulated time. If he doesn't behave, add an extra minute of time-out from the moment he does act right. For instance, if he's been

misbehaving in time-out for twelve minutes and then finally sits quietly, add one more minute for his perfect behavior and then let him out.

- Don't peek in or respond to any attempts for attention. Any interaction with your child will only reinforce whatever misbehavior he is displaying. This is the time for your child to think for himself.
- Implement time-out *anywhere* your child displays the inappropriate behavior whenever possible: "You were hitting. Go sit on Grandma's bed for ten minutes." If you're not in an appropriate place, try to find one as soon as possible.
- Following the time-out, the child must still complete what you asked him to do. If he still doesn't comply, then double the time-out length.

AFTER THE CONSEQUENCE

When the consequence or time-out has been served, ask your kid to describe what she did wrong and what she will do differently next time. If she can't remember or won't agree, she goes back to time-out, or the consequence is implemented again until she can. With younger kids or those who have difficulty remembering, you will need to guide them with their answers. Remember that a crucial part of an effective makeover is helping your kid learn what she did wrong so she won't be as likely to repeat the same misbehavior.

Some parents ask their child to draw or write a description explaining what they did wrong. Kids can also be required to prepare a "statement of intent"—a drawing, sentence, paragraph, or essay that explains how they plan to make over their own bad behavior so they don't repeat it.

If your kid does not comply with the consequence or doesn't complete the length of time-out correctly, go to Code

DID YOU KNOW?

Did you ever wonder if how you discipline has anything to do with how your kids turn out? Leonard Eron, a research psychologist at the University of Illinois, was interested in just that. He studied 870 eight year olds in rural New York State to find out how their parents disciplined them, from using no physical punishment at all to slapping and spanking, and if it had any correlation to whether the kids became aggressive. He discovered that the more severely their parents punished them, the more aggressive they were with other kids. Twenty years later, Eron studied the same kids as adults. Those who were the most aggressive as kids became aggressive adults with aggressive children themselves.

Red, the highest level of punishment. She now loses the privilege of something she *really* cares about for a specified time period—an hour for little tykes and twenty-four hours for bigger kids. Make sure the possession or privilege is something you personally can control, such as use of the phone, computer, skateboard, video games, or TV. You and your kid agreed to the Code Red consequence previously, so *now you must follow through*.

PART 5

Don't Forget to Tell Your Kids You Love Them!

The most beautiful sight in the world is a child going confidently down the road of life, after you have shown him the way.
—Confucius

"I've been scolding my son so often that he told me today that I don't love him anymore."

"I have to discipline my daughter so much that it's ruining our relationship."

"I'm afraid the only childhood memory my kid will have is sitting in time-out."

Of course, we want our kids to be well behaved. It's part of what good parenting is all about. But in our quest to shape up bad behaviors, we may overlook all the good parts of our kids: a kind heart, a quick humor, a frisky nature, a never-give-up attitude, a melting smile. And the real danger is that our kids may begin to perceive that we love them more for how they act instead of for who they are.

It can be discouraging to hear nothing but reprimands and lectures and to see our stern looks and frustrated sighs. What's more, such messages can be disastrous to the formation of our kid's self-confidence. So the last part of any behavior makeover is essential: don't forget to tell your kid you love him. What could possibly be more important than making sure your children know just how much you cherish and adore them—despite their misbehavior?

HOW ARE YOU DOING?

Here are a few questions to help you assess how well you're doing in making your kid feel cherished, especially when he's misbehaving. Check any potential problem areas:

_____ Does my kid overhear me talk about her to others in positive, loving terms and not about her misbehaviors?

_____ Do I avoid comparing her to siblings or peers?

_____ Do I avoid berating her in front of others?

_____ Do I always discipline my child privately and
with dignity?

_____ Do I have reasonable expectations, based on the
age, personality, and development of my child?

_____ Do I stop and consider my child's point of view
and listen openly to his opinion?

_____ Do I remember to compliment and encourage
my kid when he is good?

_____ Do I stay calm whenever I discipline my child,
never raising my voice, yelling, or hitting?

_____ Do I schedule one-on-one special time to enjoy
being with my kid and give my full presence?

_____ Do I avoid taking sides when there's a conflict
between my kids, or would my child say I show
favoritism?

_____ Do I lash out at my kid because I've had a tough
day?

_____ Do I accept my kid's natural temperament, and
have I made peace with his personality?

_____ Do I always insist on having my way because
"I'm the parent"?

_____ Do I try to eliminate a behavior in my kid
because I see it as a problem in myself?

_____ Do I end each discipline episode by letting him
know I love him and forgive him?

_____ Do I acknowledge to my kid whenever I was
unfair or acted inappropriately?

In your Makeover Journal, write what you commit to
doing to create a more positive, affirming relationship with your
child. On the lines that follow, write the one thing you pledge
to do within the next twenty-four hours to start that change.

_____

_____

_____

DISCIPLINE THAT PROTECTS
YOUR CHILD'S SELF-BELIEFS

All kids misbehave at one time or another. How we react to our children's misbehavior can be destructive or productive to their self-beliefs, and it makes our job especially tricky. Here are a few positive discipline practices to use in correcting your kid's misbehavior while still protecting her dignity.

Get Calm, Then Respond

The first part to correcting any discipline problem is often the hardest: you must stay calm despite how your kid behaves. If you feel yourself getting heated, walk away from your kid until you're calm. Take a deep, slow, cleansing breath, count slowly to ten, or drink a glass of water. Lock yourself in the bathroom if you have to, but don't respond to your kid unless you're calm.

Use *I* Messages to State Disapproval

When you're not pleased with your child's behavior, it's helpful to declare your disapproval starting your message with the word *I* instead of *you*. Notice how just changing *you* to *I* turns a critical, belittling message into one focusing on the kid's misbehavior, and not on a child's self-worth:

You message: "You sound just like a crybaby. Nobody will like you if you keep it up."

I message: "I don't like to hear you whine, because people don't like to be around whiners."

Focus on the Behavior, Not the Kid

The corrective message should focus only on your kid's misbehavior, never on your child. It's one of the most important ways to preserve your child's dignity and still let him know you will not put up with inappropriate behavior:

No More Misbehavin'

Kid focused: "Stop whining. Can't you behave? Your sister doesn't do that!"

Behavior focused: "I want to hear your idea, but tell me without a whiny tone."

Make Your Correction Be Instructive

We often tell our kids to stop a bad behavior but neglect to tell them what they should do differently. The right kind of discipline should help children learn right from wrong, recognize consequences, discover how to improve the misbehavior, and still protect their dignity. The corrective message tells a child what's wrong with her behavior, and what new behavior is expected:

Corrective: "That was rude: you interrupted me when I was talking. Wait patiently until I'm done, or if it's really important first say, 'Excuse me.'"

Encourage Your Child's Attempts

Although we should always be concerned about our kids' inappropriate behavior, remember that if you focus only on the bad behavior, you run the danger of overlooking times when your child acts right. So do acknowledge any effort, big or little, your kid makes to improve. Your attentiveness will help her believe behavior change is really possible:

Effort encouragement: "You tried to wait without interrupting. It's hard, but I saw you make the effort."

Use Praise to Encourage Good Behavior

Praise is one of the oldest strategies parents use to encourage good behavior, but not all praise improves behavior. Use the following five points to make your encouragement more effective in changing your kid's behaviors:

Specific. When you observe good behavior, word your message so that your child knows exactly what was done well: "You were mad and didn't pinch Kim. You used your words."

Repeated. To help your kid make the new behavior a habit, repeat the praise a few times.

Deserved. Kids know when they have really earned the praise they receive, so be sure the praise you give is deserved: "You took your time on your work; it looks so much neater."

Genuine. The best reinforcement is always sincere and genuine and lets the kid know exactly what he did that was right: "It took effort to stay calm, but you did it! Good job!"

Individual. Effective praise is directed to the deserving child. Do not make comparisons, especially with siblings! Doing so can lay the seeds of resentment and jealousy.

Nurture Positive Qualities

A kid who misbehaves is bound to be discouraged; after all, our kids do want to please us and receive our approval. Sometimes in our quest to improve their misbehaviors, we may overlook their good qualities. The result is an even more discouraged kid. That's why nurturing your child's positive strengths and qualities is an important part of any behavior makeover. Here are four points that help kids recognize their personal talents and areas of excellence:

- Choose one to three positive qualities to strengthen. Refer to the list of one hundred strengths and positive qualities on pages 312–314, and choose one or two attributes you want your child to recognize about herself. Make sure the strengths are already present in your child and are not ones you wish were true about her. Write the terms in your Makeover Journal—such as *kind, artistic, clever, creative*—and then use the same term every time you praise the quality.

- Find opportunities to point out the strength. You can start giving one strength message a day and gradually work your way up to two to four strength reminders. If you flood your child with too many compliments a day, though, they begin to lose their effectiveness and become too predictable. Usually it takes at least three weeks for a new image to develop, so keep praising your child's specific strengths for at least twenty-one days.
- Praise the strength only when deserved. Compliment the child's strength only when his actions deserve recognition. Kids are great at picking up the insincere from the genuine.
- Describe specific examples of the strength. Point out examples when your child displays the strength. He may not be able to see these strengths on his own. Here are a few examples of how to describe strengths, so your child knows exactly what he did to deserve recognition:

  Artistic ability: "You're so artistic; your drawings always have such great details and color combinations."

  Positive: "You always seem to have something upbeat and positive to say about people. It brightens everyone's day."

100 STRENGTHS AND POSITIVE QUALITIES TO ENCOURAGE

Check off the areas you feel best describe your child's innate skills, positive character traits, or special talents. Then write them in your Makeover Journal so you can include them in your makeover plans. As you discover new attributes, add them to your list.

Visual Talents

_____ drawing

_____ photography

_____ recall for
details

_____ painting

_____ active
imagination

_____ visualizes

_____ map skills

_____ directionality

_____ creative

Logic and Thinking

_____ computer
savvy

_____ organized

_____ problem solver

_____ abstract
thinking

_____ math and
numbers

_____ thinking
games

_____ deciphers
codes

_____ common sense

_____ science

_____ quick thinker

_____ learns quickly

_____ keen memory

_____ knowledgeable

_____ intelligent

Bodily Kinesthetic and Physical Strengths

_____ role
playing

_____ acting

_____ creative
movement

_____ dancing

_____ dramatics

_____ a specific
sport

_____ running
athletic

_____ strength

_____ graceful

_____ endurance

_____ balance

_____ dexterity

_____ coordinated

Musical Talents

_____ instrument

_____ singing

_____ rhythm

_____ remembers
tunes

_____ composes
music

_____ reads
music

_____ responds
to music

Personality and Character Traits

_____ creative
_____ initiative
_____ follows through
_____ trustworthy
_____ patient
_____ reliable
_____ sensitive
_____ courageous
_____ caring
_____ hard working
_____ adaptable
_____ easy going
_____ responsible
_____ generous
_____ confident
_____ independent
_____ neat
_____ determined
_____ truthful
_____ insightful
_____ gentle
_____ mature
_____ happy
_____ open
_____ prompt
_____ dependable
_____ optimistic
_____ loyal
_____ serious
_____ honest

_____ disciplined
_____ affectionate
_____ strong character
_____ faithful

Social Skills

_____ friendly
_____ leader
_____ helpful
_____ good-natured
_____ good sportsmanship
_____ courteous
_____ fair
_____ takes turns
_____ team player
_____ cooperates
_____ shares
_____ empathetic
_____ understanding
_____ peacemaker
_____ fun
_____ charming
_____ encouraging
_____ humorous
_____ good listener
_____ likable

Linguistic Talents

_____ reading
_____ vocabulary
_____ speaking

	remembers		posture
	facts		special
	creative		feature
	writing		
	poetry	**Nature and**	
	debate	**Outdoor Abilities**	
	humor and		observer
	joke telling		loves
	storytelling		animals
			curious
Physical Appearance			hiking
	neat		science
	attractive		collections

HAVE A FAMILY MEETING

A great way for families to solve family conflicts and work on behavior makeovers is by holding family meetings. They are also a wonderful way for families to get together at regularly scheduled times and enjoy each other's company, boost family harmony, and share ideas and concerns in a supportive atmosphere.

There are many possible topics for your family meetings. Here are just a few:

- Settle sibling conflicts.
- Handle repetitive problems or inappropriate behaviors.
- Set television or bedtime hours.
- Plan vacations.
- Announce family activities or menus.
- Celebrate positive happenings for individual family members.
- Voice concerns.
- Establish or revise family rules, curfews, computer times, chores, and allowances.

Principles of Successful Family Meetings

You could begin meetings by announcing any special upcoming family events and clarify everyone's schedules, such as game times, field trips, test dates, doctor's appointments, parties, or school projects. Many families set aside a small box for members to suggest family issues or topics they'd like to address at the next meeting. Here are the five most important principles of successful family meetings; do modify them to fit your family needs:

1. *Make it democratic.* The goal of the family meetings is to get your kids involved, so it's important to make sure they feel

their ideas count. This is a time to encourage your children to speak up while you hold back your judgments. During family meetings, each member's opinion is considered equal, everyone has a right to be heard, and anyone can bring up any sort of problem or concern.

2. *Determine decision making.* Usually decisions are based on majority vote, although some experts feel agreement should be made by unanimous consensus. Any decisions made in the meeting must be kept at least until the following meeting, when they can be changed.

3. *Schedule regular meetings.* Most experts suggest holding meetings once a week, lasting twenty to thirty minutes for younger kids and slightly longer for older ones. Post a meeting reminder on your refrigerator or bulletin board, and mandate attendance.

4. *Rotate meeting roles.* One way to help kids take an active part in meetings is to assign different roles that can be rotated weekly. A few possibilities might be: a chairperson to start and stop meetings and stick to the agenda; a parliamentarian to make sure rules are followed; a meeting planner to post the meeting date and time; and a secretary to keep meeting notes. Younger kids can use a tape recorder to record the meetings.

5. *Create a fun meeting spirit.* Don't hold meetings just to hash out problems; after a while, kids will dread coming. Instead, try to keep meetings fun and upbeat. One family told me they always start their sessions by having family members take turns complimenting each other's good deeds during the week. End your meeting on a fun note: serve a dessert; have a family game of cards, Monopoly, volleyball, or football; or rent a great family video to watch together.

Using Family Meetings to Solve Behavior Problems and Conflicts

Family meetings can be one of the best ways to solve family problems. It's also a great way to teach your kids the process of conflict resolution by using a real family or behavior problem. The steps are included below. Each letter in the acronym

STAND represents one of the five problem-solving steps; teach them to your kids so they can use them to solve their own dilemmas when you're not around.

1. **S** = *State the problem.* Choose a conflict that is reoccurring between two or more family members, such as chores, curfews, phone use, computer use, TV, kids getting along. Gather facts to determine who really is involved in the issue and how the rest of the members feel about it. Post a family meeting time; then at the meeting, state the problem—for example: "There have been complaints about the computer. Some people are using it longer than others or playing games on it when others need it for homework. Let's find a solution for using it that everybody thinks is fair." Many families have a Problem Box—any small box with a lid—where a member can insert a description of a home problem he wants discussed at a family meeting.

2. **T** = *Tell your view, and listen to others.* Each member has a turn to express his opinion and listen to others. Review the meeting rules: no interrupting, everyone's ideas are respected, and no put-downs. Then take turns hearing each other's ideas. It helps to restate each speaker's main point following each turn: "Ben feels people shouldn't play computer games when he needs the computer for homework" or "Dad thinks that the kids who have earlier bedtimes are not having a chance to use the computer."

3. **A** = *Ask for solutions.* Now comes the chance to solve the problem. Begin by restating the problem (sometimes it changes after everyone has shared), and then ask for possible solutions. Someone can serve as secretary and write down all ideas until kids run out of possibilities or you notice their interest fading. Here are computer solutions: have computer sign-ups, younger kids use it after school, set a timer, buy another computer, pull straws each day, rotate the order.

4. **N** = *Narrow the choices.* Review all possible solutions, and then begin eliminating choices: "Is there any solution you really couldn't live with? If so, tell us which one and why."

The question helps everyone understand each other's feelings and concerns. Any choices that members object to and can justify why are crossed off. Choices parents consider nonnegotiable are automatically eliminated. For instance, buying another computer may not be an option; it affects you financially and not the rest of the family.

5. D = *Decide on a behavior solution.* The final step is to decide on the best solution and have everyone commit to it. The best solution is the one that the majority of the group agree to. Many families write or draw the chosen solution, have everyone sign it, and post it as a reminder. A follow-up meeting is set to determine if the solution is working, and the plan may then be altered if needed. Here's how the computer problem was resolved: "Everyone signs up for a computer time on Monday. You stick to that time slot until the next family meeting when you can sign up for a new time. Two hours of extra time are available after eight o'clock each night for homework. Kim and Rob use it before dinner because they don't have homework."

FINAL THOUGHTS

I wish you all the best on your battle against bad behaviors. The path is guaranteed to be rocky and at times may become quite arduous, but that's what parenting is all about. It may well be your most challenging role and is by far your most important.

One of the most critical roles in our lives is to help our children become happy, self-reliant, well behaved, and decent human beings. There is no reward more fulfilling that knowing you have made an enduring difference in your child's life. In fact, it's our ultimate reward.

So hang in there. Fight the good fight. Consider this book a necessary resource and me your continuing ally. Look for my Web sites: www.micheleborba.com or www.moralintelligence.com for further makeover ideas and tips. I wish you well.

REFERENCES

All books cited in References are available on Amazon.com.

PART ONE:
PREPARING TO MAKE CHANGES

Percentage of parents who spank: H. S. Glenn, *Developing Healthy Self-Esteem* (Orem, Utah: Empowering People Books, Tapes, and Videos, 1989). Videocassette.

PART THREE:
THIRTY-EIGHT BEHAVIOR MAKEOVERS

1 Anger
Students hitting out of anger: CHARACTER COUNTS! and Josephson Institute of Ethics *1998 Report Card on the Ethics of American Youth* [www.josephsoninstitute.org/98-Survey/98survey.htm]. Oct. 19, 1998.

2 Anxiety

Anxiety rates in children: J. S. Dacey and L. B. Fiore, *Your Anxious Child* (San Francisco: Jossey-Bass, 2000).

3 Biting

Homicide rates of U.S. and Canadian adolescents: A. Blumstein, *Youth Violence, Guns, and the Illicit Drug Industry* (Pittsburgh, Pa.: H. John Heinz III School of Public Policy and Management, Carnegie Mellon University, 1994). R. A. Silverman and L. Kennedy, *Deadly Deeds: Murder in Canada* (Scarborough, Ontario: Nelson, 1993). American Academy of Pediatrics, "New AAP Policy Addresses Violence and Children" [www.aap.org/advocacy/archives/janviol.htm]. Jan. 5, 1999.

4 Bossiness

Findings from the National Center for Clinical Infant Program cited in D. Goleman, *Emotional Intelligence* (New York: Bantam Books, 1995).

5 Bullied

Yamamoto's study cited by E. McCoy, *What to Do When Kids Are Mean to Your Child* (Pleasantville, N.Y.: Reader's Digest, 1997).

Survey on percentage of teens contemplating suicide due to bullying cited by J. Middleton-Moz and M. L. Zawadski, *Bullies: From the Playground to the Boardroom* (Deerfield Beach, Fla.: Healthy Communications, 2001).

6 Bullying

Middle schoolers bullying classmates cited by D. Espelage in "Me? A Bully?" *Family Life,* Feb. 2000, p. 19.

Bullies rated popular by peers from a study published in the *Journal of Developmental Psychology* and cited by A. Dickinson, "Bad Boys Rule," *Time,* Jan. 31, 2000, p. 77.

Eron research tracking eight hundred eight year olds cited by N. Wartik, "Bullying: A Serious Business," *Child,* Feb. 2001, p. 82.

Research on the percentage of kid bullies with criminal records cited by K. S. Peterson, "Bullies, Victims Can Grow into Roles," *USA Today* [www.usatoday.com/life/health/child/lhchi071.htm]. Sept. 8, 1999.

Long-term effects of bullying cited by K. Zarzour, *Facing the Schoolyard Bully: How to Raise an Assertive Child in an Aggressive World* (Buffalo, N.Y.: Firefly Books, 2000).

Research by Leonard Eron finding one in four bullies end up with criminal records cited in S. Fried and P. Fried, *Bullies and Victims: Helping Your Child Through the School Yard Battlefield* (New York: Evans, 1996).

7 Chore Wars

Study on chores from E. Crary, *Pick Up Your Socks and Other Skills Growing Children Need* (Seattle, Wash.: Parenting Press, 1990).

8 Cynicism

M. Seligman, K. Reivich, L. Jaycox, and J. Gillham, *The Optimistic Child: A Revolutionary Program That Safeguards Children Against Depression and Builds Lifelong Resilience* (Boston: Houghton Mifflin, 1995).

9 Defiance

P. Coleman, *How to Say It to Your Kids: The Right Words to Solve Problems, Soothe Feelings, and Teach Values* (Upper Saddle River, N.J.: Prentice Hall, 2000).

American Psychiatric Association cited by N. I. Bernstein, *Treating the Unmanageable Adolescent: A Guide to Oppositional Defiant and Conduct Disorders* (Northvale, N.J.: Aronson, 1996).

10 Doesn't Listen

Parents magazine poll cited by L. Lambert, "From Chaos to Cooperation: A 21 Day Discipline Makeover," *Parents,* Oct. 2000, pp. 142–145.

Wait-time study conducted by M. B. Rowe, "Wait-Time: Slowing Down May Be a Way of Speeding Up!" *Journal of Teacher Education,* 1986, *31*(1), 43–50.

11 Fighting

Studies correlating TV viewing to violence from American Medical Association, *The Physician's Guide to Media Violence* (Chicago: American Medical Association, 1997).

D. Shrifrin, "Three-Year Study Documents Nature of Television Violence," *AAP News* [www.aap.org/advocacy/shifrin898.htm]. Aug. 1998.

12 Giving Up Easily

Terman's study cited by J. N. Shrunken, *Terman's Kids: The Groundbreaking Study of How the Gifted Grow Up* (New York: Little, Brown, 1992).

13 Hitting

Hitting has become an American habit cited by A. P. Goldstein, *Violence in America: Lessons on Understanding the Aggression in Our Lives* (Palo Alto, Calif.: Davies-Black Publishing, 1996).

Research showing that kids who hit today are much more likely to grow up to be aggressive was conducted by Leonard Eron: L. D. Enron, J. H. Gentry, and P. Schlegel (eds.), *Reason to Hope: A Psychosocial Perspective on Violence and Youth* (Washington, D.C.: American Psychological Association, 1994).

14 Homework Battles

Study citing the benefits of homework by H. Cooper, *Homework* (White Plains, N.Y.: Longman, 1989). J. Bempechat,

Getting Our Kids Back on Track: Educating Children for the Future (San Francisco: Jossey-Bass, 2001), p. 66.

15 Hooked on Rewards
Lavish praise produces tentative student responses: M. B. Rowe, "Relation of Wait-Time and Rewards to the Development of Language, Logic, and Fate Control: Part II—Rewards." *Journal of Research in Science Teaching,* 1974, *11,* 291–308.

16 Impulsivity
Famous marshmallow test conducted by Y. Shoda, W. Mischel, and P. K. Peake, "Predicting Adolescent Cognitive and Self-Regulatory Competencies from Preschool Delay of Gratification," *Developmental Psychology,* 1999, *26,* 978–986.

Carnegie Corporation study cited in A. Kipnis, *Angry Young Men: How Parents, Teachers, and Counselors Can Help "Bad Boys" Become Good Men* (San Francisco: Jossey-Bass, 1999), p. 16.

17 Intolerance
American youth are displaying intolerant actions at younger ages cited in M. Borba, *Building Moral Intelligence: The Seven Essential Virtues That Teach Kids to Do the Right Thing* (San Francisco: Jossey-Bass, 2001), p. 192.

S. Bullard, *Teaching Tolerance: Raising Open-Minded, Empathetic Children* (New York: Doubleday, 1996).

G. Allport, *The Nature of Prejudice* (Reading, Mass.: Addison-Wesley, 1954).

18 Lack of Friends
S. Nowicki Jr. and M. P. Duke, *Helping the Child Who Doesn't Fit In* (Atlanta, Ga.: Peachtree Publishers, 1992).

19 Lying and Cheating
Rates of student cheating as cited in C. Kleiner and M. Lord, "The Cheating Game," *U.S. News and World Report,* Nov. 22, 1999, pp. 55–61.

20 Materialistic

Average American kid sees fifty to one hundred TV commercials a day from M. Ellas, "Ads Targets Kids," *USA Today,* Mar. 22, 2000, p. D5.

Three billion dollars spent on advertising directed at kids from a Time/CNN poll cited on CNN News July 30, 2001 [www.money.cnn.com/2001/07/30/living/v_smart_assets].

Kids spending $36 billion annually and study conducted by Pennsylvania State University's Smeal College of Business conducted by Marvin Goldberg: M. Goldberg, "Understanding Materialism Among Youth," *Journal of Consumer Psychology,* Aug. 24, 2001.

Survey that kids measure self-worth based on amount of possessions cited in N. Gibbs, "Who's in Charge Here?" *Time,* Aug. 6, 2001, pp. 39–48.

Limiting TV viewing reduces materialism cited in T. Robinson and others, "Reducing Television Viewing on Children's Requests for Toys," *Journal of Developmental and Behavioral Pediatrics,* 2001, *22,* 179–184.

Study finding that parents who are more materialistic tend to have kids who are more materialistic conducted by Center for a New American Dream [www.newdream.org/campaign/kids/]. Aug. 21, 2002.

21 Meanness

Research on impact that parents play in developing children's kindness cited by N. Eisenberg, *The Caring Child* (Cambridge, Mass.: Harvard University Press, 1992), p. 96.

Study finding that parents who call attention to the harm done and encourage reparations increase empathy conducted by M. Hoffman, "Development of Prosocial Motivation: Empathy and Guilt," in N. Eisenberg (ed.), *The Development of Prosocial Behavior* (Orlando, Fla.: Academic Press, 1983).

Centers for Disease Control study results show increase in peer cruelty cited in K. Peterson, "Bullies Shove Their Way into the Nation's Schools," *USA Today,* Sept. 7, 1999.

22 Negative Peer Pressure

Survey of 991 kids and peer pressure cited by A. Goldstein, "Paging All Parents," *Time,* July 3, 2000, p. 47.

23 Overperfectionism

H. W. Stevenson and J. W. Stigler, *The Learning Gap* (New York: Simon & Schuster, 1992).

24 Poor Sportsmanship

National Association of Sports Officials concerns reported by S. Smith, "Is the Choice Sportsmanship or Death?" Knight Ridder/Tribune Information Services [www.youthdevelopment.org]. July 23, 2000.

25 Put-Downs

National Parent-Teacher Organization findings on ratio of parent put-ups to put-downs cited in S. Marston, *The Magic of Encouragement* (New York: Morrow, 1990).

26 Rudeness

Poll of 1,005 adults conducted by KRC Research and Consulting with assistance from U.S. News pollsters, cited in J. Marks, "The American Uncivil Wars," U.S. News Online [www.usnews/issue/civil.htm]. Apr. 22, 1996.

27 Selfishness

Survey by Time/CNN citing parental perception of spoiled children in N. Gibbs, "Who's in Charge Here?" *Time,* Aug. 6, 2001, pp. 39–48.

28 Short Attention Span

Ritalin use: A. Kipnis, *Angry Young Men: How Parents, Teachers, and Counselors Can Help "Bad Boys" Become Good Men* (San Francisco: Jossey-Bass, 1999).

Use of stimulants: International Narcotics Control Board, cited in P. R. Breggin, *Reclaiming Our Children* (Cambridge, Mass.: Perseus Books, 1999).

29 Shyness

P. G. Zimbardo and S. Radl, *The Shy Child: A Parent's Guide to Preventing and Overcoming Shyness from Infancy to Adulthood* (New York: Doubleday, 1999).

One-on-one play date opportunities: F. Frankel, *Good Friends Are Hard to Find: Help Your Child Find, Make and Keep Friends* (Los Angeles: Perspective Publishing, 1996).

30 Sibling Battles

Research results on the benefits of problem solving cited in M. B. Shure, *Raising a Thinking Child* (New York: Holt, 1994).

31 Stealing

Survey on prevalence of shoplifting conducted by CHARAC-TER COUNTS! and Josephson Institute of Ethics, *1998 Report Card on the Ethics of American Youth* [www.josephsoninstitute.org/98-Survey/98survey.htm]. Oct. 19, 1998.

32 Swearing

Report on vulgarity, *ABC Nightly News,* June 19, 2000.

Increase of swearing on school campuses cited by N. Hellmich, "Today's Schools Cursed by an Increase in Swearing," *USA Today,* May 20, 1997, p. D4.

Harvard University study cited by M. Borba, *Building Moral Intelligence* (San Francisco: Jossey-Bass, 2001).

33 Talking Back

Survey of adults on whether kids are raised to be respectful reported by A. Siegler, "What a Nice Kid," *Child Magazine,*

1997, cited in R. Taffel, *Nurturing Good Children Now* (New York: Golden Books, 1999).

34 Tattling
Survey of teen willingness to report threats cited in "For the Record," *Time,* Apr. 22, 2002, p. 18.

35 Teased
National Education Association statistics on rates of bullying cited in S. Fried and P. Fried, *Bullies and Victims* (New York: Evans, 1996).

F. Frankel, *Good Friends Are Hard to Find* (Los Angeles: Perspective Publishing, 1996).

36 Temper Tantrums
T. B. Brazelton, *Touchpoints: Your Child's Emotional and Behavioral Development* (Reading, Mass.: Addison-Wesley, 1992).

37 Whining
A. Ricker and C. Crowder, *Whining: Three Steps to Stopping It Before the Tears and Tantrums Start* (New York: Fireside, 1998).

38 Yelling
Murray A. Straus study cited in R. Sobel, "Wounding with Words," *U.S. News and World Report,* Aug. 28, 2000, p. 53.

PART FOUR:
HOW TO USE CONSEQUENCES

Eron's research was cited by I. A. Hyman, *The Case Against Spanking: How to Discipline Your Child Without Hitting* (San Francisco: Jossey-Bass, 1997).

PART FIVE:
DON'T FORGET TO TELL
YOUR KIDS YOU LOVE THEM!

S. Coopersmith, *The Antecedents of Self-Esteem* (New York: Freeman, 1967).

ABOUT THE AUTHOR

Michele Borba, Ed.D., has worked with more than 750,000 parents and teachers over more than two decades. A dynamic and highly sought-after speaker, she has presented hundreds of keynote addresses and workshops throughout North America, Europe, Asia, and the South Pacific on enhancing children's character development, self-esteem, achievement, and behavior. Her down-to-earth speaking style, inspirational stories, and practical strategies appeal to audiences worldwide.

Borba is the author of eighteen books for parents and educators, including *Building Moral Intelligence,* selected by Amazon.com as "one of the top ten parenting books of the year," and cited by *Publishers' Weekly* as "one of the most noteworthy of 2001"; *Parents* Do *Make a Difference,* selected by *Child Magazine* as an "outstanding parenting book of 1999"; and *Esteem Builders,* used by over 1.5 million students worldwide.

Borba appears as a frequent guest expert on television and National Public Radio talk shows, including *The View, ABC Home Show, Fox & Friends,* and *The Jenny Jones Show,* and has been interviewed in numerous publications, including *Newsweek, Parents, Redbook, First for Women, Family Circle, Working Mother,* the *Chicago Tribune,* the *Los Angeles Times,* and the *New York Daily News,* and serves as a columnist for Oxygen Media and as honorary advisory board member for *Parents* magazine. Her numerous awards include the National Educator Award, presented by the National Council of Self-Esteem.

Borba and her husband were partners in a private practice for troubled children and adolescents in Campbell, California. She received her doctorate in educational psychology and counseling from the University of San Francisco, her M.A. in learning disabilities, and her B.A. from the University of Santa Clara.

To contact Borba regarding her work or her media availability, or to schedule a keynote or workshop for your organization, go to www.MicheleBorba.com or www.moralintelligence.com.

INDEX

Honesty. *See* Dishonesty
How to Say It to Your Kids
(Coleman), 81
Hurried Child, The (Elkind), 30

I

I message, versus *you* message,
123, 308
Impulsivity: behavior tip for,
129; three steps to reduce,
130–132; makeover plan for,
132–134; overview of, 130;
and thinking through possible consequences of wrong
choice, 131–132
Internet, 250
Intolerance: behavior tip for,
137; four steps to squelching, 138–140; makeover plan
for, 140–142; overview of,
138; resources for, 143–144

J

Josephson Institute of Ethics, 21

L

Language: encouraging, 104;
and feeling vocabulary, 20;
and nonverbal communica-
tion, 149
Likeability quotient, 41
Limits, 212
Listening: behavior tip for, 88;
makeover plan for, 91;
overview of, 89; resources
for, 93; six tips for, 89–90
Lying. *See* Dishonesty

M

Manners, 205–206. *See also*
Rudeness

Marijuana, 177
Materialism: behavior tip for,
160; makeover plan for,
163–164; overview of, 161;
resources for, 165–166;
seven tips to squelch,
161–163
Meanness: behavior tip for,
167; common reasons for,
171–172; four steps to
reduce, 168–170; makeover
plan for, 170–172; overview
of, 168; resources for,
173–174
Media consumption, 60, 75, 97,
141, 161, 162, 250, 300
Methamphetamine, 221
Mischel, W., 130
Monetary penalty, 299
Moorman, C., 198
Moral questioning, 154–155
Motivation, internal, 123

N

Narcotics Control Board,
221
National Association of
Sports Officials, 193
National Center for Clinical
Infant Program, 43
National Education
Association, 270
National Institute of Mental
Health, 97
National Parent Teacher
Organization, 200
Nature of Prejudice, The
(Allport), 140
Nonverbal communication,
149
Nowicki, S., Jr., 149

O

Oppositional defiant disorder, 83

Optimistic Child, The (Seligman), 76

Overindulgence, 212. *See also* Selfishness

Overperfectionism: behavior tip for, 182; makeover plan for, 184–186; overview of, 183; resources for, 188; six strategies to reduce, 183–184

Ownership, 239

Oxygen Media, 2

P

Parental behavior: and discipline that protects child's self-beliefs, 308–311; and parent makeovers, 14–16; and potential problem areas, 306–307; related to shyness, 228

Parents magazine, 2, 89

Peer pressure, negative, 60; behavior tip for, 175; makeover plan for, 177–179; overview of, 176; resources for, 181; role playing examples for, 179; six strategies to resist, 176–177

Penn State Smeal College of Business, 161

Perseverance. *See* Giving-up attitude

Pick Up Your Socks . . . and Other Skills Growing Children Need (Crary), 69

Play dates, 227

Poor sportsmanship: behavior tip for, 189; five steps to squash, 190–192; makeover plan for, 193–194; overview of, 190; and principles of good sportsmanship, 190–191; reasons for, 194; resources for, 196

Positive qualities: list of, to encourage, 311–314; nurturing, 310–311

Praise, 124, 125, 162, 309–310

Prejudice, 140

Prioritizing, 161–162

Privileges, loss of, 300

Problem box, 317

Problem solving: in family meetings, 317–318; teaching, 262

Profanity. *See* Swearing

Put-downs, 96; behavior tip for, 197; five strategies to squelch, 198–199; makeover plan for, 199–201; overview of, 198; resources for, 203–204

R

Real, versus make-believe, 155

Reporting, versus tattling, 261, 263

Respect, 89, 96

Respectful behavior, 256

Responsibilities, 66–67. *See also* Chore battles

Restitution, 170, 241

Rewards, dependence on: behavior tip for, 122; makeover plan for, 124–126; overview of, 123; resources for, 127–128; six strategies to wean from, 123–124

Rewind method, 82

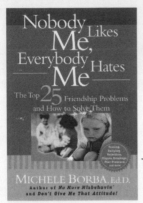

Nobody Likes Me, Everybody Hates Me: The Top 25 Friendship Problems and How to Solve Them

Michele Borba, Ed.D.

Paperback

ISBN: 0-7879-7662-8

"Michele Borba has written the ultimate parent-friendly guide to kids and friendship."
—Ann Douglas, author, *The Mother of All Parenting Books*

Nobody Likes Me shows parents and teachers how to teach the 25 most essential friendship-building skills kids need to find, make, and keep friends, as well as survive social pressure from peers.

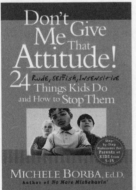

Don't Give Me That Attitude: 24 Rude, Selfish, Insensitive Things Kids Do and How to Stop Them

Michele Borba, Ed.D.

Paperback

ISBN: 0-7879-7333-5

"Michele Borba is an inspiring educator, an experienced parent, and a terrific writer."
—Michael Gurian, author, *The Wonder of Boys* and *Boys and Girls Learn Differently*

Building Moral Intelligence: The Seven Essential Virtues That Teach Kids to Do the Right Thing

Michele Borba, Ed.D.

Paperback

ISBN: 0-7879-6226-0

"If you care about the future of our children and our nation, read this important book!"
—Jack Canfield, coauthor, *Chicken Soup for the Parent's Soul*